THE GERMAN AIR FORCE
I KNEW
1914-1918

MEMOIRS OF THE IMPERIAL GERMAN AIR FORCE IN THE GREAT WAR

COMPILED BY MAJOR GEORG PAUL NEUMANN
(LATE OF THE GERMAN AIR FORCE)

FROM THE RECORDS AND WITH THE ASSISTANCE OF
TWENTY-NINE OFFICERS AND OFFICIALS OF THE
NAVAL AND MILITARY SERVICES

TRANSLATED BY

J. E. GURDON

EDITED AND INTRODUCED BY

BOB CARRUTHERS

Pen & Sword
AVIATION

This edition published in 2014 by

Pen & Sword Aviation
An imprint of
Pen & Sword Books Ltd
47 Church Street
Barnsley
South Yorkshire
S70 2AS

This book was first published as 'The German Air Force in the Great War'
by Hodder & Stoughton Ltd., London, 1921.

Copyright © Coda Books Ltd.
Published under licence by Pen & Sword Books Ltd.

ISBN: 9781783463138

A CIP catalogue record for this book is available from the British Library

Printed and bound in England
By CPI Group (UK) Ltd, Croydon, CR0 4YY

Pen & Sword Books Ltd incorporates the imprints of Pen & Sword Aviation, Pen & Sword
Family History, Pen & Sword Maritime, Pen & Sword Military, Pen & Sword Discovery, Pen
& Sword Politics, Pen & Sword Atlas, Pen & Sword Archaeology, Wharncliffe Local History,
Wharncliffe True Crime, Wharncliffe Transport, Pen & Sword Select, Pen & Sword Military
Classics, Leo Cooper, The Praetorian Press, Claymore Press, Remember When, Seaforth
Publishing and Frontline Publishing

For a complete list of Pen & Sword titles please contact

PEN & SWORD BOOKS LIMITED
47 Church Street, Barnsley, South Yorkshire, S70 2AS, England
E-mail: enquiries@pen-and-sword.co.uk
Website: www.pen-and-sword.co.uk

CONTENTS

TRANSLATOR'S NOTE 4

PREFACE 5

INTRODUCTION 7

PART I

CHAPTER I
OBSERVATION BALLOONS 12

CHAPTER II
AIRSHIPS, NAVAL AND MILITARY 18

CHAPTER III
ARMY AEROPLANES 41

CHAPTER IV
NAVAL AEROPLANES 58

CHAPTER V
PERSONNEL AND TRAINING 76

PART II

CHAPTER I
LIGHTER-THAN-AIRCRAFT 90

CHAPTER II
TYPES AND THEIR APPLICATION 117

CHAPTER III
BOMBING BY DAY AND BY NIGHT 137

CHAPTER IV
FIGHTING EQUIPMENT 166

CHAPTER V
THE GERMAN AIR FORCE ON THE WESTERN FRONT 182

CHAPTER VI
GERMAN AIRMEN IN MANY THEATRES OF WAR ITALY 202

CHAPTER VII
SEAPLANES 227

CHAPTER VIII.
ANTI-AIRCRAFT AND HOME DEFENCES 239

CHAPTER IX
A GLANCE INTO THE FUTURE 245

TRANSLATOR'S NOTE

THE ORIGINAL WORK, *Die Deutschen Luftstreitkräfte im Weltkriege*, is approximately three times the size of this English version. As Major Neumann points out in his Preface, his object has been to accumulate records concerning everything that appertains to the German Air Force, not only with regard to its history, but also with regard to its development in technical design and organisation.

He has been assisted in this endeavour by twenty-nine contributors, each one of whom is a specialist in some branch of the aircraft industry or flying service, and it is well to mention that the result is a very comprehensive and accurate survey.

Having to confine myself within certain limits, I have been obliged to recast the work and omit a great deal that did not seem to be of direct interest to English readers. For this purpose I have divided the book into two parts, of which the first concerns itself with the German Air Force as a unit of power, and describes the machines used and the training of *personnel*; the second part deals with the application of this power, and is therefore mainly historical.

From this selection of essentials I hope that the reader will be able to form a definite mental picture of the strangely paradoxical German Air Force.

I have endeavoured to preserve the individual style of each writer as far as is possible in English, but here and there the recasting of the work has necessitated slight alterations.

To Captain W. F. J. Harvey, D.F.C., late Squadron 22, R.A.F., I wish to express my gratitude for his assistance and criticism, which have been of exceptional value on account of his wide experience of service flying.

J. E. GURDON.
LONDON, 1920.

PREFACE

Man sits ever on the sands	*Sitzt das arme Menschenkind*
Washed by Time's abysmal sea,	*An dem Ozean der Zeiten:*
Gathering with puny hands	*Schöpft mit seiner kleinen Hand*
Drops from its immensity:	*Tropfen aus den Ewigkeiten;*
Sits and deems the flotsam cast	*Sitzt das arme Menschenkind,*
Shoreward - waifs and strays of	*Sammelt flüsternde Gerüchte,*
myth -	*Tragt sie in ein kleines Buch*
Is the History of the Past,	*Schreibt darüber; 'Weltgeschichte.'*
So he makes a book therewith.	

THE WORDS OF this stanza whispered a soft admonishing rebuke to me in the days when this work was first conceived and took its shape. It seemed as though they foretold the arduous journey which lay between my desire and its fulfillment, my object and its attainment. Perhaps even they hinted at the impossibility of painting on so small a canvas the entire picture of our Air Force, its development and its achievements. But then war would never have scaled the heavens had not a generation of pioneers led the way, and the airmen, before whose eyes the world lies revealed like an open book, would never have conquered space in its third dimension had they admitted the existence of impossibility; the aeroplane would never have arisen godlike from land and sea.

And so the attempt has been made to gather from many sources such vivid pictures of past events as will portray the growth of our Air Force in organisation and knowledge, and also the use to which it was put during the war. It is hoped that this book may serve as a nucleus later for a complete history of the flying service, since a record of aerial achievement in the war should never suffer from the restrictions imposed by lack of space. My present aim, however, is to select from the multitude of events, and rescue from oblivion all which we should remember concerning our struggle in the air. All that work accomplished by intense and concentrated thought, and by world-wide labours from Boulogne to Bagdad, most surely deserves immortality. And so this book shall stand for a monument, not only to all those who served with our aerial forces by land and sea, but also to the whole German nation, which used to follow their glorious deeds with wonder and amazement.

For this purpose much new material will be employed, and I shall reveal to the world many things which hitherto have been guarded as official secrets. With the aid and criticism of others it will be possible not only to outline essentials, but also to place events in their order of merit or importance. Furthermore, we may bring about an appreciation of those methods which solved for our Air Force the many problems of organisation and design, and piloted it through so many grave crises.

To the rising generation, upon whom lies the burden of carrying out the plans for that future aerial development which is to be the harbinger of peace and unity among the nations, perhaps this book may prove a source of enthusiasm and inspiration. In time to come, those who turn these pages may remember with a thrill of gratitude that during the bitter, bloody struggle for the mastery of the air was laid the foundation of peaceful aerial navigation.

INTRODUCTION

MAJOR GEORG PAUL Neumann was a former German Air Force officer who had served in the Great War. He produced his outstanding survey of the German Air Force in 1920 while the events were still recent history. He was able to draw on his own experience and his contacts to compile a large number of personal accounts from officers and men who had so recently fought in the cause. The result is an accurate, faithful and comprehensive review of the aircraft, personnel and organisation of the force which began life in 1910 as the Imperial German Army Air Service and ended the war as the *Luftstreitkräfte*.

This comprehensive and compelling review is highly recommended for anyone interested in the history of the Great War in the air and includes a series of primary sources dealing with some of the unusual and lesser known aspects of the Luftstreitkräfte including a gripping account of defending a Zeppelin against attack by British fighters.

Major Neumann's indispensable work has never been surpassed and in my opinion this English language translation is essential reading for anyone with an interest in the realities of the war in the air in the Great War.

The first military aircraft to be acquired by the German Imperial Army entered service in 1910, forming the nucleus of what was later to become the famous *Luftstreitkräfte*, which was formed in October 1916. Initially all German and Austro-Hungarian military aircraft in service used the ornate Maltese Cross insignia however the *Balkenkreuz*, a plain black cross on white, officially replaced the earlier design from late March 1918, although the last order on the subject, fully standardising the new national marking, was dated 25th June 1918.

In the era before the possibilities of air to air combat had been realised the duties of aircraft were already familiar to the armies of the day. Those duties, provided in support of armies on the ground, were initially intended to be twofold, providing reconnaissance intelligence and also an artillery spotting function. There were a number of precedents for these activities as balloons had been used during the American Civil War of 1861-1865, Franco-Prussian War of 1870-1871 and even as far back as the Napoleonic Wars. The importance of aircraft was soon apparent and France's embryonic army air service (*Aviation Militaire*), which eventually became the *Armée de l'Air*, was instituted later in 1910 while the Air Battalion of the Royal Engineers (later re-organised as the Royal Flying Corps) was formed in November 1911.

The initial units of the Luftstreitkräfte, dedicated to observation, were known as *Feldflieger Abteilungen* (Field Flier Detachments), and had an official establishment of six two-seat aircraft apiece, with each "FFA" unit assigned to an army unit in their local area. As the war progressed however the *Luftstreitkräfte* organisation changed substantially to accommodate the new types of aircraft, doctrine, tactics and the needs of the ground troops, in particular the artillery and the *Luftstreitkräfte was born in 1916*. It was also during 1916, that the German High Command, in response to the then current Allied air superiority, reorganised their forces by creating several types of specialist units, most notably single seat fighter squadrons, or *Jastas* as the contraction of *Jagdstaffel* (literally "hunting squadron"), in order to counter the offensive operations of the Royal Flying Corps and the French *Aviation Militaire*.

The Jagdstaffeln, or *hunting squadrons*, established by the reorganization that started by the late summer of 1916 were fielded by four kingdoms of the German Empire. The Kingdom of Prussia was predominant, with a force eventually comprising 67 Jastas. However, the Kingdoms of Bavaria, Saxony, and Württemberg had their own fighter squadrons: Bavaria had ten; Saxony, seven; and Württemberg, four.

On 24th June 1917, the *Luftstreitkräfte* formed its first fighter wing, Royal Prussian Jagdgeschwader I, incorporating Jastas 4, 6, 10, and 11, and set the pattern for using Roman numerals in the *Luftstreitkräfte* for designating such units. Manfred von Richthofen was moved up from command of Jasta 11 to command JG I. After his death in action, by order of the Kaiser, it was renamed to honour him.

Interior of a Zeppelin, showing the hexagonal rinds and longitudinal tie-girders.

The Prussians followed the successful re-organisation by establishing three more Jagdgeschwaders. On 2nd February 1918, JG II was formed from Jastas 12, 13, 15, and 19, and Adolf Ritter von Tutschek assumed in command. On the same day, JG III consolidated Jasta 2 *Boelcke*, and *Jastas* 26, 27, and 36 under Bruno Loerzer. Finally, on 2 September 1918, the Royal Prussian Marine Jagdgeschwader was formed from Marine Feld Jastas I through V, and placed under the command of Gotthard Sachsenberg. Bavaria also established their own Royal Bavarian Jagdgeschwader IV on 3 October 1918. It consisted of Jastas 23, 32, 34, and 35 under Eduard Ritter von Schleich.

During the war, the Imperial Army Air Service utilised a wide variety of aircraft, ranging from fighters, such as those manufactured by Albatros-Flugzeugwerke and Fokker, specialist reconnaissance aircraft, manufactured by the likes of Aviatik and DFW, and heavy bombers manufactured by Gothaer Waggonfabrik, better known simply as Gotha. In addition there were the lighter than air-ships manufactured by and Zeppelin-Staaken.

Despite the large variety of tasks undertaken by the military air forces it was the fighters which inevitably received the most attention in the annals of early military aviation. The most romanticised of all services produced high-scoring "aces" such as Manfred von Richthofen, popularly known in English as "The Red Baron" (in Germany, he was known as *"der Rote Kampfflieger"* (Red Air Fighter)), Lothar von Richthofen, Ernst Udet, Hermann Göring, Oswald Boelcke, Werner Voss, and Max Immelmann (the first airman to win the *Pour le Mérite*, Imperial Germany's highest decoration for gallantry, as a result of which the decoration became popularly known as the "Blue Max" . Like the German Navy, the German Army also used Zeppelin airships for bombing military and civilian targets in France, Belgium and the United Kingdom.

By the end of the war, the German Army Air Service possessed a total of 2,709 frontline aircraft, 56 airships, 186 balloon detachments and about 4,500 flying personnel. Casualties in the Great War totalled 8,604 aircrew killed, missing or taken prisoner. A further 7,302 were wounded. Some 3,126 aircraft, 546 balloons and 26 airships were lost during the course of the war while some 5,425 Allied aircraft and 614 kite balloons were claimed to have been shot down.

After the war ended in German defeat, the service was dissolved completely on 8 May 1920 under the conditions of the Treaty of Versailles, which demanded that its aeroplanes be completely destroyed.

Major Georg Paul Neumann has produced a masterful survey which encompasses all of the diverse activities of the German Army Air Service. Thank-you for buying this book I hope you will enjoy reading it as much as I did and I trust it will repay your investment of time and money.

BOB CARRUTHERS.
ISLE OF MAN 2013.

PART I

CHAPTER I
OBSERVATION BALLOONS

T HE KITE BALLOONS which were built by von Parseval and von Sigsfeld in 1896 were introduced into the German Army to take the place of the spherical captive balloon. In spite of the rapid development in aircraft design, no particular improvement had been effected up to the outbreak of war either in design or in equipment. The interest in the observation balloon had waned with the appearance of the airship and the aeroplane, both of which occupied the attention of the Army and aircraft industry to a far greater extent. It was assumed that the observation balloon would soon be replaced by the aeroplane. In short: *When war broke out the balloon was an obsolete means of observation and seemed likely to become extinct.*

The *personnel* itself, composed almost entirely of volunteers and skilled mechanics, was well drilled and trained, and of excellent quality. The officers were recruited from every branch of the service - highly efficient officers, some of whom had been trained at the Staff College - and were finished by a one-year's course at the Airship Training School. In addition to that, twenty officers every year underwent a four months' course to qualify them as balloon observers with the Airship Defence Corps.

In spite of all, the observation balloon service was but little heard of in the Army, which was never instructed in the uses to which balloons would be put. At manoeuvres it played only a very small part, and, on account of its limited mobility, usually arrived too late to participate in those hurried battles. It was not therefore expected to be of much use in open warfare, but in the more immobile defensive manoeuvres it had already proved to be most valuable and had won commendation from the higher command.

When the campaign on the Western Front became stationary on account of the development of trench warfare, the balloons rendered such valuable service by locating concealed hostile batteries and by similar work, that many senior officers supported the proposed retention of the observation balloon.

DEVELOPMENT DURING THE WAR

Very soon there arose the demand for an improved type of balloon. The balloon (of 21,000 cubic feet capacity), which theoretically was Supposed to ascend to 2500 feet, in practice would never rise above 1600 feet whenever there was a slight wind blowing. This was not high enough to maintain an efficient watch over the hostile artillery, particularly as the enemy soon began to take the observation balloon into consideration when selecting their positions. In order to attain greater heights many of the appliances that were fitted to the heavy basket were removed; in fact, the observers resorted to the flimsiest of mounts - a kind of stiff saddle slung beneath the envelope or some similar arrangement. At the beginning of 1915, however, balloons of 28,000 and 35,000 cubic feet capacity were sent to the front. These balloons could ascend to 3300 or 4000 feet, and as they did not rock so badly in the wind it was easier to observe from them. However, they presented no fundamental change in their design.

It was found that it was more difficult to haul in these balloons. A good hour's work was necessary in order to bring them down from a height of 3300 feet, and this involved a heavy strain on the men. The balloons were therefore usually wound in by a trolley drawn by a horse. This necessitated an open area on every side of at least 1600 yards, which was all the more difficult to find as it had to be concealed from hostile artillery observation. As a consequence the balloon could not always ascend at the points of greatest tactical advantage, since its position was limited to open country. This evil was only remedied by the introduction of mechanical winches. The balloon units at first helped themselves by constructing mechanical winches out of material captured from the enemy. In the spring of 1915 most of the units were equipped with what was in those days considered a most serviceable and efficient limbered-winch, driven by a petrol engine.

Along with the development of the balloon itself, the science of observing had undergone a considerable improvement. In particular an effective collaboration with other flying units and the application of photography to the investigation of the positions of hostile batteries were brought into practice. The heavy artillery, as a rule, supplied officers who were also trained as balloon observers so that they might be able themselves to direct the fire of the batteries.

The observation balloons therefore combined with their previous usefulness the ability to perform new tasks, consequently the whole front, and in particular the heavy artillery, demanded that they should be increased in number. At the end of 1915 there were more than forty balloon units on active service.

In the spring of 1915, during the attack on Verdun for the first time a large number of balloons were concentrated at one spot and centralised into one organisation, which was directly under the Supreme Army Command.

Our opponents, who soon came to realise the valuable work which was being accomplished by the balloons, made special efforts to destroy them by aeroplanes, and began to employ incendiary ammunition for this purpose. The losses among the balloons became very heavy in comparison to the time when darts, grenades, and incendiary bombs were the means of attack.

The remarkable tactical usefulness and the excellence of the liaison between the balloons and the artillery during the attack on Verdun resulted in a further increase in the number of field units, also in the number of places of ascent. However, this had the disadvantage of making each balloon party too weak in the matter of men and horses, and consequently they were almost immobile in spite of assistance

An A.E. Balloon ready to ascend.

from the infantry. This was particularly inconvenient during big offensives when from tactical reasons, or on account of heavy artillery bombardment, it was advisable to change the positions of the balloons with rapidity. To overcome this difficulty a special transport system was organised, which was provided in both the Western and Eastern theatres of war. In the East the transport units were made sufficiently strong to work efficiently under the conditions of open warfare, but in the West they were only organised to meet trench warfare and defensive actions. With all armies alike the organisation of the balloons was centralised.

In the meantime the design of the balloon itself had been improved. Furthermore, on account of the increasing violence of aeroplane attacks, it became necessary to accelerate the descent of the balloons, and motor winches of 24 H.P. or even 50 and 60 H.P., were employed.

The parachute, which had already been introduced in the autumn of 1915, was at first very little used, but it became an indispensable part of

Naval airship, L. 15, about to land. The pilot's gondola is in front, and the machine-gun platform can be seen on top of the envelope.

the equipment when the attacks by aeroplanes became so frequent and so bitter; and there is no doubt that the parachute contributed much towards the practical efficiency of the observation balloon.

Whereas formerly only senior officers from the staff or the artillery were accustomed to go up in the balloons, it now became a common practice for officers of other branches to test the capacity of the parachute and perhaps to experience the sensation of jumping from a burning balloon. Naturally these officers learned to realise how useful the balloons were as a means of observation and for directing artillery fire. They also appreciated the possibilities of photography, and came to the conclusion that the observation balloon could be usefully employed in conjunction with the infantry as well as with the artillery, a fact which had not previously been recognised. Later on, in both offensive and defensive actions, much excellent work was done by the balloons and the infantry operating together: it was a matter of great satisfaction to the balloon observers as well as to the latter that they were able to assist the infantry commanding officers in their work.

The greatest improvement that was made, however, consisted of a new type of balloon. On the Somme Front the French and English produced a new pattern, and we succeeded in capturing one of these balloons (Claquot, Caco). It was copied, slightly altered, and produced by us under the name of the A.E. balloon. This balloon was oblong in shape, of 30,000 c.f. capacity, and was provided with air-filled balloonets instead of planes for the purpose of stability. This balloon remained almost motionless in the air instead of rolling to 30 degrees as the old type used to do. It did not drift so far to leeward, could attain a height of 5000 feet, was very steady, and could even ascend with a wind velocity of 65 feet/sec, whereas the 'Drachen' type was useless for observation purposes in a wind velocity of only 45 feet/sec.

But a more powerful engine was required for the winch of an A.E. balloon on account of its greater lifting power and its ability to ascend in high winds. Engines of 80 or 100 H.P. were employed, and the equipment consequently became so heavy, together with its tackle, that it could only advance over hard dry ground. As this winch was unsuitable for open warfare the lighter type was also retained. Although the latter was more mobile, one had to take its limited winching speed into account.

We have now enumerated the principal points in the development of observation-balloon design. There still remains the lack of raw material to be considered, a factor which exercised considerable influence on the construction of balloons. Natural rubber, which was so important for the manufacture of balloon fabric, soon became so scarce that synthetic and waste rubber had to be used as a substitute. Eventually rubber was given up altogether, and balloons were made of 'doped' fabric, and in the final types gut membrane was inserted between the inner and outer layers of the envelope.

Proportionally with technical development the efficiency of observation from balloons rapidly improved, its range of application was thereby extended, and consequently it was decided to develop the organisation of the lighter-than-air craft *personnel* in a corresponding manner.

(STOTTMEISTER.)

Chapter II
Airships, Naval and Military

A T THE OUTBREAK of war Germany stood supreme among the nations of the world in the matter of airship design. The rigid type - as distinct from the semi-rigid and non-rigid types - was especially favoured, and had already achieved a high standard of excellence in the Zeppelin and 'Schütte-Lanz' airships. Yet how insignificant they seem in comparison to the types that now exist! During the four years of the war, beneath the pressure of dire necessity, more technical improvements were effected in airship design than would otherwise have been accomplished in ten years.

The German public knew little of this progress as it was kept secret for military reasons, consequently their enthusiasm for airships gradually grew weaker, and, owing to ignorance, false ideas rose concerning their value, their contemporary efficiency, and their future prospects, for only experts were in a position to arrive at a correct judgment on these points. The irony of the affair lay in the fact that our enemy, England, at the same time fully recognised the importance of the airship as a weapon in time of war and a means of international transport in time of peace. The English therefore made every effort to copy those German airships which fell into their hands during the war. This masterpiece of German engineering was eagerly studied and imitated in every detail. In spite of that they did not succeed in building a serviceable airship until after the Armistice, when they made the first trans-Atlantic flight while Germany was condemned to inactivity.

All the same, Germany has no cause to be jealous because an English airship made the first flight to America, Without any boasting she can claim that this success is not due to English engineering, but entirely to

German inventive genius and design, German work was quietly made use of in foreign countries, 'appreciated' and copied. A German airship, with no assistance, made a flight during the war which was even more remarkable and considerably more difficult than that which the English accomplished under present day conditions and with every modern means of assistance.

In the autumn of 1917 a naval airship, the L. 59, was sent from Bulgaria to the assistance of our troops in East Africa. A large quantity of munitions, arms, medical stores, and other goods had to be carried. The ship was obliged to fly over hostile territory, without the aid of wireless weather reports, and without the support of a base in case of danger; across the deserts of the equator which were unknown to airship travel; and constantly menaced by hostile forces. There is no doubt that she would have reached her goal in safety had she not been recalled by wireless when over Khartoum in Upper Egypt, because of a false rumour concerning our position in East Africa, and on account of the pusillanimous politicians who considered that the ship was not competent to deal with the situation. This was only one of the many errors made by politicians during the war, errors which varied from weak-mindedness to exaggerated confidence. Even if the airship had fallen into the hands of the enemy on its arrival because of the altered conditions on that front, the loss would have been nothing in comparison to the gain, owing to the moral effect of such a flight on the whole world. The importance of airships would have been increased a hundred - or a thousand-fold, not only in the esteem of the savage races of Africa and the imaginative people of the East, but also in that of our cool-headed enemies, particularly the Americans, a result most valuable to us. One remembers the impression made on America by the first voyage of the U-boat *Deutschland*. However, the case of the L. 59 only repeated the same old story of bureaucratic blunders and lost opportunities in world-politics, A bitter subject, this, for all Germans.

In the matter of skill the homeward voyage was an even finer achievement than the flight to Africa. The L. 59 covered 4500 miles in a flight lasting roughly ninety-six hours without any delay whatsoever,

The bows of the gondola of the P.L. 19, showing the arrangement of the propellers.

and could have continued for a long distance without difficulty. That fact will demonstrate to the uninitiated better than many words the pitch of excellence attained by Germany in the design of rigid airships.

At the beginning of the war the German Army had set great store by the power of the airship as a factor in land fighting, and had constructed what was in those days a strong fleet of ships. Unfortunately the airship fleet of the Navy was only in its very early stages. A private company, the 'German Airship Travel Co.' possessed three passenger airships, which were placed at the disposal of the Government when war broke out.

All existing rigid airships were similar to these in size and performance. The gas-capacity of a Zeppelin lay somewhere between 650,000 and 800,000 c.f., while that of the Schütte-Lanz of the same period was about 860,000 c.f. The performance of these ships was comparable to the smallness of their size.

At the beginning of the war the Army possessed the Z.4, 5, 6, 7, 8, and 9, all of them Zeppelins; of other types, the Sachsen, Victoria-Louise, and Hansa; the S.L.S., S.L. 2, a semi-rigid ship, the M.4, and a small Parseval.

The Navy only had one ship, the L. 3, a fact that one might consider somewhat strange when one thinks that the airship must have seemed the most suitable means of carrying out observation patrols over the sea, and raids on countries otherwise oat of reach. No doubt, however, the reason for this meagre provision of airships lay in the fact that they were clearly not competent to work under the exacting conditions demanded by the Navy, conditions which made it necessary that long distances should be covered. Although the naval authorities recognised this fact, they also saw how useful airships of a better type would be, and they were in negotiations with the building yards of the Zeppelin and Schütte-Lanz for the construction of bigger ships when war broke out.

Quick action was necessary. It was obvious that a greater number of airships was urgently required. The three existing yards, Zeppelin - Friedrichshafen, Schütte-Lanz - Mannheim-Rheinau, and the 'Luftfahrzeug-Gesellschaft,' were at once commissioned to build ships to the utmost limit of their ability, and to extend the facilities they had for building as quickly as possible.

One half of the ships that were built went to the Army, the other half to the Navy, Naturally only those types which had been already designed and tested could he built at that time, even if one had not to be content with types of an inferior quality. It was soon discovered, however, that these types were not able to meet the requirements of the Navy. The designers therefore had to draft new plans, which were carried out in practice as soon as possible.

While before the war it had been the Army which engaged most actively in airship design, it was now the Navy, on account of the number of skilled workmen they were in a position to supply. This skilled labour, assisted by the building yards, brought about that high standard of excellence which exists today. The Army adapted the types produced by the Navy for their own purposes. New types of ship appeared in rapid succession. The realisation of the means chosen by our enemies to combat the airship, namely the aeroplane, compelled us ever to increase the lifting power and climbing ability.

The opinions of the men at the front as to what was the most desirable

The revolving sheds at Nordholz, showing how the ends were lengthened.

factor in the performance of an airship varied with the changing phases of the war. At one time stress was laid on the necessity for great speed, at another it was climbing power.

But although new demands were always being made, they were always met, and so German airship design always succeeded in maintaining its position of superiority over our enemies. We suffered heavy losses, for much had to be learnt concerning this new science.

The opposition of our enemies, the forces of nature, human limitations and errors, all militated against further development, but Germany can say with truth that no airship was ever lost during the war on account of faulty construction. This statement applies equally to rigid and to non-rigid types. All three of the German airship-building yards distinguished themselves equally, and it is impossible to praise any one of them more highly than the others.

The influence of the skilled labour introduced from the Navy moderated the keen competition which existed between them, and so, through each one adopting the best designs of its neighbours, the highest possible standard of excellence was eventually attained.

An approximate review of the best types produced during the war brings forward the following facts: -

	Airship	Length (ft.)	Diameter (ft.)	Capacity (cub.yards.)	Lift (lbs.)	Engines (H.P.)		Air Speed (ft.per sec)	ft.
1	L.3 (L.7)	518	48	29,430	19,180	3	210	69	6,560
2	L.10 (L.Z.38)	536	61	41,725	34,390	4	210	85	9,185
3	L.20 (L.Z.97)	585½	61	46,825	39,240	4	240	84	10,500
4	L.30	643	78	71,940	62,830	6	240	88	12,470
5	L.60	643	78	73,050	87,300	5	240	100	19,680
6	L.71	743	78	89,595	112,435	6	260	111	21,650
7	L.100 (Planned)	781	96	141,260	180,780	10	260	121	30,180
8	S.L.3	513	64	42,375	29,100	4	210	74	7,870
9	S.L.6 (S.L.7)	534	64	45,780	34,835	4	210	85	8,530
10	S.L.8 (S.L.10)	571	65	50,615	42,990	4	240	85	11,485
11	S.L.20	651	74	73,245	77,825	5	240	93	16,405
12	P.L.19	302	51	13,080	7,275	2	180	71	8,200
13	P.L.25	369	52	18,440	13,230	2	210	72	9,840
14	P.L.27	515	60	40,740	39,685	4	240	82	14,765

This table requires no elucidation, and shows plainly enough how rapidly airship design improved. For example the L. 3 type, which existed at the beginning of the war, compared with the L. 100, which was designed though never built, had a net lift of 8-1/2 tons as compared with 80 tons. The L. 71, which was the last ship to be actually built, had a net lift of 50 tons. The percentage of net lift to total weight increased from 33% to 64% - almost double. The speed of the L. 3 was 45 M.P.H., of the L. 71, 75 M.P.H., and the L. 100 would have possessed a speed of 40 yards/sec, at a height of 6500 feet - U. 83 M.P.H. The 'ceiling' of the L. 3 with a full load was only 6500 feet, whereas the L. 71 could attain a height of about 21,500 feet, and L. 100 a height of at least 26,650 feet. It is not possible to give data concerning the maximum distances that could be covered by these ships, as these depend on circumstances such as height, speed, and the number of men, bombs, etc., that are carried. However, we may give as an example the fact that the L. 71, travelling at a speed of 65 M.P.H. at a height of 1600 feet, with a full war load and 2 tons of ballast on board, can travel a distance of 11,250 miles, always supposing that it is not compelled to rise to a height at which its petrol consumption would be greater. (The distance from Hamburg to New York by air is approximately 3750 miles.)

The Schütte-Lanz type developed like Zeppelin in size and standard of performance.

In this case also the latest Admiralty designs have never been put into practice, nor yet the method of constructing the framework of hardened aluminium (duralumin) rods, a method which doubtless would entail a striking improvement.

The development of non-rigid airships received a serious setback through the accidental destruction of the P.L. 26, and any further advance was rendered impossible through lack of rubber.

I will now consider the principal demands made by war conditions on the qualities of an airship.

The first of all these was reliability. Both ship and engine had to be built for endurance and for flights entirely free from trouble, because

Lengthening the L. 59. The airship is shown cut in half.

the airship often had to remain in the air for several days on end. In this respect it differed very considerably from the aeroplane. Again, appliances designed to assist and safeguard the ship on these long flights, such as a long-range wireless apparatus for keeping touch with the base, were indispensable. The wireless was relied on to obtain information concerning the ship's position from the direction-finding stations, and was employed by night over the sea, in clouds, and in mist.

The airship had to be as small as possible. The bigger it was the more difficult and hazardous became the handling of the vessel on the ground, and the processes of housing and bringing it out of its sheds. Furthermore, great size required the employment of large crews, with the result that more valuable gas, petrol, and oil had to be used.

The airship had to be fast in order to reach its objective without delay, outstrip its enemies, and make way against a strong head wind. It is worth mentioning experience proved that wind velocities increased with altitude.

The actual net lift had to be considerable, for it offered the pilot the choice either of saving his petrol by flying low when engaged on long-distance flights, or else of climbing to a great height where ho was immune from hostile attacks. In addition to this, the net lift regulated the quantity of bombs and the armament which could be earned.

Every one of these considerations was important, and in the course of the war first one, then another, was considered most vital. No matter what fresh demands might be made upon them, the airship designers always rose to the occasion and satisfied the immediate want.

In spite of the adverse criticism of the ignorant, airship designers achieved all that was humanly possible during the war. Steadily they worked, and steadily advanced; the complete consummation of their designs was to them no matter for comment, but a matter of course.

The ever-changing objects with which airships were planned cannot be described here in detail. Over and over again the same thing happened. A specific type was constructed, and meanwhile, perhaps, the enemies' defensive measures had been developed. Consequently the airship had to be able to climb more rapidly, and therefore the lift had to be increased. As soon as a new type was built to meet these requirements, instructions were received that some other quality, such as speed, must be improved because the ship designed for rapid ascents was too slow.

The untechnical critics responsible for these unceasing demands never realised that every airship is a compromise between conflicting qualities, and that frequently, beyond certain limits, one quality can only be improved at the expense of another.

A problem which proved particularly knotty to our engineers was provided by the aero-engine, for it developed only a fraction of its full power at great altitudes on account of the lack of oxygen. In order to overcome this difficulty they built engines with an abnormal compression, and supplied them with compressed air carried in cylinders. Unfortunately, it was not possible during the war to submit all the theory dealing with this problem to practical tests.

The aim of every airship designer was always this - 'light construction.' Every unnecessary scrap of material had to be discarded. Economy in weight was systematically developed until it affected every detail of the vessel. Every angle or corner, no matter how small it might be, was cut away, and every girder was constructed as open as possible for the same purpose of lightness. General design and detailed construction were continually being improved and refined by practical experience and theoretical science, until every scrap of material used was indispensable and was employed to its greatest advantage. The internal framework, for example, was constantly being improved and lightened. The lattice girder design was perfected, and every two grammes pared off some small rod amounted to a considerable weight when the process was continued throughout the entire structure of the ship. Indefatigably new materials were tested and adopted.

There was a tendency for economy in the matter of detail to be carried too far and for indispensable appliances and instruments to be discarded. Designers and flying men came into conflict over this point. The latter wanted their ships to be as fully equipped as possible, and for every conceivable instrument to be fitted. The designer, seeing the urgent necessity of economising weight, strove for simplification and wished to dispense with everything that was not absolutely necessary to war flying. Thus it often happened that some new instrument deemed necessary by the authorities could only be fitted after sacrificing some existing appliance. By patient work and forethought the weight of the airship was reduced in this manner. For example, the net lift of the 2,000,000 c.f, type was increased from 28 tons when equipped with six engines, to 38 tons with only five engines.

Wind resistance was another problem which required concentrated attention, for upon its reduction depended greatly increased speeds for the same engine power. At the beginning of the war the value, of this science was but little appreciated. The expert naval ship designers to whom from long experience of the lines best suited to ships' hulls, the necessity of stream-lining was already obvious, found in this science a wide field for research. With the assistance of the airship builders they produced a shape of envelope that gave the maximum efficiency; uninterrupted lines and sharp-pointed ends, particularly to the stern, served to reduce wind resistance very considerably. Every possible cause of wind resistance was discarded unless quite indispensable. The open type of gondola, which was not even comfortable to the inmates, soon disappeared: the closed gondola, which at first was angular and awkward in shape, was carefully streamlined to follow the natural flow of the surrounding air. Direct-driven propellers superseded the early complicated system of rods and stays. Even the ladders to the gondolas were made so as to fold up and thereby present less surface to the wind.

By treating the outer envelope of the airship with 'dope' not only was the surface friction and wind resistance decreased but also the troublesome absorption of moisture was put a stop to. Even the antenna of the wireless apparatus were fitted with a view to avoiding wind resistance: in brief, every detail of the ship was taken into consideration and improved.

Although these improvements were fraught with good results, they did not suffice to meet the requirements of war conditions, which grew more and more severe as time went on. It became necessary to build ships larger and larger, for only thereby was it possible to increase speed and lift simultaneously. At the front, ships of the L. 10 class with a capacity of about 1,130,000 c.f. had proved very serviceable. They were easy to handle on the ground, and could even be taken in and out of their sheds with a cross wind blowing without much danger. This operation, in spite of specially designed mechanical appliances, was most hazardous in the case of large ships. Unfortunately there was also a serious shortage of revolving sheds. Before the war the Navy had foreseen that airships would be useless without suitable housing, and therefore built the revolving sheds at Nordholz, but even these proved too small for the gigantic ships that were designed later.

Although airship designers ever and again urged the necessity of providing revolving sheds for the further development of airships, the Admiralty took no steps in the matter, for they did not imagine that the

'Tauibo' (A-type). 100 H.P. Argus 'reconnaissance' machine.

war would last so long, and considered that, as it took at least two years to build a revolving shed, they would not be finished in time. The Army authorities began building a few sheds, but they were never completed, for airships were abandoned in the spring of 1917, principally on account of the amazing development of aeroplanes.

This lack of sheds was a serious drawback to the naval airship service. It frequently happened that on account of cross winds the ships were unable to leave their sheds on those very occasions when they were required to take part in some important naval operations. As a result of this, certain military authorities grew to doubt the efficiency of airships because they did not understand the real cause of the trouble, and wrongly attributed it to the ship itself.

The Navy, at any rate, made an effort to overcome the shed difficulty, and constructed aerodromes at various places in which the sheds faced different directions, in order that at least the ship whose shed faced the direction of the prevailing wind would be able to take the air.

However, in spite of the lack of airship sheds, the improvements in types and increase in size proceeded apace. War conditions necessitated an ever increasing standard of efficiency, and there was no means of attaining this except by building larger ships. The only alternative would have been to abandon airships altogether. The size of the ship grew first to 2,000,000 c.f., then to 2,400,000 c.f. With that displacement, even allowing for a fairly high turn of speed, it would have been possible to reach a height of 26,000 feet if hard pressed by hostile aeroplanes. This particular ship was however never constructed.

It is not the object of this book to give a detailed description of how a big modern airship is built; I must be content merely to touch on such an interesting and important subject. My description therefore will be limited to the essentials of rigid and non-rigid airship construction.

The chief problem presented by the rigid type is the combination of strength and lightness in the framework. On one hand there is the lifting power of the gas, and on the other the weight of the framework itself and all the other additional weights, such as gondolas, bombs, ballast, petrol, etc. Both of these opposing forces must be distributed as evenly as possible along the entire length of the ship in order to ensure equilibrium. This point must always be kept in mind, not only while the ship is being built, but also when it is in flight. It might be just as dangerous for all the bombs or ballast to be released from one point as it is for two adjacent gas compartments to lose their gas. (In the one case there is a force acting upwards on the point from which the weight was dropped; in the latter a force acting downwards at the point from which the gas was lost.) The outer hull of the ship consists of main systems of girders 11 yards apart, arranged round the angles of a polygon and braced by cables in order to keep them rigid transversely. These polygonal rings are linked at every corner by longitudinal tie-girders which run the whole length of the hull. Between the main girder rings there is a series of auxiliary rings, 5½ yards apart, whose function is to brace the longitudinal tie-girders. Both rings and tie-girders are braced together by diagonal cables to prevent any shifting. Along the middle of the ship is the main central girder, which passes through the gas compartments and is connected to each ring by trestles. In the event of one gas compartment losing gas this girder prevents the adjacent compartments from being forced through the bracing cables of the rings on either aide, by the difference in pressure. If the compartments were thus forced against the bracing cables they would tend to draw the ring inwards, and would severely strain its girders. The quadrilaterals formed by the girders of the rings and the longitudinal tie-girders are also braced in order to withstand the great pressure of the gas within the compartments.

Along the whole length of the bottom of the ship is a gangway carried on triangular trestles, which serves as a means of communication from one point to another. Placed along this gangway are the fittings and controls such as the gas cylinders, rudder, control cables, bomb releases, telegraph and telephone wires, electric lighting system, speaking tubes, tanks for petrol and oil, the water ballast containers, each one of 1 ton capacity, etc. The ship is so constructed that all these weights are principally carried by the main rings, as are also the gondolas. This gangway is further supported by cables passing obliquely upwards through the gas compartments and attached at the top to the main rings. In the neighbourhood of the pilot's gondola there is a vertical passage communicating with a platform on top of the ship on which several machine guns are fitted. This platform also serves as a point from which astronomical observations can be carried out. The envelope consists of linen, strong but light, which is stretched tightly against the framework in order to offer as little resistance as possible to the wind. The gas compartments lie in the spaces between the main rings, and in the modern types have a capacity of about 210,000 c.f..

The safety valves, which used to allow the gas to escape into the central gangway itself, are fitted on to the top deck of the ship; they open directly into the air, and are connected with the compartments by a shaft passing between the walls of each compartment. This system was not originally used on the Zeppelin, but the gas used to be allowed to escape into the space between the compartments and the outer envelope, through which it gradually filtered. The dangerously explosive mixture produced by mingling hydrogen and air was thus rendered harmless through its rarefaction on escaping from the ship. The disadvantage of this arrangement, however, lay in the fact that the leaking compartment was enveloped in an explosive oxyhydrogen mixture lying between it and the outer hull of the ship.

When the practice of treating the outer envelope with 'dope' was adopted, this system of valving had to be discarded, for the 'dope' rendered the linen of the envelope impermeable to gas. The plan of fitting shafts leading to the top deck was therefore copied from the

Schütte-Lanz. Even this system had its drawbacks, for it frequently happened that an explosive mixture was formed outside the ship which took some time to become diffused and harmless. Neither of the two methods therefore was an ideal means of valving gas.

Trouble was caused by the safety valves themselves becoming coated with ice when they were opened in the cold, moist atmosphere of high altitudes over the sea, consequently it became impossible to close them again sufficiently to prevent leakage of gas. This difficulty was never really overcome. It is true that quite useful special devices were fitted, but even then it was necessary to watch very carefully for the formation of ice, and to remove it in order to be certain that the valves closed properly. For this reason the valves on the top deck were made accessible, so that if necessary they could be closed by hand. These valves were necessary in order to discharge gas before landing, when, on account of too great lift - strange as it may seem to the layman - it was not possible to bring the ship back to earth by any other means.

This question of the gas compartment was, and still is, one of the moat difficult in the science of airship construction. The compartment must be as light as possible, impermeable to gas, and unaffected by moisture. Before the war, compartments were made either of one or two layers of rubber, or else of seven thicknesses of gold-beater's skin. The rubber compartments were unsuitable on account of their weight and their electrical properties. Pure gold-beater's skin could not be used owing to an insufficiency of the raw material. Besides, it had the additional disadvantage of being very easily rent when once even a small hole had made its appearance. It therefore became necessary to make compartments of fabric, the so-called 'fabric' consisting of one layer of linen and several layers of gold-beater's skin, superimposed and glued together. Finally linen and a light kind of silk were used in conjunction, when once it had been established that silk possessed no dangerous electrical properties.

All varieties of compartments had the same disadvantage, namely their tendency to absorb moisture, for the latter made them heavy and thus burdened the ship unnecessarily. Furthermore the gas inside the compartments became saturated and lost some of its buoyancy. It is to be hoped that in the future, when raw material of good quality is again obtainable, these difficulties will be removed.

The compartments were manufactured by the 'Ballonhüllen-Gesellschaft', one of the branches of the Zeppelin works, and by the Balloon Fabric Co., Riedinger-Augsburg.

Another serious problem closely connected with airships is the question of the supply of gas. During the war, when efficiency rather than economy was the main consideration, it was impossible to economise in gas. After every raid or patrol the compartments were refilled with pure gas; but in the future, when airships are used for peaceful purposes, this practice of replenishing the gas will be a serious matter. Out of regard for running expenses there cannot be an unlimited consumption of gas. An attempt will therefore have to be made to keep the ships with compartments not completely filled when in their sheds, and to prevent the diffusion of gas through the walls of the compartments, as such diffusion causes deterioration of the gas. This affords much material for further research and ingenuity. The question of raw materials during the war also seriously affected the construction of the outer envelope. In peace time a Zeppelin hull was made of an alloy of zinc and aluminium. As tho ships increased in size that substance proved not to be strong enough, and so 'duralumin' was employed. The great strength of 'duralumin' made it possible to attempt constructions for which any other substance would have been quite inadequate. It was also obvious that only the finest quality of material could be used in the manufacture of other parts such as bracing wires, nuts, bolts, pins, etc.

With regard to the building of the 'Schütte-Lanz' type, where girders are made of wood, another difficulty was encountered. Naval ships of this type used to absorb moisture from the sea air; the wood, therefore, became heavy and lost its strength. Various adhesive substances used in the construction were also affected. This inconvenience was obviated by a new and ingenious method whereby the wood was smoked, treated with resin, and saturated with a special preparation. In spite of this, wood was discarded as material for constructing the new and large-sized airships,

Junker-Fokker CL I, all-metal machine. Exceptionally good field of fire. No external bracing.

and thin 'duralumin' plates were used exclusively. Although difficult to produce and work with, weight for weight: the latter substance is twice as strong as wood. A consideration concerning airship design which was placed above all others, was the necessity of removing everything which could possibly kindle sparks as far away from the gas as possible.

Everything of this description had to be enclosed in the gondolas, while they in turn were suspended far enough from the hull to ensure free passage to the wind, for the draught caused by travelling through the air was a valuable safeguard in itself. Between the hull and gondolas there was no connection whatever through which gas or inflammable vapour might be conducted to the engines.

Naval designs departed from this practice, and in the semi-rigid M type the gondolas were mounted inside the hull along the central gangway. Eventually every airship was provided with the same number and arrangement of gondolas; two gondolas, each equipped with one or more engines, were suspended underneath the ship fore and aft, the former also being used as an under-carriage for landing.

A further two gondolas were carried, each containing an engine, one on each side of the ship. The position of these gondolas was calculated so that they never came into contact with the ground on landing.

There was, however, a difference between the Schütte-Lanz and the Zeppelin in that the former had a special gondola for the pilot built aft close up under the hull of the ship, whereas the Zeppelin was piloted from the foremost engine gondola. In the latest designs the former system was exclusively adopted for the reason that, with the ever increasing difficulty of handling large ships, especial care had to be taken to protect the vital parts such as the engines, because it was found that the gondola which had to take the shock of landing was very easily damaged. It is true that such gondolas were protected by mats and skids; frequently enough, however, these were not sufficient to prevent damage when a bad landing was made, through clumsiness on the part of the pilot, bad weather, or some other cause. In order to prevent the framework of the ship also from being damaged by a bad landing, the bottom gondolas were attached to the ship by struts of such a nature that they would only stand a certain strain and broke if subjected to a force in excess of that strain. Landing a ship in heavy weather, or taking it in and out of its shed when a cross wind is blowing, is a most difficult operation to effect without causing any damage. The bigger the ship the more dangerous it becomes, for the gondolas, under such conditions, are not sufficient to hold it by. On those occasions, therefore, a species of frame is used which grips the gangway tightly, and is detached when not in use. There was very little difference between the engines used on airships and those that were fitted to aeroplanes, only in the case of airship engines a longer life was desirable as they had to be depended on for longer spells of running. Reliability was therefore of more importance than great power. In order to look after these properly, they were enclosed in gondolas of sufficient size to hold the mechanics as well. Some of the critics complain of the fact that types other than the Meybach engine were never used. Those people forget that during the war there were not limitless industrial facilities, and that it was necessary for one factory to specialise in the design of airship engines, for other factories were too overburdened with work to undertake their study and development. It is true that from time to time difficulties were encountered, but that was only to be expected in so new a branch of engineering, and one can truthfully record that all defects were eventually removed. The power of these engines increased from 210 to 240 and 260 H.P., while eventually they were all designed to develop their full power only at high altitudes. Great improvements were also made in the construction of propellers.

The problem of driving one propeller off two engines was solved, and an attempt was made to fashion the blades so that the pitch could be varied. Each engine gondola was a self-contained power unit which could work independently. Petrol was carried in tanks situated on the central gangway as nearly as possible vertically over the engine they were intended to feed. Because of the necessity of economising weight the tanks themselves were made of thin aluminium plates, and could be dropped from the ship in case of emergency. In the pilot's gondola a cockpit was reserved for the wireless telegraph apparatus. A very simple form of wireless aerial could be lot out from the gondola by means of a cranked drum.

An airship on active service is useless without wireless, and therefore, because it was so vitally important that the wireless should be absolutely reliable, the most elaborate precautions were taken in the shape of auxiliary dynamos, etc. Several different engines could be used as a source of electrical power, and, in addition, various electrical machines and accumulators were carried. Should the engines fail, the necessary power could be obtained from a propeller driven by the wind. For various military reasons the 'damped' system of transmission was used. Telegraphic direction-finding enabled the ship to discover its whereabouts at any time, and was independent of drift. The land direction-finding stations, and the system of calling up two home stations in order to obtain the position of the ship by triangulation, suffered from a great disadvantage in that the enemy could also pick up messages or interfere with the signals. Thereafter, instead of the signals being transmitted by the ship, they were only received and the signals were despatched from stations on the earth. In addition to the wireless, the pilot's gondola was fitted with controls and various instruments to enable the commander to navigate and direct his ship. These included a telegraphic system to the other gondolas, microphones, speaking tubes, instruments for navigation such as the compass and an arc for measuring the angle with the horizontal; the variometer for measuring the rate of ascent or descent, an electric thermometer to register the temperature of the gas; ballast controls, electric controls, searchlights for night landings, lamps for signalling, the oxygen apparatus for high altitudes, etc. Furthermore, in order that the instruments could be used at night when any display of light would betray the ship's whereabouts, all the dials and pointers of these instruments were rendered self-luminous. In the matter of these details both rigid and non-rigid airships were identical.

The distinctive feature of the non-rigid type is the envelope, whose form is not supported by any internal framework but is preserved entirely by the pressure of the gas inside acting directly against the rubber skin. The engine gondolas were fitted with mechanical pumps, whose function it was to supplement the internal pressure by forcing gas into the ballonets. The ship was divided into various partitions by sheets of material permeable to gas, which were set obliquely along its length. Whenever any part of the ship was damaged or tended to become deflated, it was possible to preserve its shape by pumping ay: directly into the gas chambers.

An ingenious arrangement of springs inside the upper part of the envelope automatically closed any small holes such as might be caused by bullets. The pressure in the gas chambers and ballonets was automatically regulated so as to be correct under all conditions. An auxiliary regulator, operated by hand, was also fitted. Weight was distributed over the entire ship by a system of cables, in such a manner that it was borne by the envelope itself without undue pressure at any specific point. A semi-rigidly constructed gangway was suspended immediately beneath the envelope and carried the petrol tanks, bombs, water ballast, etc., as well as the engines and controls. Outside this gangway were the two big pipes, one on each side of the ship, which connected the ballonets with the automatic gas regulator. An extraordinarily difficult piece of work was necessitated by the fact that the outer envelope and the internal partitions had to be made from one piece of material The Balloon Fabric Co. at Augsburg undertook this work with unqualified success. The outstanding qualities of the non-rigid type, namely lightness and economy in the matter of gas, together with the remarkable improvements effected during the war, have given

Fokker Dr 1. Single-seater fighting scout. Triplane, with rotary engine. No external bracing wires.

rise to the hope that the non-rigid as well as the rigid airship will prove to be of great use in the future.

Along with the development of the airship itself there appeared a host of other problems which had to be solved. It was not only necessary to build airships in large numbers but also to supply them with the substances they required, especially gas, in sufficiently large quantities.

Before the war the military authorities had distributed their aerodromes along the frontiers, and had provided each with a small gas plant and the necessary appliances. During the war they built a few new aerodromes of a similar description in addition to some in the more remote theatres of war, in Ghent, Brussels, Warsaw, Russia, Bulgaria, and in other places. The sheds were constructed of canvas and were easily transportable, as were also the gas plants.

In peace time the Navy only possessed the aerodrome at Nordholz, which, however, was of the most modern description, A revolving shed for two ships made it possible for the ships to take the air in any wind, even during bad weather. In the course of the war, when it became necessary to provide sheds for a large number of ships, the question arose as to whether the Army practice of building only one shed to each aerodrome should be followed, or whether several sheds should be grouped together at one place.

On account of the numbers of men it was necessary to station at each aerodrome, the latter plan was adopted by the Navy, and rows of sheds were set up at Nordholz, Hage, Namur, Tonderan, Ahlhorn, Seddin, and Seerappen.

The great drawback to the double shed was the possibility of losing two ships simultaneously in case of fire. Even building sheds close together was (inadvisable, for at Ahlhorn it once happened that an explosion in one shed destroyed several others together with the ships they contained.

The sheds had to be of the most up-to-date design, with mechanical aids for taking the ships in and out, methods of suspending deflated or damaged ships, gas apparatus, and so forth. Unfortunately revolving sheds were not built during the war. The only existing shed of that type, which was at Nordholz, was lengthened in order that it might house the bigger type of airship. Even then it was not large enough for the latest types, but a further lengthening was not possible.

Stores, repair shops, and other buildings were situated alongside the sheds, while the quarters for the men were always close by. Telegraph and meteorological stations, beacon fires, and an observation balloon to mark the aerodrome when it was obscured by clouds, together with every safeguarding device that human ingenuity could produce, were part of the equipment of every aerodrome.

As the war progressed the question of the gas supply to airships became of paramount importance. The demand for gas was ever increasing with the number of ships and the great heights at which they worked. Every ship on landing had to be refilled with gas and made ready for another flight as quickly as possible. Naval airships alone, for example, required 5,650,000 c.f. of gas daily. This vast amount was supplied mainly by private firms who set up quantities of new plant and greatly increased their output. In the case of those stations where the existing plant produced an insufficient quantity to satisfy the daily demand, gas was supplied by rail on trucks specially designed for the purpose.

In the early stages of the war the insufficient and poor quality of gas was the cause of much trouble and many accidents. These difficulties, however, like all others, were overcome by indefatigable labour and research.

Little can be said concerning the recent development of airships among our enemies, as we do not possess the necessary information, England, more than any other country, recognised the value of the airship as a weapon of offence and for coastal and ocean patrols. She therefore undertook the further development of the airship with the greatest energy, and produced a large number of ships of different types, principally non-rigid, A type of small ship which appeared to be very useful, incorporated the design of both airship and aeroplane, for it consisted of an aeroplane fuselage and engine suspended from a non-rigid envelope. Also the rigid type, which has been unsuccessfully employed since the war, was built by several English firms who used as models the German airships which were brought down. As far as one knows at present the modern English rigid airship is an exact copy of the German.

Little is known of American airship design. There have been rumours of a small rigid type of special construction and that larger ships were to be built on the same lines. No details, however, have reached us yet.

Non-rigid ships are supposed to have been used by Prance in the early stages of the war for both observation patrols and for raids. It is also claimed that, like England, she has constructed a large number of non-rigid ships for similar work.

Although, on account of the meagre information at our disposal, it is difficult to arrive at an estimate concerning the airship designs of our enemies, it seems certain that Germany still leads, and it is to be hoped that she will continue to do so in the future.

(ENGBERDING.)

CHAPTER III
ARMY AEROPLANES

I T IS MORE than doubtful if the aeroplane would ever have attained such importance as a means of attack and a decisive factor in warfare if the Great War had continued as an open campaign, and consequently ended in a short time.

We took the field in 1914 with a 'reconnaissance machine' fitted with a 100 H.P. engine. This machine could remain in the air for four or five hours, its 'ceiling,' when fully laden, was about 5000 feet, and its speed from 55 to 60 M.P.H. On the Western Front in the autumn of that year we brought out a biplane L.V.G., which had a somewhat better lift, but was particularly distinguished iu that it could climb and travel faster. Unarmed, without wireless apparatus, and with the observer's seat in front, this machine during the first few months of war did good and useful service, principally reconnaissance and artillery observation. However, as the war on the ground concentrated more into trenches, and the struggle became stationary with a closed system of opposing lines, this type proved to be unsuitable under the changed conditions. The incessant elaboration and development of the tactics and science of trench warfare called so urgently for rapid production of efficient aeroplanes that one might truthfully say that trench warfare was the mother of the modern flying machine.

As early as the winter of 1914 these new forces were themselves felt, and their influence was shown in the development of aeroplane design. Engine power increased from 100 to 120, 150, 160, 200, to 220 H.P., while pilot and observer changed place. The multiplication and improvement of stationary aircraft batteries forced machines to fly at a height of 7000 or 8000 feet instead of the original height of 2500 to 4000 feet, for the latter height was not even safe against rifle or machine-gun fire. The ever increasing difficulty of observing the enemy's positions and materiel, with the ever changing details all concentrated along one tip of land, was considerably increased when machines were compelled to fly higher. Yet it was of the greatest importance that these observations should be made, and this necessity called for the assistance of cameras, which rapidly developed in efficiency, size and weight. Again, the rocket pistol was in-accurate in directing the fire of our artillery with speed and accuracy, so it was superseded by wireless telegraphy. The increasing number of targets suitable for bombing, and their improved resistance to our explosives, necessitated heavier projectiles and increased the desirability of carrying several bombs, when machine guns were mounted, principally as a means of defence, it became necessary to add a considerable quantity of ammunition. Such heavy loads could only be carried by the more powerful craft in which the only position which gave the observer the unrestricted view required for artillery observation and photography, as well as a good field of fire for his machine gun, was behind the pilot. It must be remembered that the observer's gun was movable and fitted to a swing mounting. For the purpose of providing a good field of fire, for rapidity in assembling the machine, and in order to make it possible to attach new planes without difficulty, it became necessary to simplify and to diminish the number of struts and bracing-wires between the wings. Development next led to a further increase in engine power which rose to 260 and 300 H.P., while the observation and reconnaissance machines, which were so constantly menaced by hostile scouts, were provided with a second machine gun. In the case of reconnaissance patrols far over the lines, for example, our machines could only break through the enemy's defences at a high altitude (19,000 to 22,000 feet), and similarly the photographic machines, when engaged on the construction of photographic maps, could only carry out their work and escape by being faster than their pursuers. All this was the direct result of trench warfare.

The continual contraction and concentration of the actual fighting zone, and the increasing number of aeroplanes employed by both sides, brought about a kind of open warfare in the air, and the original type of machine, the reason for whose existence was purely strategic, found itself incessantly compelled to engage in aerial combats. In fact it became necessary to fight in order to accomplish any work at all, for not only did our machines have to overcome a strong resistance whenever they crossed the lines, but it was also imperative that hostile reconnaissance, bombing, and artillery observation machines should be chased off our territory. Consequently it became necessary to evolve a type of machine specially designed for fighting, and aerial fighting was ever demanding a higher standard of performance, even higher than that which was required of the 'working aeroplanes.' In order to be a match for the excellent French and British fighting machines, we had to build aeroplanes to climb higher and more rapidly, aeroplanes that were extremely fast, quick on the controls, and quick in their manoeuvres so as to make immediate use of an opponent's error or weakness in these lightning duels in the air.

In the spring of 1915 it became clear that the original standard type, in spite of all improvements, would have to be replaced by types designed for special purposes, since it could not satisfy the new requirements of war, which demanded, among other things, a much greater radius of action. Furthermore, the old type could never have carried 1000 or 2500 lbs. of bombs or undertaken raids on the enemy's dumps and camps behind the lines; nor could it have attacked the ports on the coast of England and France, or penetrated into the heart of England to bomb her industrial centres and shipbuilding yards. In short, the standard type, designed for general purposes, became obsolete.

Trench warfare itself brought into existence a specialised type of machine, the 'contact machines', which frequently flew at a height of only 30 or 40 feet. Heavy armour was required to protect the engine, tanks, pilot, and observer from the withering rifle and machine-gun fire to which they were subjected, and this armour could only be carried at the expense of climbing power, flight duration, and quickness of movement. On the other hand, the two-seater fighting machines which attacked infantry directly with machine guns, bombs, and hand grenades, had to be as fast as possible and very quick on the controls. For that reason this type was only lightly armoured or else carried no armour at all. All these many considerations laid emphasis on the desirability of specialising types according to the work they had to carry out. Speed, rapidity of climb, and quickness of manoeuvre could never be combined with capacity for carrying heavy loads and flight duration. As I have said, the result was the production of many types, each one designed for a special purpose. Therefore in the course of time aerial operations became classified into four main categories:-

    a.   Reconnaissance and observation.
    b.   Attacks on the infantry and other work connected with fighting on the ground.
    c.   Aerial combats.
    d.   Bombing.

The German aircraft and aero-engine industries never failed to fulfil the wishes of the fighting forces, and kept them constantly supplied with the most modern and specialised machines. This achievement is all the more remarkable because of the lack of material at home and other industrial difficulties, particularly from tho spring of 1917 onwards, when the Allied forces had the advantage over us in these respects.

Forty-seven thousand six hundred and thirty-seven aeroplanes were taken over from the factories by the Air Force between August 1914 and the end of December 1913. Approximately 150 different types (excluding experimental machines) were designed during that period. At the end of the war 35 firms were engaged in aircraft construction in stead of the 12 which undertook it when war broke out; in addition to these factories there were 90 parks for the assembling and repair of aeroplanes. To sum up briefly the line along which the design of aeroplanes developed, one might say that progress was made towards two diametrically opposite goals; on the one hand, design endeavoured to produce machines of incredible size and power; on the other, to produce machines so small that they were almost like toys.

(NEUMANN.)

Types Used for Photography, Artillery Observation, Long-Distance Reconnaissance, & Contact Patrols

From the spring of 1915 onwards the C-type aeroplane with a 160 H.P. engine was used for reconnaissance, observation, and similar work. A machine gun on a swing mounting was provided for the observer, and during the summer of 1915 a wireless receiving set was fitted. Although serviceable, and fitted with machine guns, it can bear no comparison with the later fighting and bombing machines. At the beginning of the long series of C-type machines was the first German 'battle-plane,' which made its appearance at the front in the spring of 1915, In addition to excellent flying qualities, this machine was easy to take off and land. The French monoplane of that period, armed with a fixed machine gun, was helpless against the C type except in the improbable event of its being able to attack from behind, or more particularly from underneath the tail.

Small differences between the machines destined for different branches of reconnaissance and observation work soon appeared and gradually led to subdivisions of the C type.

The old normal C type, however, with a 200 or 220 H.P. engine, was still used for short-range photography and artillery observation. It was sufficiently fast, easy to control, and stable. The observer's field of view was excellent, and the machine could be flown in bad weather for a considerable time without involving any undue strain on the pilot. For artillery observation the observer's cockpit was altered and improved with a view to convenience in handling the wireless.

An airman engaged on artillery observation should not have to depend on wireless alone, but must be provided with several auxiliary means of communication. The observer's seat should allow sufficient room for movement in order that every region of the sky and earth can be watched, and so that the machine gun can be swung freely and without constraint. All the following instruments had to be fitted into the narrow space of a cockpit: wireless transmitting and receiving set, amplifier, etc.; a drum for winding 40 yards of wire aerial in or out; a Morse key, ammeter, electric flash lamp, various cartridges for coloured lights, smoke signals, etc., the whole outfit weighing about 220 lbs. Everything carried in the aeroplane had to be conveniently placed and easily accessible, since a disorderly arrangement would detract greatly from the efficiency of the most skilled observer.

In addition to these means of communication every observer's cockpit was provided with a board for his maps, a stop watch, a writing pad, coloured pencils, etc. Electrical power for the wireless apparatus was provided by a dynamo, either driven direct from the engine or else mounted on a bracket and operated by the force of wind causing a small propeller to revolve.

The weight of the wireless installation and other appliances, together with the increasing size of the cameras that were employed, made it necessary to increase the engine power to 200 and 220 H.P. and to effect various improvements in the construction of the machine itself.

LONG-DISTANCE RECONNAISSANCE MACHINES

As has already been pointed out, the progress of the war made it more and more necessary to build fast machines capable of reaching high altitudes, where they could break through the enemy's aerial defences to reconnoitre and photograph the areas far behind their lines.

When the original low-powered C type was found unsuitable for this work, 260 H.P. engines were installed, and a special photographic machine was designed. The twin-engined G type, which was already projected in 1915, was peculiarly suited to this work, and was, in fact, employed with very satisfactory results after it had been considerably lightened and improved in various ways.

Machines for contact patrol and other work associated with the infantry came more and more into use, and for this purpose the C type also was originally used. In 1917, however, on account of the very heavy losses inflicted by fire from the ground, the machine had to be extensively altered, although the main design was still adhered to. The forward part of the fuselage encased the occupants, engine, and tanks in strong armour-plating of chrome nickel steel. An entirely new departure in aeroplane construction in 1917 produced a most interesting type, the Junker-Fokker, which was entirely built of duralumin and had a monoplane wing with internal bracing. The wings of this machine were remarkable for their exceptionally thick camber.

The necessarily high ratio between speed and wind resistance, a factor that causes much trouble to designers, was hero reduced to a minimum, for the abnormal thickness of the planes prevented the formation of those eddies in the air which give rise to 'drag,' while their lift was quite as efficient as other wing constructions with their complicated systems of struts and bracing wires.

The all-metal construction was a great protection against fire, and the armour plating, which consisted of one-fifth inch chrome nickel steel, was impenetrable at the closest range. This armour also completely encased the engine.

(NEUMANN.)

'TRENCH-STRAFING' MACHINES

With the growing practice of harassing the infantry by low-flying aeroplanes, there arose the necessity of developing the 0 type especially for this purpose. It was equally important that a machine designed with this object should be fully equipped with offensive weapons such as machine guns, bombs, etc, and also exceedingly fast and quick on the controls. As a consequence, climbing power and flight duration had to be sacrificed. At first armoured machines with quick-firing guns were experimented with, but they were abandoned later in favour of the new CL type, which was a lighter variety of the C type. The CL machine, on account of its speed, could attack and escape quickly, and it was also more suitable for aerial fighting.

Albatross G 3. Twin-engined bombing machine. Crew consisted of rear gunner, pilot, and observer; pilot's seat in center.

The Hannoveraner and the Halberstadt were among those specially designed to answer this purpose. The former did not survive so long as the Halberstadt because it was not so light on the controls, and because a considerable area of ground was invisible to the observer on account of the excessively wide fuselage.

The Halberstadt CL 4 and the Hannoveraner CL 5 were built on lines very similar to the D-type single-seater fighter.

An all-metal machine, the Junker-Fokker CL 1, was an exceedingly fast monoplane two-seater whose planes were unsupported by any external bracing wires. One advantage of the all-metal construction was the fact that there was no tendency for the wings to tear when punctured by bullets; also, the additional protection afforded to the vital parts and the occupants rendered the machine almost secure from attack.

The duties of contact machines necessitated a heavy armament. Two fixed machine guns were therefore mounted in the pilot's cockpit, both synchronised to fire through the propeller. The observer was armed with the usual Parabellum machine gun on a swivel mounting. In spite of the lightness of the CL type they were able to carry a considerable load of bombs and ammunition. As a rule, in 1916, they carried four or five 22 lbs. torpedo-shaped, high-explosive bombs, and of course the special 'trench-strafing' bombs, which were fitted with exceptionally sensitive detonators. These bombs would explode when dropped from a very low altitude, whereas the former required a fall of at least

1500 feet before they would detonate. Ten or twenty high-explosive grenades were also carried, usually suspended from a wire cage which was provided with a simple form of bomb sight. Another variety, which was, however, exceedingly unpopular, was the 'Flying-Mouse.' These little bombs, only 4 or 5 inches long, "were slung on to rods attached to the machine. As soon as one had been removed from its rods it was 'live' and had to be thrown overboard immediately. Their detonators were very sensitive, and the bombs were therefore dangerous to handle. Four rods, each bearing about six bombs, could be mounted on one machine.

The formation and squadron leaders also carried a wireless installation for the purpose of transmitting any important information they might acquire, or for registering our artillery on some moving target.

SCOUTS

Like the reconnaissance, artillery, and 'trench-strafing' machines, the fighting scout was also evolved from the original C type. It is true that all scouts bore a resemblance to each other and had developed distinctive features in the matter of general construction, engine power, and performance in the air. All the same, neither in outward appearance nor yet in the essentials of their design, did they depart much from the old B type, the ancestor of the C family. The fighting machine set out to select from the conflicting qualities of an aeroplane, such as lift and speed stability and quickness of manoeuvre, those qualities most suitable for the purpose of fighting in the air; and the scout, therefore, was built for speed, rapidity of climb, quick movement, and great strength of construction. Machines whose common daily task consisted of diving, rolling, looping, and performing aerial evolutions that are not even possible to birds, must be sound in every detail. In comparison to these acrobatics, the ability to carry a heavy load was unimportant, consequently it became the custom for scouts to be single-seaters. The original Fokker monoplane, with its planes braced by cables and its fixed guns synchronised by the engine to fire through the propeller, gave way to the biplane and triplane types. These last two types were entirely free of external bracing wires. Finally another Fokker monoplane was designed with the internally braced wing construction which had proved so excellent on the Junker-Fokker.

A stationary engine was installed in the biplane type, while rotary engines were fitted to the triplane and monoplane. All types were armed with two fixed machine guns firing through the propeller off a synchronising gear driven by the engine. The decrease in external measurements and the consequent diminution of wind resistance, when combined with a corresponding increase in engine power, yielded great speed and rapidity of climb.

Careful construction secured the necessary agility. Whenever any particular quality was desired, the model was altered. For example, at the request of the military authorities, the camber on the planes of the Siemens D 3 was slightly lowered, with the result that the speed of the machine increased to over 90 M.P.H. and the climbing power diminished, although the wing span and engine remained unchanged.

(NEUMANN.)

BOMBING MACHINES

The vast accumulations of war material of every description, the concentration of troops into camps, the railway stations and harbours with their multitudes of laden trucks and ships, all constituted excellent objectives for bombing expeditions. Open warfare would never have permitted these conditions to exist, and therefore it is to trench warfare that the development of the bombing aeroplane must be attributed.

When it became possible to hit objects from a great height on account of the greatly improved bomb sights, much larger areas could be destroyed. It was found, therefore, that even when raids were carried out by several squadrons together, the light 20 or 40 lb. bombs did not effect as much damage as might have been possible.

An early seaplane: Friedrichshafen type with central float. Note the numerous bracing wires.

When attempts were made to bomb the coasts of France and the interior of England, the C type of aeroplane proved quite ineffectual because it was not able to carry bombs and the quantity of petrol necessary for such long flights. Furthermore, the enemies' defences were proof against all but the heaviest projectiles. Consequently, like scouts, special types were evolved from the original model, only with this difference, that the former strained after speed, height, and agility, whereas the bombing machine was designed for carrying heavy loads, for stability and capacity.

The fighting machines tended to become ever smaller, while the bombers increased in size and grew into twin-engined machines, of which the earlier types were mostly constructed with an open fuselage, and were fitted with engines of 150 H.P. The engine power was increased later to 260 H.P..

With this power the speed of the machine was about 95 M.P.H., and its net lift approximately 45,000 lbs. A strong armament consisting of about four machine guns could therefore be carried, and the crew included two gunners in addition to the pilot and observer. A powerful long-range wireless set was invariably provided, and experiments were made with a 2-inch quick-firing gun. Bombs of 110, 220, and 660 lbs, in weight were carried on racks under the wings, and an individual G-type aeroplane could even labour along with the concentrated weight of a 2200 lb bomb, the heaviest that was ever used in the war.

Night-Bombing Machines

The N type, or family of night-bombers, first appeared as a compromise between the original C type and the G or day-bombing machines. The abnormal camber of the wings enabled the machine to carry exceedingly heavy bombs for short distances, and also made it possible to take off and land in a small space, a most important consideration for night-flying machines.

Giant Aeroplanes

Before the war the project of building giant aeroplanes was seriously and carefully considered at the Zeppelin works and the Bosch factory in Stuttgart, but subsequently the idea was dropped. The idea was again put forward in 1915, and was realised in actual fact by the Gothaer Waggonfabrik, who constructed the first experimental Gotha-Ost. During the war sixty-four giant aeroplanes (R type), of twenty different designs, were built, six separate factories being engaged in the work. The first were used on active service in the summer of 1916, Of these about twenty have travelled over 3000 miles, and have dropped over 100 tons of bombs.

The first R had already been designed in 1912 by the Russian engineer Sikorsky, who was the first to risk attaching four engines to an aeroplane, and who moreover made a great advance by fashioning the forward part of the fuselage in the shape of an enclosed cabin to shelter all the occupants. Another machine was designed by him in 1915. This also was equipped with four engines, and was truly of gigantic size. Later, however, he adopted the twin-engined model.

The primitive Sikorsky machine was to a certain extent the precursor of the first German giant aeroplane, the experimental SSW R, which was built by the Siemens-Schuckertwerken in the winter of 1914. The many improvements and the increased strength of this experimental machine were obvious, and foreshadowed the growth of a merely big aeroplane into the modern giant aeroplane, but the twin-engine system was shown to be too weak and unreliable to carry the enormous weight of the new types.

In 1915, therefore, Siemens-Schuckert produced a machine in which the two engines at the side were supplemented by a third placed in the centre of the fuselage. This engine was linked up with both the two propellers at the sides.

Almost all subsequent R machines have followed the lines laid down by this first SSW R, only the engine power has gradually been increased to 1800 H.P. In fact, from that period the development has been principally concerned with the number of engines and the most efficient arrangement of the propellers.

(NEUMANN.)

A GENERAL REVIEW OF THE DEVELOPMENT OF THE MILITARY BRANCH OF THE AIR FORCE DURING THE WAR

A period of barely ten years is traversed by a curve representing the growth of our Air Force, from the inception to the culminating point of a mighty aerial power, a decisive factor in battle, and from that culminating point down again to Germany's collapse.

The word 'flying' has always been synonymous with fighting, first against prejudice, then against wind, weather, and the malice of inanimate matter, then for the laurels of records for height, speed, and duration: finally against a host of enemies. Our young Air Force seems to have been cursed almost throughout its whole Life by the spirit of bad luck, but here I shall confine myself to a rough sketch of the extent and force of that amazing development in the flying service which was occasioned by the wan The German Army took the field in 1914 with 49 flying units, including those on home defence. In the winter of 1918, 350 'Formationen' were demobilised, not including the 77 'Feldstäbe' which had not been on active service. At the beginning of the war there

A machine about to leave the seaplane carrier

were 15 reserve training centres: when the Armistice was signed there were 64. The aircraft and aero-engine factories were turning out 50 to 60 aeroplanes per month in the autumn of 1914, while in the autumn of 1918 over 2000 aeroplanes were built monthly. When war broke out the flying *personnel* at the front consisted of 550 men: at the end of the war a good 5500 were actually on active service, and a similar number was employed at home for training and other purposes.

The aeroplane in use at the beginning of the war might almost be compared to the archaeopterix of prehistoric days, or, to use a more modern simile, to a kind of flying wire entanglement. With their engines of 80 or 100 H.P. the machines at that time could only attain a speed of 60 or 70 M.P.H. Instead of the obsolete complicated system of bracing, we have nowadays the 'self-supporting,' or internally braced, wing. Wind resistance diminished as the lines of the aeroplane became more and more graceful. Engine power in the normal reconnaissance machines was increased threefold, and in the larger types fivefold. The total engine power of a modern giant aeroplane is over 1500 H.P. and the span of these machines more than 100 feet. Air speed increased to 90 or 100 M.P.H., and in certain highly specialised types rose to 130 M.P.H..

At the beginning of the campaign there was an incessant repetition of a certain catchword - 'Limited tactical height' - at which all aeroplanes were to carry out their work, I doubt if the inventor himself knew what exactly was meant by this phrase. Two thousand five hundred feet was selected as the magic height, and the aeroplane was then supposed to be protected from hostile fire of every description by some mysterious agency. The height limit, however, removed itself to 18,000 or 20,000 feet. The English bombers in particular, having dropped their bombs and being lighter by the amount of petrol they had consumed, used to return over the Channel at this height in order to avoid interference. The 'lone patrol' reconnaissance machines made a practice of flying at the same height in order to reach their objective unseen by the enemy.

But the understanding had also to be enlightened on the subject of height from a diametrically opposite standpoint. In a small pamphlet published in December 1912, I dared to throw doubt on the hallowed infallibility of 'limited tactical height,' and I pointed out that the infantryman's axiom 'get to close quarters, no matter what it costs,' applies equally well, under certain conditions, to the flying man. That made the aged armchair pilots wag their heads! It remained for the contact patrol and trench-strafing pilots to correct the error of the wise. An order given to an infantry observation machine, ascertain for certain whether white or coloured troops are in possession of Maisonette, will demonstrate the heights, or rather depths, at which machines had to fly, heedless of fire from the ground, in order to obtain such information.

A few words concerning the increase in reliability during the war. One thinks of the Prince Heinrich flight in 1914, in which all the best pilots and machines were represented. Forced landings and crashes at the landing stages defeated most of those expert airmen.

When on active service in the spring of 1915, the squadron attached to General Headquarters was ordered from Ostend to Metz. Twenty-nine machines left Ostend, and in the evening of the same day they had arrived at their new aerodrome and were ready to participate in the attack on Verdun. In those days it was not permitted to immortalise the story in an epic. 'The infantry march, and the flying man flies'! That was the only thought of the experts who had never been either in the trenches nor yet in a pilot's seat.

Although the armament of the aeroplane was totally inadequate at the time of mobilisation, the science rose later almost to perfection. In the spring of 1914 a vast quantity of literature appeared dealing with the possibility and practicability of carrying cavalry swords in aeroplanes. For our first flights in the face of the enemy they gave us automatic pistols fitted with shoulder pieces. Today it sounds as though I were speaking in a dead language when I recall that in August 1914 I flew over Belfort with a carbine as my only weapon. I had nailed a gramophone horn on to the stock, so that in the event of meeting an enemy, I might at least dismay and terrify him with its illusory caliber.

Later, rocket pistols and Mausers were brought into use. Yet as early as the summer of 1916, aerial combats were daily taking place in which many hundred machine guns were used on both aides. Even guns of a heavier calibre became part of the aeroplane's equipment.

The development of aerial photography followed similar lines. Focus increased from 25 cm, to 120 cm. The science developed from photographs, that resembled picture puzzles more than anything else, to stereoscopic clarity of the most minute details: from the crude, inaccurate confirmation of maps to the exact science of topographical surveying from the air; from the single exposures of the hand camera to the cinematographical series of many hundred exposures: from complete dependence on sunlight to the possibility of taking photographs by night.

The development of wireless telegraphy cannot be alluded to without calling to mind the difficulties that were put in the way of its application to the aeroplane. The enthusiasm, the daring, and the desire for experimenting were all provided by our young pioneers and the aircraft industry as early as 1910, But again our old friend, the querulous godmother of this Sleeping Beauty, bestirred herself and shook an admonitory finger, saying, 'Do you wish to add an electric chair to the present dangers of the aeroplane?' War rendered the pilot articulate by means of wireless telegraphy. In the full sense of the word it became a bridge linking sky to earth.

We flew into the war burdened with the somewhat ironical title of 'fair-weather warriors.' Soon, wind and rain, clouds and snow lost their terrors for us beneath the relentless pressure of war. Flying by night, that much derided practice, followed on the day, and the sole remaining insuperable obstacle to the aeroplane was ground mist, in much the same way as a quagmire renders cavalry attacks impossible. But the airman will eventually find a means of overcoming even ground mist, for whenever he has set out to accomplish a certain object he has invariably succeeded.

It is with pride that I now undertake the task of analysing the various human elements whose combination brought into existence our mighty Air Force. Most of the credit lies with those enterprising individuals among our young officers who took up flying, and to those few seniors who, though occupying responsible positions, concealed a subaltern's spirit beneath the uniform of a General Officer.

A far-seeing and daring industry served the flying man through thick and thin, in spite of all prophecies of disaster and the never-ending agitation of the pessimists. More is due to the Government and the Press - especially in respect of pre-war flying - than to many of the officials whose department was supposed to exist solely for the purpose of developing flying. I will, however, admit that now and then airmen subordinated practical design to a kind of nebulous fanaticism.

From the beginning of the war onwards we had to fight against superior odds. The markets of the world were open to our enemies, and the Allies could make use of the good weather of the Colonies during the entire winter for the training of their *personnel*. We could form no reserves, nor could we relieve any of our flying units by allowing them to rest periodically. Even darkness and the forces of nature, which at first automatically afforded the airman brief respites, quickly enough lost their power in this respect. In spite of all we stood up to our man. In November 1918 there were still isolated formations - attacking their enemies!

(SIEGERT.)

Chapter IV
Naval Aeroplanes

BEFORE THE WAR, seaplanes were like step-children to the Navy, for practically nothing was expected of them; it was on airships that the Navy relied for reconnaissance and observation patrols. If seaplanes were not exactly thought of as playthings, they were at any rate not taken seriously, and were very badly off for men, material, and money. The Naval Air Service, to which the seaplane section was attached, had its base at Putzig. There were also seaplane stations at Kiel, Heligoland, and Wilhelmshaven. The total strength of the *personnel* before the war was about 200, so only Putzig and Kiel could be maintained at full strength. Heligoland and Wilhelmshaven were only used as landing places during naval manoeuvres. About twenty flying officers, almost all of whom were young naval officers, had been fully trained before the war, but among them there were no observers. In case of general mobilisation, it was assumed that young officers should be taken from the Fleet, and that they should be relied on to carry out observers' duties without any special training.

The existing supply of aeroplane material was not sufficient to satisfy the most modest demands either in quantity or in quality. Money for further enterprise and research had to be found as soon as seaplanes showed signs of promise. One might ask how any promise at all could be found, since we did not possess a single serviceable machine. When we first attempted to build seaplanes, along with the other Great Powers, no endeavour was made to design a special type for the purpose owing to the need of economy; floats were therefore fitted to land machines. Often enough it happened that, instead of being able to rise from the water, the machine had to content itself with skating along the surface. It soon became clear that this state of affairs would lead nowhere. Seaplanes were brought from England and America, and

French racing machines were investigated: then we set to work building types of our own.

The result of this was the existence of many different types at the beginning of the war. The hangars at Holtenau were like a museum. Between German machines with fuselages and tail booms there stood the productions of English, American, and Austrian designers. In those days the seaplane was still in its very early stages of development, but even then flying officers were unanimous in prophesying that the twin-float fuselage type would prove superior to all other designs, and particularly in the matter of seaworthiness would quite outclass the flying boat. By seaworthiness I mean the ability of rising, descending, or travelling over the surface of the sea in bad weather. Our first service machines were anything but seaworthy. A forced descent on the open sea caused damage at the very least, and frequently involved the loss of both machine and men. We have only the reliability of the German engine to thank for the fact that the entire Naval Air Service was not annihilated in the early days of the war. The German aircraft industry was situated in the interior, and the designers bad frequently had no experience of the sea except as bathers. Seaplanes were therefore designed from theory alone, and were not constructed in accordance with practical experience. Only the aircraft factory at Friedrichshafen, which had a base on the Baltic, was in a position to produce seaworthy aeroplanes in peace time. One must admit that this firm led the way in seaplane design up to the end of the war.

On the experimental machines that were built before the war a 100 H.P. Mercedes, Argus, or Gnome engine was fitted. At first the rotary engine was particularly favoured because it enabled the seaplane to rise easily from the water by reason of its light weight. The rotary engine was, however, later abandoned in favour of the stationary, since on long flights its petrol consumption was greater and it was unreliable. As a matter of fact only Mercedes engines of 100 H.P. were used in the North Sea machines during the first few weeks of the war because of their well-established reliability.

The indefatigable labour of the senior officers of the Naval Air

Service, combined with the faith of the flying men themselves in the great future that lay before them, succeeded, in the last month before the war, in attracting the attention of the highest Government authorities to the importance of their work, and consequently the foundation of the German Naval Air Service was laid. And yet, in Heligoland during the first weeks of the war there were only six machines ready to operate with the High Sea Fleet, and only three machines were serviceable for observation work over the fairways of the Baltic.

The performance of the first seaplanes was not remarkable. When fully laden with petrol for four hours, two occupants, the necessary appliances for signalling, but without either armament or bombs, these machines could only attain a speed of 65 m.p.h. and could not rise above 3000 feet. On special occasions, when more petrol, bombs, or anything else had to be carried, they were not powerful enough to rise from the water should there be even a slight wind blowing.

Our principal enemies in naval warfare, England and France, were more advanced than ourselves in the matter of seaplane design before the war, Russia, who played an auxiliary part in the Baltic, originally employed French types. France also had endeavoured to transform land machines into seaplanes in the same way as we had, and met with the same misfortune; however, she succeeded in getting the advantage over us before the war by spending large sums of money, and with the assistance of Naval experts, England and America were further fortunate inasmuch as most of their factories were by the sea, and consequently the results of their experiments could quickly be made use of for further development: both countries had therefore produced types greatly superior to our designs before the war. Many seaplanes which we had purchased from them were the foundation of the types which we produced later. England, as a shipbuilding nation, at first laid special stress on the importance of seaworthiness, and even before the war had produced types which were as good in this respect as those which we were building in 1915. Apart from the value of this early recognition of the importance of seaworthiness for observation patrols over the ocean, the English aero-engine, like our own Mercedes, served them in very good stead on account of its reliability. It was probably for reasons of seaworthiness that they developed the types with fuselages or tail booms, whereas France and America specialised in flying boats.

England had also hit upon the right pattern of wireless apparatus, for she adopted the hanging aerial, while our experiments in peace time had been unsuccessful on account of the evil effect of the aerial mast on the flying qualities of the machine.

The performance of our seaplanes was first confined by their limited petrol capacity to a radius of action of 75 nautical miles, and therefore to a total flying limit of 150 nautical miles. As they carried no wireless, they could only communicate information to the ships at sea by means of signalling lamps. These machines were not strong and consequently were unable to stand against bad weather. In spite of that fact our pilots, fired by the spirit of war, frequently undertook flights which did much to improve their general efficiency, and, thanks to the excellence of the engine, tended greatly to strengthen the faith of the pilots in their machines.

The once desultory research was now pushed forward with every means at our disposal, but it was a hard task. Practical design was in an embryonic form, the number of flying officers was small, and furthermore, at the beginning of the war, the military authorities took control of the aero-engine factories. The Navy was therefore compelled to adapt the Army aero-engine to its seaplanes, consequently the chance of producing a powerful engine, which is of paramount importance to the seaplane on account of the difficulty of rising from the water, was temporarily lost. This disadvantage, however, had to be put up with on account of the necessity for avoiding any cleavage in the aero-engine industry, and in order to ensure the necessary mass production. Fortunately for the development of seaplanes the rivalry which had existed between the land and sea forces still remained, and the Navy therefore was in the position to make use of the best material afforded by its sister arm, and to adapt it for its own purposes.

From these beginnings there arose the seaplane experimental department, and this gradually took over most of the work connected with further development. As has already been said, it was at first only a creation of necessity, and consisted of officers and men who had no practical experience, and who had to carry out their work without suitable appliances. It is easily understood why the men on active service were at first extremely dissatisfied with the work of this department. On account of the demand for aeroplanes many machines had to be made use of in the first few months of the war which suffered from serious defects - defects which although quickly discovered and corrected by the designers, could only be remedied in the machines on active service by laborious research on the part of the flying officers themselves. This state of affairs was not altogether desirable, but it at any rate had the advantage of raising the technical efficiency of the flying officers, and consequently the experimental department could be supplied with highly skilled officers who had had practical experience at the front. It must be admitted that the Aircraft Department of the Admiralty and its auxiliary branches, in spite of initial difficulties, undoubtedly succeeded in its object; for it not only overtook our enemies in respect of seaplane design, but also secured the superiority of the German Naval Air Service up to the end of the war, even though in the last two years our enemies had better quality of material available.

As I have already said, the stations at Heligoland and elsewhere, which had existed before the war, were very badly equipped with machines at the outbreak of hostilities.

Mobile flying units, according to the Army's conception of the phrase, were never formed in the Naval Air Service because all seaplane stations were of necessity stationary. Only the amphibious flying units might be considered mobile.

The first seaplane unit on active service was formed on 4th of December 1914 at Wilhelmshaven. It consisted of three flying officers, one ground officer, 55 men, and two 120 H.P. Friedrichshafen machines. On the rooming of December 6th it arrived at its destination, the bleak mole at Zeebrugge, which still bore traces of the last bombardment in November. At first the station buildings on the mole served as hangars. The train, which still kept up steam, was used as the chilly quarters for the *personnel* and a mobile base for the whole unit, for the seaplanes could quickly be mounted on low-lying trucks in the event of a bombardment, and men and machines could be moved inland to a place of safety. During the first two months the weather was bad, and the time was therefore used for the erection of workshops and shelters, and for carrying out short trial flights and observation patrols with the machines. The observation patrols and raids into the Channel, and the attacks on French and English coast towns which were carried out from the end of the year onwards, will be dealt with later.

The first land Naval Air Service unit went to Flanders on the 20th December 1914. This unit participated in the fighting round the Yser, first at Snaeskerke, and later at Mariakerke. On the 20th February 1916 it was reinforced by a second unit. Both units maintained an unceasing watch over hostile territory, and carried out very rapid and successful photographic patrols over Boulogne, Calais, and Dover, as well as successful bomb raids, in the first months of their existence. As early as November 1916 one of their machines flew over London and destroyed a position of military importance with six bombs.

DEVELOPMENT DURING THE WAR-AEROPLANES ON BOARD SHIP, AND SEAPLANE CARRIERS - THE 'FERNLENKBOOT'

Observation Patrol Machines - Only 100 H.P. reconnaissance machines were available for the early operations of the war. These machines were two-seaters, and carried enough petrol for four hours' flying. The first step forward brought with it the 120 H.P. engine, which made it possible to carry enough petrol for six hours' flying, and also greatly improved the speed, climbing power, and seaworthiness of the machine.

Particularly when attacks were made against submarines, 20 kg. of bombs could also be carried. But even this type was unable to carry out

Siemens-Schuckert R 8, the largest and most powerful German Giant Aeroplane. A pair of two-bladed propellers are in front, and a pair of four-bladed propellers behind the radiators are on either aide of the fuselage, as are also the ladders communicating with the machine guns on the top plane.

the most important duty of a seaplane - namely, rapid transmission of intelligence concerning hostile forces - for it was not capable of carrying a wireless installation. This was first made possible by the 150 and 160 H.P. engines. The reconnaissance machines working in the North Sea were then equipped with a wireless transmitting set, and later with a receiving set. Furthermore, anchors and driving anchors were supplied, tools and spare parts were carried, while a serviceable set of navigation and signalling instruments was installed. Also the performance in the air and on the water was greatly improved.

The final type of reconnaissance machine was a Friedrichshafen design fitted with a 200 H.P. Benz engine, a type which, at the end of the war, was performing all the work possible to a single-engined machine without any difficulty. This machine could carry out reconnaissance patrols 130 nautical miles away from its base without any intermediary landing. It was equipped with a complete wireless installation, improved armament, bombs to be used against submarines, and a movable machine gun for defensive purposes. The machine was so seaworthy and reliable that it could rise and descend when a wind-strength of 5 was registered over the North Sea.

It was principally in the matter of seaworthiness that the development of the reconnaissance machine had to overcome such tremendous difficulties. Good performance in the air necessitated the lightest possible structure; strength, on the other hand, which was so essential to seaplanes, involved a considerable weight. It was necessary to find a compromise between these conflicting qualities, and this compromise could only be discovered by laborious practical research. Above all things the seaplane must be strongly constructed in every part. Any small weakness, such as would only cause some trivial damage to a land machine, would mean the certain loss of the seaplane in the event of a forced landing, and in case of help not arriving in time would also involve the death of its occupants. Even the types already in use on active service were constantly being tested on the sea, and weak points were strengthened or the design was altered.

Fighting Machines

The valuable experience that was obtained by the aeroplanes operating over the North Sea was made use of in the design of machines for other theatres of war such as Flanders, Kurland, and Turkey, where reconnaissance patrols over the sea could not be accomplished without a certain amount of aerial fighting, and consequently where the machines had to possess speed, climbing ability, quickness of movement, and armament at the expense of seaworthiness and a long radius of action. Single-seater fighting seaplanes were built on lines similar to the Army scouts, and their work over the sea was similar to that of the scouts over land. Even though a certain degree of seaworthiness were sacrificed, they naturally could not reach the same standard of excellence as the fighting scouts on account of their heavy floats, although they were designed on the same principles. When, however, the enemy, troubled by the heavy casualties caused by our fighting seaplanes, began to employ their land machines for defensive patrols over the sea, the single-seater seaplane was outclassed and it had to be replaced by two-seater fighters. It was not possible for our land-fighting machines to undertake work of this description, because our patrols took us far out over the English coast, or among the islands of the Mediterranean, and our machines were therefore compelled to fly long distances over the sea in order to carry out their observations, whereas our enemies had only to defend the neighbourhood of their bases against our observation. Industrial research, assisted by the Navy, succeeded in producing a two-seater fighter which could carry out any manner of reconnaissance over the enemies' coasts, which outclassed their seaplanes in every kind of warfare, and which was so efficient that even their scouts never attacked except in superior numbers. These fighting machines, which were usually armed with two fixed and one movable machine gun, were of the twin-float type. They were provided with a 180 H.P. engine and carried enough petrol for 3½ hours' flight; their speed was 100 M.P.H., and they were sufficiently seaworthy by reason of their aluminium floats to rise from the sea or land with a wind-strength of 3.

FLYING BOATS

The flying-boat type was principally favoured by Austria, America, France, and Russia, Its chief advantage was a diminished wind resistance, for the slim boat's hull took the place of the fuselage and floats of the seaplane. Consequently a flying boat was able to fly faster and climb quicker than a seaplane of the same engine power.

On the other hand, the disadvantages of the flying boat might be enumerated as follows:-

1. They are not seaworthy because the planes are close down to the water, and also they are not so stable laterally as the seaplane, in which the weight is distributed over two floats lying some distance apart.
2. For aerial combats there is no protection in front such as is afforded to the seaplane pilot by his engine.
3. In the case of single-engined flying boats, even when they carry an observer, it is impossible to ward off any attack from the rear because the propeller, being situated in the middle of the boat, occupies all the field of fire.
4. A restricted power of manoeuvre, because the pilot of the flying boat, who sits some distance out in front, can never control his

machine as well as the seaplane pilot who sits above the centre of gravity.

One would not be far wrong in claiming that the twin-float seaplane is fundamentally superior to the single-engined flying boat, and that our development of the former type during the war was well justified. This statement is supported by the combined evidence of tests both in peace time and during the war. We had purchased, tested, and copied English, American, and Austrian flying boats, and had also produced types constructed by our expert yacht designers, From time to time on active service we employed both single-seater and two-seater flying boats with every degree of seaworthiness, and we invariably returned to the twin-float seaplane. In spite of its being faster and able to climb quicker, the flying boat with only one engine could never gain a footing in the German Naval Air Service.

The balance, however, changed in favour of the flying boat when big aeroplanes with two or more engines made their appearance. Protection in front was not so important, as it is really only small and quick machines which engage in aerial combats. Also a certain, though somewhat limited, field of fire was opened up towards the tail of the machine between the two engines. Also in the case of big flying boats seaworthiness is not so essential because, with the greater reliability of two or more engines, forced landings become less important factors in one's calculations.

Giant Seaplanes - 'G' and 'R' Types

In the last year of the war the Naval Authorities ordained that aeroplanes should be used instead of airships for the purpose of observation patrols over the North Sea, as airships were unable to fly westwards during the day at a height favourable to observation on account of the enemy's defensive patrols and the danger of incendiary ammunition to lighter-than-air craft. As a result of this the construction of long-distance reconnaissance machines, carrying a larger crew and petrol for eight or ten hours, and also of large flying boats and seaplanes with two or more engines such as the G and E types, came more and more to the foreground. Unfortunately the giant flying boats were never actually used at the front, yet the preliminary tests have already shown that in this branch also our theory was leading us in the right direction.

TORPEDO-CARRYING AEROPLANES

The designs for the early long-distance reconnaissance machines were developed from the practical experience which was obtained in the first year of the war with torpedo-carrying aeroplanes, a type which originally was intended to be highly specialised but which was ultimately converted into a normal machine. The idea of discharging torpedoes from aeroplanes is an old one. Even before the war experiments were made in America and Italy, but as a matter of fact were quite unsuccessful During the war every means had to be used to sink any hostile ship which came near our shores. Every resource of science and skilled design was incorporated in the construction of torpedo-carrying machines, principally with a view to employing them in Flanders and the Dardanelles.

At first, efforts were made to attach torpedoes beneath single-engined land aeroplanes capable of flying short distances over the sea. The idea was that the torpedo should obtain its initial velocity from the actual speed of the machine, and should be discharged at short range against any hostile ship. Bronze torpedoes were also constructed for reasons of weight economy, and were carried by single-seater land machines. However, one could hardly expect any of these methods to prove successful. The enemy was soon able to recognise such machines, and, quite apart from that fact, taking-off from land with a live torpedo on board was certainly not free from danger. Nothing therefore ever came of the torpedo-carrying land machine. We then tried to build aeroplanes which were able to fly long distances over the sea and carry a heavy torpedo and two men, the pilot and the torpedo man. This could never be done with only one engine, and the result was the construction of twin-engined seaplanes for this purpose. The discharge of the torpedo was to he effected by the velocity of the machine, and it was quite expected that the aeroplane would be lost if it crashed on landing while still carrying the torpedo. One had to be resigned to a short life and no seaworthiness. On account of the necessity for economising weight the construction of the machine had to be exceedingly frail, as otherwise even two 100 H.P. engines were not able to carry the heavy torpedo.

Things were made more difficult by the fact that anything linking up the two floats, such as was fitted to the normal seaplane, had to be discarded to make room for the torpedo. In spite of every effort to make them light, the first torpedo-carrying machines seemed rather to hang in the air than to fly, and only extraordinarily skilled pilots were able to attack under such conditions.

After the first tests had been carried out at the front, it became clear that the chances of such an attack being successful were not nearly as good as at first one had been inclined to believe. Many ineffectual flights were made, and in most cases the torpedo was brought back to land. From this we learnt that the aeroplane had been made too light, but when all the corners and angles were strengthened the weight of the machine increased. The appearance of more powerful engines, the 200 H.P. Benz and the 260 H.P. Mercedes, required a stronger and safer machine, but only improved the flying qualities to a slight degree, so that, even for the most up-to-date type, very skilful pilots, highly-trained torpedo men, and a long course of training were necessary. In the last year of the war the torpedo-carrying machines were abandoned, for the results achieved did not justify the loss of men and material. After the first two torpedo attacks in Flanders and in the Gulf of Riga, the enemy's counter-measures became so effective that very little chance of success remained.

The experience we had gained, at any rate, inasmuch as it applied to the design of the aeroplane itself, proved useful in the construction of long-distance reconnaissance machines with several engines.

LONG-DISTANCE RECONNAISSANCE MACHINES

When we suddenly realised in 1917 that the airship was not suitable for work over the North Sea on account of its inflammability, there arose the demand for an efficient substitute in the shape of an aeroplane. Designers were faced with a difficult task, and several months elapsed before a serviceable multi-engined seaplane was produced, for at that time industrial congestion and paucity of material made it impossible to produce a machine capable of satisfying war conditions. That was where the twin-engined aeroplanes, which were now no longer required for torpedo-carrying, proved useful. They were strengthened, the floats were linked together, and in place of the torpedo a petrol tank was installed which could be dropped in case of necessity. The machine could keep in the air for ten hours on end, and, as was soon obvious, would have answered the purpose admirably had it been sufficiently strong and reliable. Unfortunately, however, this was not the case; it was not efficient either on the sea or in the air. As soon as one engine failed the heavy machine was compelled to descend, even after it had dropped the auxiliary tank, and in bad weather it was almost certain to be smashed. After many had been lost in this way, these machines were only employed for escorting convoys and similar work. Eventually they were given up altogether.

Unfortunately the long-distance reconnaissance machines with two or more engines and two floats were never made full use of under war conditions. It is impossible, therefore, to say how far they would have satisfied their requirements, and which types would have proved most efficient. There is, however, reason to believe that in the future the multi-engined flying boat, which has already been described, will be most commonly employed as a means for long-distance observation. A

1000 H.P. giant flying boat with four engines, constructed throughout of duralumin, although it was never tried under war conditions, was tested at Warnemunde and on the seaplane stations of the North Sea. These tests tend to show that the giant flying boat will prove a better reconnaissance machine than the seaplane with fuselage and floats.

A question of particular interest affecting all seaplanes is the possibility of their being carried on board ship. In contrast to the ever-moving flying units of the Army, the seaplane station is immobile. Both reconnaissance and fighting machines could only be stationed at fortified places along the coast. During operations with the Grand Fleet or a Battle Cruiser Squadron, it is of the greatest importance to the pilot to have some sort of base when he is engaged on an observation patrol outside the region covered by the seaplane stations. When the airship failed it became necessary that aeroplanes should be carried on board ship, or on a specially designed carrier ship, in such a way that they could take the air, and could be recovered after their work was over. The seaplane, therefore, must not only be designed for launching into the air and landing on the water, but it had also to be sufficiently strong to be hauled on to the rolling deck of a ship without danger. Even this difficult problem was solved, and eventually every type of machine used by the Navy could, in case of necessity, be taken on board ship.

The enemy also, particularly England and America, adapted cargo vessels and warships to serve as aeroplane-carriers in order that they might bring their machines nearer to their objective, England even built a special ship for the purpose, the Argus, which was extremely fast and was provided with an open upper deck, where land aeroplanes could both take off and land. Other aeroplane-carriers, as a rule, only carried seaplanes which were launched and then recovered. Some of these carriers, particularly American battleships, were equipped either with a short 'runner' situated between the forward turrets, on which the light single-seaters could take off, or else they had a catapult device which could discharge both land and sea planes from the ship. Experiments were carried out with a similar device by the German Navy shortly before the Armistice was signed, and good results were obtained.

D.C.B.'s or 'Distance Control Boats'

A few words concerning the 'Fernlenkboot.' This device, of which the practical development had been undertaken as early as 1915, had to undergo many tests and much research before it Could be employed at the front. The 'Fernlenkboot' was a kind of torpedo which travelled along the surface of the water and was under the control of the firer. It was driven by a petrol engine, and contained in the nose a large mass of explosive which would either destroy or seriously damage a ship in the event of impact. An electric cable, which unrolled as the boat proceeded, connected it with an observation post on land whence, originally, its movements were directed. As it was impossible to observe its movements accurately at a distance, an aeroplane was shortly introduced in order to direct operations. This aeroplane transmitted its instructions by wireless to the land station, whence they were automatically relayed to the 'Fernlenkboot.' Two stations were set up on the Flanders coast to test the practicability of this new invention under war conditions.

They succeeded in putting a monitor out of action by a direct hit. Other attacks were not carried out because the large warships never came within range of the 'Fernlenkboot' and it was not worth while to discharge it at torpedo boats and smaller craft because their greater speed and power of manoeuvre rendered any chance of success very small.

In conclusion I must point out that the development of the seaplane had to overcome much greater difficulties than the development of the land machine. Many different types were designed for various purposes - more almost than for the Army - although the supplies of seaplanes was much smaller (during the war about 2500 machines as against over 44,000 for the Army), The Navy and the seaplane designers had to effect as great improvements in their machines as did the Army, and they suffered moreover from this disadvantage, that the factories, on account of the vast amount of work they were called upon to produce, were unable to construct a series of any given type which had proved successful. The devotion with which officers, mechanics, and workmen carried out their duties in spite of all difficulties - duties which were often enough somewhat thankless - deserved the fullest recognition, and they eventually found that recognition when the German Naval Air Service remained steadily the best.

Organisation of the Personnel

At the beginning of the war the *personnel* of the Naval Air Service, including both sea and land units, consisted of about 200 men (combined land and sea units for land flying did not exist in those days); at the end of the war about 18,000 men.

When the Armistice was signed there existed thirty-two seaplane stations and bases in Flanders, on the North Sea, the Baltic, the Balkans, and in Turkey; four aeroplane-carrier ships, and twenty-six naval land-flying units. Of the latter sixteen were stationed in Flanders. These were composed as follows: three naval land-flying units for artillery observation and for reconnaissance with the naval forces serving on shore; two coastal squadrons, which were stationed on the coast and were used to direct the fire of the heavy guns; two escort squadrons for the protection of the latter; further back, one fighting unit consisting of five scout squadrons for fighting over the land, and one unit for fighting over the sea. In addition to that there were a staff photographic squadron and a flying unit employed on intelligence work at the park at Ghent.

At the end of the war the Naval Air Service was organised as follows: at the head there stood an officer commanding the flying service, who was subordinate in all his duties to the 'Korpskommando'[1], and,

---

1. There being no exact English equivalents to these appointments, I have retained the German nomenclature in some cases. - TRANSLATION

in the matter of *personnel* and *matériel*, the 'Marineflugchef' under the direction of the Admiralty. Under the command of the officer commanding the flying service there were the 'Group Commander' of the seaplane squadrons with the seaplane stations and the sea-front units, the 'Group Commander' of the coastal units and the artillery observation squadrons, and the 'Group Commander' of the land flying service with the units under his command.

THE DEVELOPMENT OF THE NAVAL AIR SERVICES AMONG OUR ENEMIES

As I have already said, our enemies were further advanced in all matters concerning seaplanes before the war than we were, and England in particular provided a quantity of valuable material on mobilisation. Although indeed we succeeded in outstripping our foes in a short time and keeping our lead, one must not forget that England was fully occupied in raising her Army and in satisfying the consequent demand of her Army in respect of land-flying units. Another point to be taken into consideration is the fact that England possessed the mastery of the seas, and that therefore it was not so important for her seaplanes to be seaworthy, as she was able to salve thorn in case of forced landing. The development of seaplanes in France followed the same lines, for the importance of their behaviour on the sea itself was relegated to the background.

For our enemies the most important task in naval warfare was the necessity of combating U-boats. On that account aeroplanes with a good field of vision in front were particularly required in order that bombs could be dropped with accuracy from a low height. Our enemies, therefore, specially developed and retained the single-engined flying boat. The observer in the bow of the flying boat has an excellent view over the region immediately before him, while the pilot is able to make straight for his target unhindered by the engine or the wings. The inefficiency of flying boats on the sea itself was an unimportant factor because of England's mastery of the sea. It was not necessary for the machine to be light on the controls, for in most regions they had no cause to fear interference from hostile aircraft. In Flanders, where our fighting machines were face to face with the enemy, flying boats were assisted by two-seater seaplanes armed with a rear gun, and by single-seater seaplanes modelled on the scout lines.

The fact that England eventually set no great store by seaworthiness is shown by the design of her seaplanes, which, in addition to the two principal floats, were fitted with a third at the end of the fuselage, the tail float, A machine which rests on the water on three floats is, however, never as seaworthy as a machine with long main floats and a fuselage clear of the water. This curious development on the part of English design was all the more remarkable owing to the fact that before the war she favoured the German method, which we had already devised in those days. During the last few months of the war English long-distance reconnaissance machines made their appearance in the North Sea with the object of disturbing our mine-sowing operations. These were flying boats of American design. At first one heard a lot concerning these machines; it was almost feared that the enemy had gained an advantage over us. Finally it was established as a result of aerial combats and the reports of enemy aviators that the redoubtable Curtiss boat answered its purpose as little as our long-distance reconnaissance machines with the two floats. Furthermore, they could only be used successfully in conjunction with naval forces.

(MOLL.)

Chapter V
Personnel and Training

I. General

AS THE WORK to be accomplished by aircraft was always increasing in importance and becoming more varied in character, heavier demands were continually being made on the mentality, physique, and, more particularly, the *morale* of all ranks alike. Our rapidly depleted reserves at home and in the field called for incessant replenishment, and there had to be some sort of 'pool' upon which to draw for the formation of fresh units. It wag imperative that these requirements should be satisfied, and consequently the problems of the selection and training of Air Force *personnel* became concentrated more and more upon the three qualities enumerated above, namely, mentality, physique, and *morale*. Among those on home service alone, most of whom were engaged on training duty either as pupils or instructors, we lost 1399 pilots and 401 observers between August 1914 and October 1918. These figures require no comment.

Generally speaking, all flying men should possess the following qualities: a keen pleasure in flying, a strong sense of duty, self-control, will-power, and the ability to form rapid decisions; good eyesight, physical dexterity, and a sound physique, particularly heart and nerves; no tendency to dizziness or sea-sickness; a well-developed sense of direction; a quick perception of tactical and strategical conditions; a knowledge of the principles of both open and trench warfare; familiarity with the science of gunnery and the problems affecting guns of every calibre; the ability to take aerial photographs and to interpret them; a working knowledge of petrol engines, meteorology, field telegraphy and wireless telegraphy, the field telephonic system, signalling lamps and the use of carrier pigeons. The flying man should also be familiar with machine guns and quick-firing guns, and able to understand operation orders, and orders from the higher command, and make intelligent use of them. In addition to these common qualities and general stock of information, every airman had to be trained in the special knowledge affecting his particular branch of the service, according to whether he were a balloon officer, airship officer, aeroplane pilot or seaplane pilot.

Thus, for example, balloon officers had to be acquainted with the following subjects: a knowledge of the properties and use of gas, the science of free ballooning, experience in defence against aeroplane attacks, and the proper use of anti-aircraft quick-firing guns and machine guns, practice in the use of field glasses from a swaying basket, and experience in guiding troops during an attack so as to be able to undertake operations with the infantry and similar work.

Airship officers had to be specially trained to control the elevation or direction of the ship, or as engineers, or as the actual responsible commanders.

Aeroplane pilots had to be taught how to fly the various different types, while officers of aeroplanes and airships alike had to be instructed in navigation, the mechanism of bombs, bomb dropping, etc.

This training was of a more ambitious nature than that required of any other arm. We will now consider more closely the training of each individual branch of the Air Force.

II. OBSERVATION BALLOONS

As a rule there was only one observer in the basket of an observation balloon, and it was only during training that two were sent up simultaneously.

To make better use of the balloons without increasing their number, experiments were carried out in 1917 with two baskets slung beneath one envelope, a method which, even at the front, gave satisfactory results up to a height of about 3000 feet. This practice was, however, soon abandoned, for the two baskets upset the stability of the balloon and caused violent rocking.

Generally speaking, the junior officers were not competent to undertake all the work expected of the observation balloons, and even specially qualified officers required about a year's training, although a large number of junior officers became excellent artillery observers.

It required a good deal of pluck and stamina to remain in the air for eight hours on end in bad weather, and an unusual devotion to duty and self-control to fight against sea-sickness without loss of personal efficiency. The balloon observer had to do his duty alone and unseen, without the moral support afforded to the infantry officer by his men and by the knowledge that he must set them an example when leading them into action. Thousands of feet up in the air, alone, and frequently suffering from the intense cold, he had to face shell-fire and attacks by aeroplanes without any means of defence whatsoever. He must make his observations and never allow himself to be disturbed by the thought that, if his balloon were set on fire above him, he would have a few seconds only in which to make his leap for safety with his parachute. As he was unable to see and form any judgment himself, he had to rely on the officer on ground duty to give him the order to jump. When this order came through the telephone, he had to jump from his basket into the depths below without a second's hesitation. Even then his troubles were not over. The attacking aeroplane would direct a furious fire against the defenceless man hanging from the parachute. The blazing tracer bullets would leap at him. Only extraordinary will-power, self-control, strong nerves, and a stout heart enabled him to stand the strain, and to go up again after his descent! Many an infantry officer who had applied for training as a balloon observer in order to have a rest from tho hardships of the trenches has said, after an experience of this kind, 'I would sooner undergo a five days' bombardment than make another ascent!'

It was even a difficult matter to learn how to use a pair of field glasses when the basket was rolling and rocking. The observer had to memorise the maps of both our own and the enemy's lines, for the use of a map was so difficult, especially when a wind was blowing, that it was only resorted to in cases of emergency. However, aerial photographs were a useful aid to his memory.

During the war balloon officers were recruited from the infantry and from other branches of the service, principally the artillery. Tests of their qualifications and ability - tests which resulted in the rejection of a large number - were followed by a course of technical training lasting from three to five months for officers, and about a year for other ranks. During this period, if circumstances made it possible for two observers to ascend in one basket, the pupil also was given some practical instruction in the air on fine days. He was put in the charge of an experienced observer and made thoroughly familiar with the surrounding country, but when directing artillery fire he had to make his report directly from the instructions given by the observer. Later on he was sent up in bad weather.

After one or two months' service with the balloon corps, during which he was required to perform easy work with the artillery, he was sent to the Airship Training School, where he remained from six to eight weeks. This course was followed by four to six weeks' training with the artillery. Along with young artillery observers the pupil now learnt the science of gunnery and the difference between observation from the ground and from the air, both of which were practised simultaneously on this course. An inspection of the shots on and around the target served to throw light on errors in observation.

At this point in his career the pupil returned to the front as an 'assistant observer.' On days when there was no important operation on foot he was allowed to observe by himself and to register for shoots on easy targets. Whenever heavy fighting was in progress he worked with some experienced observer, provided that it was not necessary for the balloon to ascend much above 3000 feet. The results of shoots were generally confirmed by photographic machines.

There now followed a course with a training division during which the pupil, who was now an almost fully-trained observer, learnt the methods of liaison with other arms under various conditions of warfare.

The German Fleet returning after the sortie on August 19, 1916.

By this means his knowledge of tactics was improved. He also learned how to work with the intelligence corps on their training grounds and became acquainted with the intelligence system used by the higher command.

The Airship Training School only supplied a general training in the matter of aerial photography but special instruction in this subject was given by the Aerial Photographic Section.

As time went on, balloon observers began to specialise in various branches of their work. One man, for example, might obtain exceptionally good results with the heavy artillery at long ranges, and he would pound away at the various headquarters of the enemy's command; another, having earnestly studied the enemy's ammunition dumps from aerial photographs, would bombard them until they blew up. Yet another would be unusually quick and skilful in picking up columns on the march, trains, and other moving targets, and in bringing the fire of his battery to bear upon them. A very useful observer was he who could report on the essential features of any phase of a battle, omitting the details, but at the same time drawing valuable conclusions from the results of his observations. It was the duty of the officers commanding the units of the balloon corps to see that the right work was given to the right man at the right moment. No balloon observer might ever say to himself that he had finished his training, for he must ever be acquiring fresh knowledge and wider experience.

(STOTTMEISTER.)

III. Naval and Military Airships

The crew of a naval airship consisted of twenty-three trained airmen, and a further twenty-four whose duty it was to look after the ship. Every man received some special training, either as a navigator or in a technical capacity. Included among the flying crew there were:-

1. The Commander.
2. An observation officer, who was also in charge of the wireless apparatus.
3. A steersman.
4. A chief engineer.
5. Two men in charge of the elevating and two in charge of the lateral controls.
6. Two wireless operators.
7. A sailmaker.
8. Twelve mechanics to look after the engines and the tanks.

It was the duty of the observation officer to direct the movements of the ship before ascending and after landing, for the Commander was not able to leave the pilot's gondola during those periods. When the ship was in flight, he was in charge of the wireless apparatus, coded and decoded all messages, and went the rounds of the ship. When an attack was in progress he operated the bomb sights and releases. On the ground he acted as second in command.

Navigation was in charge of the steersman under the direction of the Commander. It was the steersman's duty to keep the course and speed, and to check the ship's position on the chart. During the landing manoeuvres he used the ship's telegraphic system to communicate orders to each individual engine. On the ground he was principally responsible to the Commander for the work of all the flying *personnel*.

The chief engineer looked after all the machinery of the ship, and was responsible for the testing of the engines and the petrol before leaving the ground. On a war flight, his position was in the rearmost engine gondola.

The men in charge of the elevating controls directed the use of the ballast, and of those valves which could be opened by hand. When not otherwise engaged, they manned the machine guns and searchlights, and at the same time served as lookouts, A man was told off to keep an eye constantly on the petrol supply and to see that every engine received the necessary quantity. The sailmaker constantly inspected the gas compartments, tested the working of the valves, patched small holes in the outer hull, etc. The flying *personnel* consisted entirely of officers or N.C.O.'s.

The party in charge of the airship on the ground comprised every possible kind of craftsman that might be required; i.e. sailmakers, girder workers, mechanics, electricians, etc. They did not actually fly, but assisted the flying *personnel* in the maintenance of the ship. Every member of the crew was a volunteer who had been taken over from the High Seas Fleet, and put through special courses under the direction of the Officer Commanding the Airship Service.

Special training ships were used for this purpose, and, at the beginning of the war, the passenger snips which had already been built, such as the Hansa, Sachsen, and Victoria-Louise, were employed on this work. The training centres were at first situated at Leipzig and Dresden, then, until the autumn of 1916, in the neighbourhood of Hamburg, later at Nordholz, which had meanwhile grown to be the most important station of the Naval Airship Service, Along with a practical course on the general subject of airship flying, the personnel underwent intensive instruction and specialised training according to whatever their work was to be. Naturally the most important training was that of the Commanders for their multitudinous duties.

The naval officer brought with him, owing to his experience at sea, a quantity of knowledge which was also useful for the navigation of airships. As a rule it required about six months to complete his training, but it frequently happened that this period was cut short when ships were being built in larger numbers. Sometimes this curtailment of his training was unfortunate. Whenever possible it was arranged that an airship Commander should go on active service with the crew with which he had been trained. It was a very necessary condition for successful flying and general efficiency that the Commander and his crew should have worked together and should know each other.

Particularly during the last year of the war, when the ships were compelled to fly at great altitudes on account of the strong hostile anti-aircraft defences, the strain to which the airship crews were subjected was severe in the extreme. Men of sound constitution and strong physique alone could be employed on this work: only those who have had actual experience can realise what it is like, for example, to be boxed up in a narrow engine gondola, with the engine roaring in his ears for twenty-four hours on end. In addition to that, one must take into consideration the extreme cold, and the difficulty of working in the rarefied atmosphere of 19,000 or 20,000 feet under conditions to which our bodies are not accustomed. The effect of oxygen shortage manifested itself in various unpleasant ways, such as mountain-sickness, lassitude, etc., so that it became necessary to carry oxygen on long war flights when the ship was likely to remain at these great heights for as long as ten hours at a time.

(HOLLENDER, STAHL.)

IV. MILITARY AEROPLANES

When the design of German machines reached its highest point in the construction of multi-engined giant aeroplanes, equipped with every conceivable instrument, capable of carrying heavy loads of bombs, and manned by a crew of from six to ten men, the *personnel* included some or all of the following groups: pilot, observer, Commander, machine gunner, wireless operator, and mechanic.

V. Observers

The observer, invariably an officer, was as a rule the person actually responsible in an aeroplane. This was not only the case in giant aeroplanes, of which the Commander was generally an observer, but also in the smaller types where the pilots were frequently of non-commissioned rank. His iron will and his devotion to duty alone was all that the pilot had to rely on in a moment of great danger, for he performed his task isolated in the heights, suffering from the intense cold of 40 degrees or more of frost, and surrounded by exploding shells, without that moral support afforded to the infantryman by his comrades in battle. Well might it be said of the pilot, 'unaided he stood, and alone.' That phrase might be applied physically as well as mentally. With the increasing number and varying nature of tasks allotted to aeroplanes, new demands were constantly being made on airmen, particularly on observers. Whereas the pilots could be trained and classified for the purpose of flying some individual type of machine, the observer had to possess a general knowledge, including every branch of aerial science, and the ability to apply this knowledge under varying conditions. The war, which was indeed the father of all things appertaining to flying, has also made the observer what he is, and will remain for all time. In his comprehensive ability, his mental and physical strength, and his devotion to duty, the observer has proved himself to be indispensable under every circumstance of war, not only to the higher command, but also to the supreme command.

He had to be able to think strategically as well as tactically, as otherwise his activity was useless, both to the higher command and to the troops. He had to know how to employ machine guns of various patterns and firing every description of ammunition in his aerial battles, while he had to use bombs against ground targets. He found a serviceable weapon against tanks, railway trains, and dug-outs in the quick-firing gun. At the end of the war we were about to use flame-throwers from aeroplanes.

Unless he possessed an intimate knowledge of the science of gunnery, the artillery would have been robbed of much of its efficiency, even though it were still assisted by some sort of aeroplane observation. A knowledge of the behaviour of falling bodies, from high-explosive bombs to provisions, from propaganda leaflets to his own plunge from a flaming machine in a parachute, necessitated a profound study of trajectories and the use of exceedingly complex sights and similar pieces of mechanism.

Shortly after the beginning of the war, the officer observer, who hitherto had done work similar to that of a cavalry scout, had to undertake the study of camouflage in all its branches. Closely connected with this work was the demand for reliable aerial photography, and a practical acquaintance with every type of camera, including eventually the cinematographic camera, was essential.

He had to possess a sound knowledge of wireless telegraphy, of which the applications became more general and more diverse every day.

To complete the list we should mention that archaeological work has been projected and carried out by aeroplanes. In February 1918 the archaeologists emphasised the importance of a photographic survey of the ancient civilisation of Asia Minor, Mesopotamia, and Palestine, and suggested that this survey should be carried out by the usual methods employed by the Air Force.

We have not yet alluded to all the branches of knowledge which are necessary to the flying man, such as, for example, meteorology, with which he must be familiar not only in order to interpret the reports of the meteorological stations correctly, but also so that, in the event of bad weather arising, ho would be able to select the best line of flight. It was the duty of the observer to note every circumstance and take it into account.

The attacks on England necessitated the use of every means of navigation, including astronomy, for the purpose of locating the position of the aeroplane. Finally, the observer had to be able to take over control from the pilot should the latter be killed or incapacitated through wounds. That fact brings us to a very important point, namely, mutual trust and collaboration between pilot and observer.

(NEUMANN, SIEGERT.)

VI. The Pilot and Observer As One Individual

The pilot, far from being merely an aerial chauffeur, was the trusted comrade and the complement of the observer, and therefore it was only just to expect that the observer should assist the pilot in his many technical duties, both during and after a flight. This necessitated technical knowledge, and the observer had to be as familiar with every part of the aeroplane as he was with the mechanism of the engine, the troubles to which it was subject and the remedy for such troubles.

It was this knowledge alone which could give him that trust in his machine which was so essential to his own efficiency, enable him to examine and test every part of the machine with the pilot before a flight, and, whenever it was possible, to remedy any trouble or damage caused by bullets during the flight itself. He should also be able to assist the pilot to repair the aeroplane should it be damaged after a forced landing, and, in the event of the pilot being incapacitated, he should have sufficient presence of mind to bring the machine to earth. Even if it were set on fire, as it might be by a bullet in the tank or by the ignition of petrol vapour, he had to remain master of the situation. In a case like this the airman has but a few seconds in which to save his life, and lie can only do so by lightning-like action; such quickness as this can only be ensured by wide knowledge and constant practice.

The collaboration and mutual assistance of pilots' and observers in two-seaters, and of all the occupants in larger machines, resulted in self-reliance and confidence, both mental and physical. The two men were linked together by a bond of comradeship forged in many hours of common trouble and danger, and it was unwillingly that such a bond was ever severed. In such cases it made no difference whether it was the observer alone, or both observer and pilot, who held commissioned rank. The two must be adjusted to one another so accurately that they worked almost automatically. An instinct had to be developed by which one could understand and almost foresee the wishes and actions of the other. There was no time for deliberations or consultations, in spite of

A parachute landing. The observer is about to cut himself free from the parachute.

all mirrors, speaking tubes, and writing tablets, when the pilot wished to direct his observer's fire against the fleeting targets that presented themselves in the course of aerial combats.

Often enough during the war, a pilot, mortally wounded and with life ebbing from his body, has brought his comrade back to the friends that waited for them behind our lines. It has happened that observers have crawled out along the planes of their machine, thousands of feet up in the air, clung to the bracing wires, and remained, facing a gale of wind that almost tore them from their hold, in order to restore the equilibrium of the shattered aeroplane, and by doing so have saved their pilot's life and their own. Other observers have taken over the controls from their unconscious pilot when he was badly wounded, and thereby have robbed Death of his prey. But it was not only on such rare and extraordinary occasions that the life and liberty of the one rested in the hands of the other. The fate of the pilot, as of all the other occupants of a machine, depended on the coolness and accurate shooting of the observer in every aerial combat, in the same way as only the calm skill of the pilot would avail to save them from dangerous anti-aircraft fire.

Again, the presence of other machines should never escape the observer's notice. It was not sufficient that he should be able to distinguish and recognise friend and foe at close quarters, when the black cross or cockade was visible; the observer had to be able to decide instantly as to their nature when the machines were still far off, merely from their appearance and design. Upon this knowledge depended his ability to make use of every weakness in his enemy's position, and therefore one might say that this knowledge was the foundation of aerial tactics.

(NEUMANN.)

VII. PILOTS

At the beginning of the war only a very few naval officers had been trained as seaplane pilots. It had not been considered necessary to provide any special training for observers, but the first few weeks of the war showed clearly enough that a special course of training was necessary if all the work was to be carried out properly. Before long not only officers, but warrant officers, N.C.O.'s, and men were trained as observers. The necessary qualifications were physical and mental fitness, experience at sea, and, where possible, some knowledge of navigation and signalling.

The training of the seaplane pilot followed the same general lines as that of the Army airman, only special instruction was given in navigation, for his life frequently depended on his knowledge of this science.

The great strain of single-seater fighting, where the pilot was called upon to act entirely alone, made it preferable that scout pilots should be officers. Not only was it essential that the fighting pilot should have an absolute mastery over his machine and the ability to fly as not even a bird can fly; he had also to be versed in a good deal of the observer's lore, such as direction-finding and meteorology. It was advisable that he should have a keen sense to appreciate a strategical or tactical situation, so that he could understand the observations he made from the air and communicate them by wireless to the ground.

However, apart from the actual tactics of aerial fighting, his most important qualifications were good shooting, familiarity with the mechanism of a machine gun and its synchronising gear, and his ability to aim his fixed gun by means of the aeroplane controls themselves. The fact that exceptional skill, iron nerves, and the mentality of a sportsman or a hunter were the peculiar characteristics of the fighting pilot does not detract in any way from the excellent quality of the thousands of other pilots who were not so fortunate in their work. Day and night they performed their tasks in those suffocating heights, frequently indeed ascending several times in the course of twenty-four hours; the engine in front firing 1400 times to the minute; their eyes ever on the look-out for fighting; carrying out their duties from memory, fully recognising the fact that a wound, which would be rapidly attended to in the case of their comrades on the ground, meant a hideous crash and a flaming death, while a forced landing behind the enemy's lines meant death also, at the hands of the revengeful population.

Pilots for most types of machines were taught to fly on C and J type machines, then from the G to the R, Night flying was another matter and called for separate training. Also we must remember that much pioneer work was done by our airmen on home defence towards the development and refinement of new types. The practical experience acquired by airmen on active service was made use of for progress at home. One must not forget either that administrative work at home required considerable business, organising, and judicial ability. The old saying, 'The soldier must know how to measure a mountain range or a pair of trousers, and to weigh a loaf of bread or a point of justice' was no longer nonsensical when applied to our flying men.

Imperial German Air Force! A pebble I cast into the sea of memory creating waves in rings that joined, swept on towards the shore, and were then turned back. Today the waters of that sea lie calm and mirror-like, pitilessly reflecting the image of the past. Below there in the depths one's eye can see the sunken city of his dreams; far off one hears the ringing of bells. Atlantis!

(SIEGERT.)

PART II

CHAPTER I
LIGHTER-THAN-AIRCRAFT

IN AN OBSERVATION BALLOON DURING AN OFFENSIVE IN RUSSIA

(BASED ON THE REPORT OF A BALLOON OBSERVER)

I ARRIVED AT the balloon shed eight miles behind the lines at six o'clock in the morning. The recording officer had made all preparations for the ascent, and the balloon was already out in the open, I examined the equipment in the basket by the light of an electric flash lamp, adjusted the altimeter, and stowed away my maps and aerial photographs. Then I climbed into the basket, buckled the parachute tackle to my belt, satisfied myself that the ripping gear and valve control lines were clear, and tested the telephonic communication from the basket to the earth. At the same time the telephonist gave me the meteorological station reports, which ran as follows: Wind-strength near the ground 5m. S.; 1500 feet 11m. S.W.; 2500 feet 12 to 14m. S.W.; low clouds; wind rising and gusty; temperature -10° C. That meant bad visibility, I made a rapid mental calculation: at 2500 feet the temperature would be as low as -18° C., with a very pleasant rolling and tossing into the bargain.

'All O.K. Ready to go up,' I announced. 'Let her go! Ease up the guys!' ordered the officer in command. And then the balloon rose; the wind whistled. Before long there was a slight jerk and the balloon ascended no farther. 'They are going to let out the 200 yard cable,' the telephonist announced. I sat down on the floor of the basket to get some protection from the biting wind, for the day's work was going to be heavy. However, we succeeded that day in driving the Russians out of their advanced trenches and throwing them back across the river Dvorczak.

By 7.30 in the morning the balloon had arrived at its point of ascent, two miles behind the lines. Everything was still muffled in darkness, and all was quiet along the lines except for occasional flashes from the artillery on both sides. The ground party got into communication by telephone with the division and the officer commanding the artillery, to whom I reported and asked if there were any special instructions. This done, I gave the order for ascent. I stopped at a height of 2400 feet, close up underneath the clouds. The thermometer registered -21° C, and the wind howled through the rigging, causing the balloon to sway and roll at the end of its cable through a circle whose diameter was at least 100 yards. It was useless to think of observing through the binoculars. It was just possible to see as far as the enemy's front line trenches, and there promised to be ample scope for good observation work.

Then I heard the words 'Eight o'clock' sounding in the ear-pieces of my telephone headgear. With one accord the whole front began to spout fire; the preliminary artillery bombardment had begun. Soon the light had become so good that I was able to report on the effect of our fire: 'Good shooting on the Aloff gun pits, only two batteries are answering from there'; 'The north wing of the Nakow batteries is not receiving sufficient attention, five batteries are replying from that position' (here more precise instructions followed). Ten minutes later I was able to report to the artillery that our fire had got on to the latter position also, and the enemy's artillery fire had considerably diminished in volume. We encountered but little resistance, and it therefore seemed certain that our surprise had succeeded.

As yet there had been no new hostile batteries to report, but the enemy's infantry called incessantly for assistance by discharging rockets.

Meanwhile the day had brightened, and the visibility had become excellent. At 8.45 A.M. I thought I saw a column emerging from the village of Nakow, eight miles behind the lines. At once my binoculars went to my eyes. At first, however, I was not able to get the road into the field of vision, but finally I succeeded in fastening on this place for a second or two, and that was sufficient. It was a column of artillery on the move. Immediately I reported it to the division and the artillery, and undertook co-operation with the balloon battery (10 cm. guns), for if possible we wanted to catch the column on the march, I was quite warm now, in spite of the cold, and hardly aware of the rocking of the basket, for here was real balloon work/ From the speed of its advance I decided definitely that it was a column of artillery, and estimated its length to be 400 yards, therefore three batteries. At 9.20 A.M. the whole train passed the fork roads at 205, about 3 miles behind the lines; it, however, did not turn off, but continued along the main road.

After a short conference with the battery commander, the order was given: The battery will shell the region approximately 300 yards to the side of the road. The worthy Russians, doubtless, rejoiced over the bad shooting of the German batteries, until suddenly we set about them. The battery directed its fire upon the road itself, and shelled it to pieces. Shell followed shell, and only very few fell short or over. The advance faltered and the column broke away from the road in small groups, thereby showing themselves up all the more clearly against the snow. I immediately called on the battery commander to spread his fire over a larger area, but at that moment I received a message from the ground to the effect that the artillery should now be directed against the front line infantry trenches.

I had almost forgotten: at 9.40 A.M. there was to be the attack on the trenches themselves. A wonderful spectacle now unrolled itself before my eyes shells exploded in a continuous line like a row of pearls, save for a gap near the small wood at Pitzka. A short conference with the battery commander, and five minutes later this defect was remedied. This done, I could once more devote my attention to the previous target. The hostile artillery division had deployed on both sides of the road, and each battery of three or four guns were now blazing away as though they had gone mad. Then the 10 cm. battery, under control from the balloon, began a bombardment as calmly and deliberately as though it were on a practice ground. We soon had our enemy registered correctly, and the shells fell to such good effect that his fire weakened. Then we turned our attention to the other side of the road, but after three shots these guns also gave up the fight.

'10 A.M. The infantry are attacking.' Although I was unable to see our brave infantry as they rushed forward to the assault, I was with them in spirit, Hitherto our barrage had remained stationary on the front line trenches, but it now crept slowly forward, 65 yards to the minute. Red signal rockets invoked help and artillery support, but all in vain, for by this time the Russians had only five batteries in action, all of which were firing spasmodically, and one of these I silenced with the balloon battery, I was able to report successively: 'Our barrage has passed over the second line; now the third line'; and by 10.32 A.M., 'Our fire lies on the further bank of the Dvorczak. The attack is successful!'

As soon as the nervous tension had relaxed, I felt wretchedly overstrained. The god of the air levied his tribute, and my breakfast left my stomach as an offering.

'The Divisional General Staff Officer is on the telephone, sir.'

I knew then that I had to pull myself together, for I had to give detailed answers to questions concerning the situation. Will-power won and conquered my physical weakness. But those who know what sea-sickness means - and balloon-sickness is far worse than that experienced on the roughest sea - can realise with what I had to contend. The balloon observer who succumbs to this sickness is unsuited for his work. There are not many, however, who are always able to control themselves.

As a matter of fact, I continued my observations. The hostile artillery was now completely silenced, and consequently batteries on the section of our neighbouring northern division opened enfilading fire on the river Dvorczak. As there was no communication between the balloon and this division, the artillery commander forwarded them the results of my observation.

I then received the following message from the ground: 'The balloon will be advanced as far as our old front the trenches.' The gale was now blowing with increased violence, causing the balloon to sway and rock more and more violently. I was thrown from one side of the basket to the other, and the icy cold penetrated to my bones. Suddenly, complete silence! The wind whistled no longer; the basket swung up against the balloonets, while the nose of the balloon reared until it was almost vertical; no answer came through the telephone: clouds enveloped me. The balloon had broken loose!

At first I experienced a comfortable feeling at being relieved from the eternal rolling; but prompt action was necessary, since in six or seven minutes' time I should have drifted over the enemy's lines. Maps and aerial photographs fluttered down in small fragments from the basket; hastily I examined the tackle of my parachute, to see that it was clear, and then untied the cable of the ripping gear. On no account dared I allow the balloon to fall into the hands of the Russians, I tugged fiercely at the cable; nothing happened! A cold perspiration broke out all over me, I clenched my teeth, and felt all my muscles grow tense. Again I tugged. 'Hurrah!' I shouted out loud. The fabric gave; the balloon was ripped, and I heard the gas escape whistling into the upper air. Two more vigorous tugs at the cable; a glance at the altimeter, which showed a height of 6000 feet; then over the side of the basket, and a plunge into the bottomless abyss.

As I fell I shut my eyes and wondered whether the parachute would open or whether I should fall like a lump of lead, and be dashed to pieces on the ground below. Those three or four seconds of dead drop seemed an eternity. Then I felt a gentle strain on the harness round my breast, and above my head heard a slight crack. Looking up, I saw the parachute tight and fully opened above me. I was saved! But as yet I had no cause for jubilation, for I knew not where I might come down. I wondered whether I should land within our own lines, or if I was doomed to inglorious captivity. Soon I had dropped below the level of the snow clouds, and then I felt as though the earth was rising up to meet me, not that I was falling, I could not help thinking of my comrades on the Western Front, who, on such occasions, when they were hanging helpless and defenceless from their parachutes, were attacked by aeroplanes with machine-gun fire.

Barely 200 yards away I saw my balloon plunging down into the depths. That sight made me realise that I had to make preparations for my landing, for I knew that I should be dragged along the ground if I did not quickly release myself from the parachute. Hastily I drew my clasp-knife. Close below me I could see our own support trenches. Reaching up with my left hand, I got a good grip upon the tackle of the parachute, in order to cut myself free. But in the same instant I found myself lying on my back in a trench, and a moment later I was snatched on high again; the parachute harness tightened round my chest as though it would break the bones. Next my face hit the edge of a hard parapet and my eyes became flooded with blood. The gale had taken possession of the parachute and was rushing it along under enormous pressure. The knife; where was my knife! Surely I could not have dropped it! With my left hand I grasped the ropes, endeavouring to seize as many of them as possible: one-two cuts with the clasp-knife: the ropes snapped; the pressure relaxed and darkness closed in upon my eyes.

When I recovered consciousness I was lying in a dug-out, and two gunners were bandaging my bleeding forehead. 'Another three yards, and you would have been dragged into the barbed wire, sir!' one of them said.

Weeks later a fractured bone and round my chest a purple weal, which still caused me pain, served to remind me of my first parachute descent.

(STOTTMEISTER.)

NAVAL AIRSHIPS - RECONNAISSANCE OVER THE NORTH SEA - ESCORTING AND ASSISTING THE MINESWEEPERS

The many different kinds of reconnaissance which fell to the lot of the airship varied with the progress of the war. Experience soon taught us that, as a rule, three airships simultaneously patrolling the entrance to the Bight were sufficient to give security against unseen raids by the enemy. Consequently these patrols became established as a matter of routine inasmuch as from dawn to dusk, when weather conditions made it possible, one airship patrolled a line running north and south, of which the southern point lay slightly to the west of the Island of Texel close by the Dutch waters, and whose northern point was rather south of the Dogger Bank. Similarly a second airship reconnoitred the whole Dogger Bank from the northern limit of its companion, and a third the district from the northern point of the Dogger Bank as far as the Horns Reef Lightship on the Danish coast. The orders given to the Commanders of these airships were generally expressed briefly as: 'western defensive patrol, middle defensive patrol, or northern defensive patrol,' with indications as to the boundaries between which they were to work, and a note added to the effect that they were to remain in the air until sundown.

It was the Commander's duty to keep a sharp watch upon the district which had been allotted to him, and to report by wireless to the authorities any item of information which might be of value in our naval warfare. Naturally such information principally concerned the enemy's naval forces, but there were also several other facts which might prove useful to the authorities, such as reports on the movements of cargo vessels, particularly between Holland and Scandinavia, and on the position of any of the enemy's mine-fields which were not known to the Admiralty. I may here mention that it is very easy to detect mines from an airship at a low height whenever the sea is calm. The airship was better than the aeroplane as a means to observation, owing to the fact that, by stopping its engines, it was able to hover for a long time over its objective. This fact, combined with steadiness of the roomy pilot's gondola, made the work of observation much easier and increased its possibilities. Thus, for example, by buoys dropped from the airship, we were able to mark the boundaries of any mine-fields that were sighted, and could thereby indicate their position to our mine-sweepers.

The unceasing airship patrols up and down those three lines we have already mentioned made it possible for the mine-sweepers, which consisted of slow and not heavily-armed steamers, to carry out their arduous labours unmolested by the enemy. The airships were always sufficiently far ahead of the mine-sweeping flotillas to be able to give them such timely warning of any attempted surprise that they could escape into safety. Surprise attacks of this nature were attempted more than once, but without success. In connection with this subject it is worth mentioning that, after the beginning of the unrestricted U-boat campaign, England sought to defend herself by blocking up the whole Bight with a thickly-sown mine-field, hoping thereby to render it impossible for the submarines to emerge. It then became the duty of the mine-sweepers to clear paths through this field of mines, and constant trouble was the natural result, for the English, of course, took great pains to block up again as quickly as possible the paths that had been cleared. Laymen may perhaps be able to realise the difficult nature of this work - to which no word of publicity has been given - from the fact that during the last year of the war the English, even according to their own account, sowed on the average 10,000 mines per month. It was almost impossible to stop their activity in tins direction, since the work was done at night by mine-layers or cruisers, or by submarines specially adapted for the sowing of mines. Without reliable aerial reconnaissance it would have been impossible to control the extent of these mine-fields, and consequently it might have been impossible to continue the submarine campaign.

One has frequently encountered the following criticism, particularly from naval officers, that aerial reconnaissance was incomplete owing to the fact that it depended so much upon weather conditions. It is true that sometimes it was impossible to carry out the patrols on account of the weather, particularly in winter when the conditions were bad for weeks on end; one should not, however, forget the fact that even for modern naval warfare the old principles that held good in the days of sailing vessels are still valid, for light vessels - that is torpedo boats, etc. - can only take part in naval operations when the weather is fine. Even a slight wind and a light sea are sufficient to detract so much from the general usefulness of these vessels that no naval leader would voluntarily go into battle under such circumstances. During the whole period of the war, from the moment when there were sufficient airships in existence, no serious conflict was undertaken or met with any success without the co-operation of airships, and the fact that the English avoided coining into contact with the German fleet as much as possible can be ascribed not so much to our submarines as to the fact that they could not shake off our aerial reconnaissance. The commander of the German Fleet was kept continually informed concerning the strength, formation, course, and position of the enemy by our airships, and was therefore in the position to secure all tactical advantages, as a rule long before the enemy was even aware of the proximity of the German forces.

Sometimes the patrols over the Bight, which have been described above, were strengthened when, for special reasons, it seemed to be necessary. Thus, from time to time, individual airships were solely occupied in looking for mines, sometimes to a certain extent under the escort of other ships which were simultaneously patrolling the district so that the attention of the entire crew could be concentrated upon this work.

Other ships, either singly or in pairs, would scout the whole area of the North Sea, as far as the English coast on the one hand and the Norwegian coast on the other. This work was usually undertaken with a view to observing the cargo vessels in that region of the North Sea which was blockaded when once the unrestricted submarine campaign was started. The so-called 'neutral channel', which was a narrow belt of water lying from the Island of Terschelling northwards across the Dogger Bank, and whose object it was to make it possible that Dutch shipping should pass to and from neutral countries, was kept under continuous observation by the airships engaged on the 'middle defensive patrol.'

The efforts which the enemy made to combat our airships prove that they found our activity in the air exceedingly unpleasant. They were, in fact, almost helpless in this respect, and were unable to put similar methods into practice themselves owing to lack of sufficiently serviceable airships. The only success they could boast of was the fact that, from the summer of 1917 onwards, our airships had to abandon looking for mines, and the ships that were working on the western and middle defensive patrols were compelled to carry out their work from greater altitudes: 7000 to 9000 feet, instead of the original height, which had been 2500, This was brought about because the English gradually learnt to appreciate the weakness of airships, which was their liability to catch fire on account of the hydrogen they contained. Owing to this inflammability, an airship is almost certain to be destroyed by any aeroplane that can climb above it. Naturally reconnaissance suffered in consequence of these increased altitudes, and the flying itself put a heavier strain upon the airships' crews, particularly in winter, for the temperature of the air rapidly diminishes with increased height. However, the enemy never succeeded in putting an end to our defensive patrols.

CO-OPERATION WITH THE HIGH SEA FLEET: CRUISER WARFARE

Apart from the uses that we have already described, airships were of outstanding importance for all offensive operations undertaken by the High Seas Fleet, They were able to supply a considerable proportion of those reconnoitring forces which the German fleet required but had previously lacked, and were able, on account of their speed which was so much greater than that of all sea-going vessels, to keep in touch with the enemy. Furthermore, an airship could so regulate its distance from the enemy that, while still being able to make all necessary observations, it ran but little risk of being shot down or prevented from finishing its work. The principal source of danger was the enemy's naval forces, for the English scouting vessels were superior both in numbers and in speed, although submarines and mines greatly increased the difficulty of carrying out reconnaissance by sea-going craft. One must also remember that an airship with a crew of twenty-three men can be replaced in six weeks with but little trouble, while the loss of a cruiser was a much more serious matter since we had so few, they took so long to build, and both the men and the ship were immensely valuable.

During offensive operations the fleet endeavoured to assemble as many airships as possible on the scene in order to carry out long-distance reconnaissance. This screen, as it may best be called, should be sufficiently close for the nearest airship to remain constantly in sight so that any attempt on the part of the enemy to slip through our lines unseen might be frustrated. During a sortie, and when it seemed probable that the fleet would be at sea for several days, some of the airships remained behind as reserves.

It was not so easy to carry out this work in practice as it might seem from this description, for one must remember that up to the beginning of the war there had been no opportunities for practice because there was not a sufficient number of airships in existence, and that furthermore the difficulty of navigating airships under the varying conditions of visibility and weather over the enormous area of the North Sea, together with several other factors, gave rise to a lot of trouble. Owing to the fact, also, that the English fleet hardly ever appeared on the open sea, but, as every one knows, generally remained concealed in Scapa Flow or elsewhere, any conflict between the two fleets was so rare that our airship officers had but little opportunity of acquiring experience. On two occasions, however, when it was a question of victory or annihilation for the German fleet, the co-operation and reconnaissance of our airships were extremely important factors in the plans of the Admiral commanding the fleet. The first of these occasions was the battle of Jutland, and the second was the sortie of the German fleet on August 19, 1916.

In spite of the bad visibility, ten airships took part in the battle of Jutland. The L. 24 made the important discovery that the main body of the British fleet, which had engaged the German fleet during the day, had collected together its scattered units during the night of May 31st; while L. 11 was able to report the exact strength, formation, and the course followed by an entirely new English force, which had been cruising down in the south during the day.

It was clear that these reinforcements were intended to cut off the retreat of the German High Seas Fleet. The information supplied by these two airships, as the Admiral in charge of the German forces himself admits, caused him to continue his withdrawal southwards and develop his attack against this new adversary.

The fact that the enemy did not renew the engagement in the morning, but rapidly retreated to the west as soon as our airships had got into touch with them, can doubtless be attributed to a direct order from the British commander, who had recognised his error, and must, very justly, have feared that a resumption of the fight would complete his defeat.

The sortie of the German fleet on August 1916 led us far into the English waters, and was accompanied by eight airships which reconnoitred before the fleet in a fan-shaped formation. Of these five were actually in touch with strong hostile forces, and were able to direct the German fleet and enable it to develop its attack against these units before the enemy was even aware of the proximity of the German ships. The fact that the enemy did not engage in battle, in spite of the fact that they, as we discovered later, were at sea in full strength that day, but rather beat a retreat home at full speed, is in my opinion to be attributed to the fact that, in spite of unstinted expenditure of ammunition, they were unable to ward off our reconnoitring airships, which gave the German leader so much greater security and certainty in his position, and enabled him to make use of every tactical advantage. Also during the many attacks that the English made on the Eight, experience proved to us that as soon as the airships appeared the English forces retired and abandoned their undertaking, since the great advantage of a surprise had then disappeared. This activity on the part of our airships led to many conflicts with the enemy's naval forces, a very welcome break in the monotony of the watch that the commanders had to keep over the usually deserted North Sea, a break moreover that was practically without any danger, in spite of the fact that often enough more than thirty ships were simultaneously trying to bring the airship down, and were firing at it with guns of every caliber. Our airship crews used to derive much pleasure from the sight of the ships wildly zigzagging

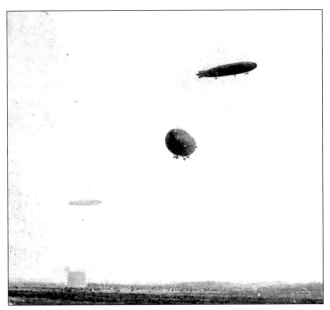

L. 35, L. 41, and L. 44 about to descend after carrying out a raid on England in August 1917.

across the sea, and scattering in order to avoid their bombs. Later, our airships frequently engaged in combat with the enemy's submarines, of which many which had light-heartedly entered into the fight instead of speedily diving, were destroyed by accurate bomb-dropping.

Airships also took a leading part in the cruiser operations against the enemy's cargo ships. The L. 40, having landed on the water, held up a steamer in order to examine its papers. On April 23, 1917 the L. 23 sighted a Norwegian three-masted barque while cruising some fifty nautical miles N.W. of the Horns Reef Lightship, When the airship approached, this vessel trimmed its sails and launched two boats. After a long and careful scrutiny, lest they should have to deal with some trap, the L. 23 landed on the water in the neighbourhood of the ship which, although unchallenged, had heaved to, and discovered that she was bound for West Hartlepool with a cargo of pit-props. The crew were ordered to return on board; the airship's steersman and two N.C.O.'s armed with pistols were sent with them, and after a voyage lasting forty-three hours this valuable prize was brought safely into a German harbour.

Exploits of this description were, however, soon abandoned, as the risk was out of proportion to the possible success, for there was always a considerable danger of the airship being destroyed, as it floated motionless on the water, by some submarine, aeroplane, or warship suddenly appearing on the scene.

'L. 59'

Airships were also used as a means of transport to districts otherwise inaccessible. Thus, for example, during the severe winter of 1916 and 1917, the L. 16 carried the necessary provisions to the inhabitants and garrison of one of our small North Sea islands, which was in danger of famine owing to the fact that all communication by sea had been cut off by the ice.

A far greater achievement, however, was the attempt made by the L. 59 in the autumn of 1917 to provide medical stores, and much other war material, to our heroic troops in East Africa, who were struggling against overwhelming odds. This undertaking, which was of quite exceptional importance on account of its moral effect on the Zeppelin airship designers and on the initiative of the Navy, was unfortunately abandoned owing to a false rumour that our garrison in East Africa had evacuated the whole of that region, The airship ascended from Jambol, in Bulgaria, flew diagonally across Egypt to the confluence of the Blue and the White Niles south of Khartoum, and, having thereby accomplished more than half its flight, was recalled by wireless and landed again at Jambol without any difficulty. It had been in the air for ninety-six consecutive hours, and had flown some 4200 miles over an entirely unexplored region. The commander, Captain Bockholt, announced in his report on the flight that he could have comfortably remained another two days in the air. In comparison with this achievement the first flight from England to America made in peace time by the English airship It. 34, an airship which, incidentally, had been copied from our design and concerning which there has been so much talk, was mere child's play, for it had been possible to our airships for many years past.

OVER LONDON IN A ZEPPELIN

The weather chart on April 25, 1916, showed favourable conditions, and we had every reason to hope that the prospective raid on England would actually take place. Instructions had been given that our ship, the L.Z. 97, was to be ready to leave the ground by 6.30 in the evening. We had only landed at dawn after a longish cross-country flight, and forthwith refreshed ourselves for the new venture by a short sleep.

All that afternoon we were busy making the necessary preparations for our expedition. The men in charge of the filling operations hurried about their jobs, and the gas streamed hissing into the compartments of the envelope, while mechanics tested the revolutions given by the engines. Clouds of dust whirled high in the blast of air from the propellers. When the Commander made his appearance through the hangar doors the officer on duty reported that all was ready. At a signal given by a blast on a whistle, the landing party, which had been standing to for some time, seized the hand-rails of the gondolas, A command - a sharp tug forward - and the ship moved slowly out of its hangar.

Gently guided by the ropes the ship glided out, its runners grating softly on their steel rails. A blast from the trumpet announced that the stern had emerged and that the ship was free of the hangar.

A signaller, instructed by the Commander, gave directions to the crew by a flag, and shortly the ship was swinging gently in the wind on the broad landing ground 200 yards from its shed.

'Hands off: ease up the guys.' The men at the ropes let go, and the landing party stepped back from the gondolas. For a moment the ship hung motionless before it soared majestically upwards. 'Hold on!' Hand-rails and ropes were seized again, and the craft was pulled down. Then the Commander went on board, and, after a hearty 'Good luck,' hundreds of brawny arms pushed the gondolas upwards into the sky.

We cast one brief glance round our home aerodrome, which lay flooded in the light of the setting sun, and then started the engines. Every man was filled with an inexpressible joy; we were off to England!

A long journey lay before us, the first section being over conquered Belgian territory. After a short time Brussels had been passed, and darkness drew on apace. It was well into the night before we reached the coast, and for hours after that we cruised over the English Channel, which could be seen dark green, almost black, beneath us. Night pressed down menacingly upon us, only millions of stars glittered in the heavens, and reflected their light in the waves. But here and there beneath us were red flecks which we knew were not the reflected images of stars. They were look-out vessels and patrol boats, through whose funnels we could see, deep down, the glowing furnaces. Except for these there was no light at all; everything was shrouded in unfathomable darkness and silence.

Thousands of feet above that waste of waters passed our narrow vessel; the deep throb of its engines sounded into the stillness of the night, causing the gondolas and flying wires to quiver.

We continually checked our course and kept an unceasing watch into the night, but there was nothing to be seen until at last we could make out the coast of England, At that moment the moon came to our assistance. It rose above the dark-green sea, a friend perhaps, but not one to be relied on, for as clearly as it showed to us our enemies below, it betrayed to them the presence of our ship in the sky. Again we made a brief comparison with the map, although we had already recognised the coastal contour as being near Blackwater, the very point which we had hoped to make. The reckoning of our course had been entirely free from error.

There is much uncertainty in these flights over the sea, as every one knows who has conducted raids which involve crossing the Channel. During the war we had to do without meteorological reports of the air above England, particularly over the west of England, and consequently it was impossible to form an accurate judgment of the weather conditions, seeing that they depend mostly upon barometrical depressions advancing from the west. We had to rely solely upon observations at the coast itself, and therefore had to take into account the possibility of a strong wind suddenly springing up which might blow the ship out of its course. This was a factor over which we had no control, and moreover when one is above the sea, particularly at night, there is no means whatever of discovering one's whereabouts.

Over England at last! Our hands are drawn to the bomb-release lever like iron to a magnet: but the time has not yet come, London is our objective, and there still remains a good two hours' flight before we arrive at our journey's end. We lean out of the gondola port-holes once more, and pick out landmarks and locate them on the map as well as we can from that height in the bright moonlight. Below us everything is as still as death, and the country is perfectly darkened. Not a gun is fired, not a search-light directed at us.

The English naturally do not want to give away prematurely the positions of their defence batteries and the towns which they protect.

Far, far away we discern a light, and soon afterwards a second. They lie on our course. A short calculation follows. We must be right over London, Impenetrable shadows envelop the gigantic city, only pierced here and there by minute pinpricks of light. Yet even so the various districts and the main streets can be unmistakably recognised in the moonlight.

On emerging from the interior, where I had been testing the bomb-release mechanism, I am amazed at the clearness with which the ground can be seen.

We know that the eyes below must also be watching us, but the silence remains unbroken. Did they really hope that we should not find their London?

At high speed we steer for the city, the Commander standing ready on the bombing platform. The electric lamps which he has now switched on glow with a dull vari-coloured light. His hand is on the buttons and levers, 'Let go!' he cries. The first bomb has fallen on London! We lean over the side. What a cursed long time it takes between release and impact while the bomb travels those thousands of feet! We fear that it has proved a 'dud' - until the explosion reassures us. Already we have frightened them; away goes the second, an incendiary bomb. It blazes up underneath and sets fire to something, thereby giving us a point from which to calculate our drift and ground speed. While one of us releases the bombs and another observes results, I make rapid calculations at the navigation table. Now the second incendiary hit is also visible. Its flames scarcely have leapt convulsively upwards in a shower of red sparks before we hear the shattering report of an explosion, so loud that it is plainly audible above the roar of the propellers. At the same time on come the searchlights, reaching after us like gigantic spiders' legs; right, left, and all around. In a moment the bright body of the ship lies in the beams.

'Hard aport!' The steersman spins his wheel, and in a moment the great ship obeys its helm. We are out of the dazzling rays and once more in the depths of night. But it is no longer pitch dark. The countless beams of searchlights fill the sky with a vivid light. They have lost us - strike, as it were, wildly past us, catch us once again, go on over us; one remains still, the others hunt around, crossing it or searching along it for the objective, while we steer in quite a different direction.

This mad frolic continues for hours on end.

We lose all idea of the passage of time as we fly on, every half-minute releasing another bomb.

Every explosion is observed, and its position pin-pricked on the map.

It is difficult to understand how we manage to survive the storm of shell and shrapnel, for, according to the chronometer, we have spent a good hour under that furious fire. When London lies far behind us, we can still recognise it distinctly; the searchlights are still stabbing the darkness - more than sixty of them - looking for the bird that had already flown. Silence closes in around us, and everything beneath seems stricken with death.

Now we have to struggle against the freshly-risen wind, but the ship luckily is undamaged, and every engine intact. We, therefore, grapple with the storm as we have just done with our enemies.

The last few hours and the events with which they had been filled are still fresh in our memories. The English coast lies behind us, receding farther and farther into the distance, and the foam on the crests of the waves beneath shimmers in the moonlight as though it is phosphorescent. A vague twilight envelops us. It is pitch dark inside the gondola, with the exception of the very faint spots of light from the pointers of the instruments. Many-coloured stars still dance before our eyes, the result of the dazzling searchlights. We are over the sea. The man at the elevating wheel rubs his eyes, blinks, quickly slides open the shutter of his lamp, and flashes its rays on his instruments. The gondola is lit up, as the light gleams on the aluminium. Then hell is let loose! They have long lain in wait for us down below there, and now the little dot of a gondola light has betrayed us. In a moment the searchlights of tho warships in the Thames estuary have caught us and hold us fast. Again a withering blast of fire is directed against us. 'Put out that light!' The Commander reaches over the steersman's shoulder and switches it off. But the ship, once caught, cannot get away from the searchlights. Shell after shell shrieks up at us, among them incendiary shells; they burst dangerously near. After ten minutes the light grew fainter, and the firing dies away. Again we travel through the gloom and silence - hour after hour.

The sky turns from indigo to grey, as dawn creeps up from the horizon. Many miles lie still before us, and the eastern horizon is red before we cross the Belgian coast at Ostend, Darkness still envelops the earth beneath, but up above already shines the light of day.

'Keep a sharp look-out for aeroplanes!' the Commander orders. Whenever a German airship was reported from England, aeroplanes ascended from the aerodromes on the coast, and flew out over the Channel to lie in wait and intercept its passage to the Belgian coast. They knew well enough the route we took on our return.

Between Bruges and Ghent two hostile aeroplanes are reported from the top platform. I take up my position with a machine gun on the starboard side of the forward gondola. I watch their approach, but they are flying too high, I cannot bring my gun to bear unless we get above them. Aloft, on the platform, the machine gun is chattering. A stream of flaming bullets flickers past us - too short.

Again and again at frequent intervals there are bursts of fire overhead. We know them of old. The Commander orders a climb: they can't cope with us at that. They are, of course, faster than we are, but we can beat them at climbing. The distance between us increases, and they are left behind. Suddenly there is another burst of machine-gun fire. The enemy has managed to overtake us, and is attacking us from below. We must not allow them to get above us at any price, because then they will be in a position to dive.

We climb higher and higher. The gas blows off madly amid the rattle of the machine guns, A minute later the blazing bullets are flashing past again. Again too short. All at once one of the aeroplanes turns, and goes down in a side-slip. It is suddenly surrounded by fleecy puffs. We are close to the Dutch frontier. Nevertheless the machine goes on down and must therefore be damaged, probably by bullets in the engine.

The other aeroplane does not like the look of things. He has, perhaps, expended all his ammunition; at any rate he sheers off and disappears.

On looking at the altimeter we find that we have broken the airship height record.

The rest of our journey home is accomplished without further mishap, and we land at our own aerodrome after a flight of nearly twelve hours' duration. Our gallant craft has left its first war flight behind it, our bombs lie in the City of London.

(LAMPEL.)

MILITARY AIRSHIPS
AIR RAIDS ON ENGLAND

Naturally the raids on England brought more recognition to the officers concerned than any other work. For one reason, the nation was made familiar with them in the newspapers.

On the night of January 19, 1915, the first raid by Zeppelins was made on the fortifications of the east coast of England, and although carried out by two ships - L. 3 and L. 4 only - it was the cause of dismay and terror throughout the whole of England, and great rejoicing in Germany. This raid proved to us that the hitherto unapproachable island was accessible to German arms, and that here too the war could be carried into the enemy's country. On the other hand, it gave rise to the most exaggerated hopes, for many were led to believe that the naval airship would be able to achieve the impossible, to reduce the whole of England to ruins in a very-short time, and thereby to decide the war. We ourselves never cherished exaggerated hopes as to the effects of our attacks, although, in spite of all English attempts to conceal the results, it was always perfectly obvious to us that the effects were extraordinarily great. Apart from the fact that we, of the Airship Service, could personally observe the results of our raids, trustworthy reports on our work were continually coming through.

If the raid were really as ineffectual as England made out, it is difficult to understand why she considered it necessary to adopt the elaborate system of aerial defence which was built up during the war. The simply fabulous defences in operation throughout the country, and especially in the neighbourhood of the East and South Coasts, almost defy description. In *personnel* alone, according to a careful estimate, at least 500,000 men were employed upon them, with a great quantity of *matériel* in the shape of guns, munitions, aeroplanes, and searchlights which otherwise could have been used on the Western Front, Thus the air raids, in addition to their destructiveness, and doubtless their very great moral effect on the population, relieved the pressure at the front. The first sign of demoralisation was the flight of all the well-to-do people from the East Coast, the depopulation of its watering-places, and a general feeling of panic in that part of the country.

Furthermore, the actual destruction caused must have been very great, when one considers that each individual airship can carry up to three tons of bombs. In clear weather the fires caused by them were often clearly seen twelve miles out to sea.

At first the raids encountered so little resistance, owing to the weakness of the aerial defences, that individual Zeppelins delivered attacks from a height of under 3000 feet. This condition, however, soon altered, for the strength of anti-aircraft defences rapidly increased from month to month. In fact, from the summer of 1916 onwards, we suffered heavy-losses, although the raids were carried out from a height of 9000 feet. Even then, in spite of a lavish expenditure of ammunition, and the use of the most powerful searchlights, anti-aircraft guns never scored except with lucky shots. Meanwhile, however, the aeroplane pilots had learnt to fly by night, and it was an easy matter, seeing that once caught by the searchlight beams it is almost impossible to escape, for them to spot an airship, and, by using incendiary ammunition, to shoot it down in flames.

It was believed in England that by this means a stop had been put to Zeppelin attacks, as there were no raids from the end of November 1916 until March 1917. This hope was soon disappointed. An entirely new type of airship had been designed during this period, a type which could attain a height of 18,500 feet, where the most powerful searchlights were utterly useless. Consequently both anti-aircraft guns and aeroplanes had to work in darkness, and the defensive measures against aircraft broke down.

Soon, however, other difficulties were encountered, the magnitude of which we had not hitherto been in a position to appreciate, and the presence of which formed the chief reason for the gradually diminishing frequency of the raids. A long flight in the intense cold - sometimes as many as 40 degrees of frost were registered - lack of oxygen, and the rarefied atmosphere, told upon the vitality of the airships' crews to such an extent that, finally, many men were unable to endure the height and had to give up flying. Particularly when high flying was first practised, and before the invention of the oxygen apparatus, it frequently happened that many members of the crew were rendered incapable by weakness or some other symptom of air-sickness. On the L. 44, for example, while making a raid on Harwich in May 1917, so many were affected by air-sickness, that the ship drifted over the town completely out of control, and without a single engine running. It was not until they were well out to the middle of the North Sea that two of the engines were restarted, and the ship was able to return to its base.

The factors which caused more trouble than anything else to the raiders were the unfavourable meteorological conditions which prevailed at high altitudes. They almost invariably encountered a strong wind blowing from the west or the north, and the airship, which developed only one quarter of its engine power at that height, could scarcely make headway against it. Frequently, therefore, even when favourable weather obtained at a lower level, our ships could not reach their objective. It was also due to this cause that the Air Force suffered its grievous loss in October 1917, when four airships were driven by a northerly gale into French territory and were lost. But even this difficulty was overcome during 1918, when the airships were fitted with more powerful engines designed to develop their greatest power at high altitudes. This gave the Zeppelins a considerably increased radius of action, and enabled them to carry out nights of much longer duration. A raid lasted from twenty to thirty hours, according to the weather and the objective. The latter was usually left to the discretion of the commanding officer, owing to the almost complete dependence upon the weather conditions, and because the weather at the base gave no indication as to what might be encountered over England When our giant aeroplanes in Flanders became able to reach London and the south of England, the airship was confined in its sphere of action principally to those industrial regions of the Midlands and the North which were beyond the range of aeroplanes. The number of airships participating in each attack varied according to the number which were airworthy; the biggest raid was successfully carried out by thirteen airships.

In the Baltic our naval airships accomplished useful work by observation patrols for the Navy, and by raids into Russian territory. Naturally, however, since England was our most powerful antagonist on the sea, the greatest number of airship operations were carried out over the North Sea. Only the few who were fortunate enough to serve with the Air Force as pilots or Zeppelin crews during the war, can realise how magnificent was the aerial arm created by German inventive genius and energy. Not one of our opponents ever achieved anything comparable to it.

My First and Most Dangerous Raid on England

At noon on November 27, 1916, three officers were sitting in the Casino at Nordholz. One of them, Lieut.-Commander Max Dietrich of the L. 34, was celebrating his birthday, and his chair had been decorated with boughs of fir trees. The weather chart for that morning informed us that the storm which for days had been blowing over the North Sea, had at last died down. Capt. Straffer, the airship's pilot, having inquired of his commanding officer whether there would be a raid on England that day, had been informed that it depended on the meteorological report which was expected from Bruges. We had almost given up hope when the adjutant rushed into the mess shouting: 'Gentlemen, orders to attack the industrial district of the English Midlands; splendid prospects; the first ship must be in the air by one o'clock at the latest!'

After that, nobody thought of eating; there was too much rushing about and excitement, and the ringing of telephone bells. First-Lieutenant Frankenberg, who was in command of the L. 21, said to his companions: Leave the birthday things as they are; we'll have our celebrations tomorrow.' At 12.45 exactly, L. 21 left its shed and set out for England. A quarter of an hour later I started on L. 22, followed by L. 34. I cannot recall what my thoughts were at that time, but I remember the glowing faces of my men, for it was our first raid. In other words, our dearest wish was about to be fulfilled.

In a short time we reached Heligoland. There was not a cloud in the sky, and the eye was met by a magnificent spectacle. On all sides were the grey shapes of these gigantic birds of prey, flying together over the water. On the left were the airships from Ahlhorn and Hage; in the middle our ships from Nordholz; and on the right were those from Tondern, I counted ten in all, each setting its course for Flamborough Head. Darkness soon set in, and they gradually disappeared from sight, only the L. 21 remained visible for a long time, right ahead of us. Great masses of vapour floated at a height of 7000 feet in the west; we climbed above them into the clear starlit sky. The Aurora Borealis shimmered

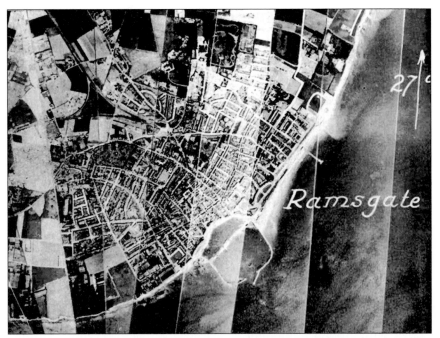

Ramsgate, photographed from a German reconnaissance machine at a height of 17,000 feet.
A 'mosaic' photograph, consisting of several exposures pieced together.

away to the north, throwing great pencils of light up to the zenith, and making the horizon as bright as day. Suddenly appearing from out of the cloudbanks, L. 36 bore clown upon us only a few hundred yards away, then disappeared again like a ghost. Nest, to our great annoyance, we were enveloped in thick mist, and the thermometer registered 16 degrees of frost. We strained our eyes to pierce the obscurity ahead, whence, in clear weather, the enemy's country should be visible.

10.15 in the evening. The slender sickle of the moon had disappeared beneath the horizon in a halo of orange light, and before me, only fifteen nautical miles away, the English coast at Flamborough Head could be seen sharply outlined. In the south a bright shaft of flame appeared, steadily increasing until it lit up the whole sky: that was where some Zeppelin had dropped its bombs, and the ship itself could be seen glistening in the beams of innumerable searchlights. Again the eyes of my men shone with pleasure, for they knew that we ourselves would very shortly be over the enemy's territory.

The next few hours slipped by like minutes. We reached our objective amid the dazzling rays of searchlights, the banging of guns, and the bursting shells which glowed as though red hot. Above it all we heard the explosion of our bombs while the airship shuddered throughout its entire length. It was like some wild phantasmagoria. Suddenly to the north of us, where one of our number had been caught by the searchlights, there appeared a crimson ball of fire, which rapidly increased in size. A minute later we recognised the glowing skeleton of an airship falling in flames. We wondered who it might be.

By 1.30 A.M. the raid was over. As we made for home darkness again enveloped us. Far behind many patches of flame on the ground bore testimony to the success of our raid. While I was contemplating the scene the pilot suddenly exclaimed that the ship was rapidly losing height, and that he was unable to prevent it. This was hardly to be wondered at, for we discovered that the compartments inside the envelope had been riddled with shrapnel and splinters of shells, and the gas was pouring out. It was a moment which demanded a cool head. Owing to the darkness no part of the ship was visible. As quickly as possible I brought her down below 2000 feet in order to ease the internal pressure and thus to lose less gas. Apart from this consideration the engines developed more power at that height. Everything superfluous was thrown overboard, and disappeared into the depths below. The machine guns, every drop of our ballast water, even the petrol, as much as we could spare, were sacrificed in this way. In spite of all I had but little hope of bringing the craft safely back to its base, and my spirits gradually sank as I thought of lying somewhere beneath the waters of the North Sea.

The men were still so enthusiastic over the raid they had just carried out that they were quite unperturbed, and did not even fully appreciate the danger, I therefore quietly ordered the officer of the watch to get into touch with the Admiral of the Meet by wireless, to report on our raid and to add these words: 'The airship has been severely damaged by artillery fire and is urgently in need of assistance/ Five minutes later we received an answer to the effect that torpedo boats and cruisers were being despatched, and in the grey light of early dawn we met the Second

Torpedo-Boat Flotilla, scouring the sea in search of us sixty nautical miles north-west of Borkum. A rising west wind helped us along, and the gas expanding as it grew warmer increased our lift. This turned the scale in our favour, for we reached the neighbouring aerodrome at Hage with the last drop of petrol in our tanks. Everything movable had been thrown overboard, and the engines could not have kept going for another half hour.

There was no return to Nordholz on that day, for both our other ships had fallen victims to the terrible fire of the enemy.

The birthday had become a day of death.

(HOLLENDER.)

Chapter II
Types and Their Application

The Influence of Trench Warfare On the Use of Aircraft and Aerial Tactics

THE COLOSSAL ARMIES which faced each other in closed lines hundreds of miles long in September 1914, when trench warfare set in, allowed no room for movement either of the armies themselves or of the attendant cavalry. Consequently both strategical and tactical reconnaissance had to be carried out over the heads of the armies. Open flanks of the old style, where the scouting bodies of cavalry were able to slip round the wings to reconnoitre the situation behind the lines and to observe the enemy's movements, disposition and the distribution of his reserves, the system of railways and roads, and the extent of his fortifications, etc., were now almost non-existent. The distances that had to be covered and the area which had to be reconnoitred increased in proportion to the numbers of the belligerents.

The longer ranges of which guns were capable, the development of indirect fire tactics, and the completely camouflaged and concealed battery positions, together with the ever increasing volume of artillery fire, made it more difficult to observe for the artillery and to carry out the necessary fire control. There arose, therefore, the need for a new means of observation. The artillery observation machine had to satisfy this want, first of all by discovering concealed targets, and then by making it possible to bombard them successfully with only a small expenditure of ammunition. The observation balloons, which, as a rule, were compelled to remain some distance behind the lines, were no longer able to cope with the situation, although their assistance was still indispensable to the infantry. Then, again, attacks on the enemy's balloons could only be carried out by aeroplanes. Thus it came to pass that the aeroplane, which originally was only used for purely strategic purposes, was now also applied tactically.

Together with long-distance reconnaissance whose tendency was ever to strive after yet more distant objectives, there developed various specialised forms of tactical reconnaissance, a type of work which called for the aid of every scientific means, particularly the camera, and therefore there came into existence special types of machine such as the artillery observation machines which we have already mentioned, and the infantry contact machines. On account of the observing eyes in the air the higher command was compelled to make use of the night more and more for moving troops and material and to develop anti-aircraft artillery both in number and efficiency. The result of this was soon made manifest; the aeroplane was obliged to undertake night flying, while its original height of 1000 or 1500 feet, which was hardly even safe against rifle or machine-gun fire, increased to a height of from 7000 to 10,000 feet, and later, in consequence of aerial fighting, to still greater heights.

Aerial fighting itself may be reckoned as a link in the chain of cause and effect between trench warfare and aerial development. Duels between aeroplanes, for which no preparation whatever had been made in Germany in peace time although England and France had already foreseen its possibility, were a product of the second year of the war. The first phase of the Great War knew nothing of them. In the days of open warfare it was necessary to avoid any conflict with hostile machines because the principal work expected of aeroplanes in those days consisted of scouting and long-distance strategical reconnaissance on account of the rapid movements and far-reaching attacks associated with that style of warfare and in consequence of the long time taken by cavalry to perform this work. The cavalry then took over the work of co-ordinating the movements of the Army: i.e. tactical reconnaissance. The advent of trench warfare altered all this entirely, and all reconnaissance and screening operations were taken over by aircraft from the cavalry.

In the old days mounted troops had to force a way through the enemy's screen of scouts in order that the reconnoitring patrols might carry out their work, and, similarly, now fighting machines, assisted by anti-aircraft guns, had to overcome the enemy's aerial defences in order to open up a way for our own observation machines. Also the artillery observation machines at the front, and the areas behind our lines and at home, had to be protected from attack or from the designs of the enemy's bombers; on the other hand, the way had to be kept clear for our own squadrons, and protection afforded against attack. Aircraft, therefore, had to undertake new work. Aerial tactics came into existence, and very shortly brought about the use of formations or squadrons for aerial fighting to replace the single fighting machines.

Co-operation with the infantry became ever closer until eventually the aeroplane, in the shape of contact patrol machines, actually took part in operations on the ground, and became indeed a decisive factor in battle. The influence of trench warfare therefore gradually extended the scope of aerial activity from purely strategical reconnaissance to work in the neighbourhood of our front line trenches and those of the enemy, until eventually, in big offensives, the aeroplane became tho only reliable link with the fighting troops.

Finally, the vast accumulations of war material of every description, of ammunition dumps, of troops concentrated into camps; the stations and harbours crowded with trains and ships behind the stationary lines of trenches; all provided such targets for aerial bomb-raids as would never have existed under the conditions of open warfare. Although the raids carried out by individual machines which were only capable of carrying small loads of bombs produced a moral though, rarely, material effect, in the second year of the war it became necessary to organise bombing on a large scale, and to make use of the big machines which had been designed in the meantime. This led from the combination of various small units, a method which at first was only occasionally employed, to the systematic use of large bombing squadrons, for which a special science of tactics was evolved as in the case of the fighting and infantry contact machines. The use of great height, in other words the full inclusion of the third dimension, was the most peculiar feature of this science, and was the factor which principally distinguished it from that to which we had previously been accustomed. AH the various kinds of work which we have described in this brief review produced their own special type of machine, each type having been developed by experience, frequently altered, and perfected to suit those general purposes which we are now about to consider.

(NEUMANN.)

LONG-DISTANCE RECONNAISSANCE

The principal work of aircraft consists of strategical reconnaissance. That fact remained true throughout all the changes which the young service naturally had to experience during four years of war. Because at the beginning of the war this work was exclusively carried out by flying men, it happened that, in spite of the greater numerical strength and differentiation of the units that were formed later, purely strategical reconnaissance was only allotted to the oldest and most experienced airmen, who, in order that they might be able to satisfy the requirements of the higher command, were generally senior officers of exceptional experience.

In detail, the development of long-distance reconnaissance varied with the demands made by the operations on the ground. According to whether the ever-changing situation on the ground caused the higher command to attach more importance to observation of the enemy's intentions, or to the working out of our own plans, long-distance reconnaissance became the principal consideration, or else receded into the background. In the long run it became principally a question of the material available, and at times even depended solely upon this factor. The region to be reconnoitred by these machines was sharply limited between the strip of ground which could be observed by infantry patrols, and the enemy's back areas, from which we could only obtain information through the unreliable sources of the Press or of paid agents.

In open warfare, both on the Western and Eastern Fronts, it was the flying man's duty to explore that area which was inaccessible to horses and therefore to the eyes of the cavalry, to report on the disposition of the enemy's troops and to reveal his intentions by observing movements on the roads and railways. At first, however, neither the infantry nor the higher command perceived the value of the aeroplane as a means of observation, and even in the most urgent cases but little use was made of it. But it always happened that whenever a commanding officer, with due understanding of the limitations of aerial observation at that time, made use of this means, the aeroplane exercised a predominating influence on the operations. Particularly before and during the battle of Tannenberg much good work was accomplished, and the disposition of the small forces at our disposal was based upon aerial reconnaissance which early obtained information concerning the movements of the Russian hordes. One can say the same of the decisive operations of the German attacking flank on the Marne.

When the German Army on the Western Front was compelled to take up the defensive in the beginning of October 1914, the new methods of trench warfare at first exercised but little influence on the duties of the flying man. However, the work of tactical reconnaissance was allotted to aeroplanes because the operations of infantry patrols were so restricted under these conditions. Even then strategical reconnaissance remained of fundamental importance, in fact gained in importance on account of these new conditions, because a reliable survey of the disposition of the enemy's troops was even more to be desired since our defensive operations had to be carried out with such inadequate forces.

When the fighting became more and more concentrated into the trench system during 1915 and 1916 - we were acting principally on the defensive, and only attacked once (at Verdun) - new demands were made upon both the infantry and the higher command, and consequently the Air Force had to undertake new tasks. Reconnaissance was almost entirely confined to the area within range of our own artillery; battery positions and points of concentration close behind the enemy's trenches became the principal targets for our guns, and consequently artillery observation and contact patrol work grew in importance.

As the *personnel* of the Air Force did not grow numerically in proportion to the ever increasing amount of work it was called upon to perform, the flying units devoted themselves almost entirely to the service of the infantry and long-distance reconnaissance was practically abandoned. During that period of the war neither side achieved any strategical success, and the considerations of the higher command were principally tactical. During the bitter fighting around Verdun and in the battle of the Somme, we were content to deal with the front line only, and the necessity for back area information seemed hardly pressing. This state of affairs was altered after Field-Marshal von Hindenburg took control during the later phases of the battle of the Somme, As the general situation was unfavourable to any offensive operations in the coming spring our energies were concentrated on preparing to meet the expected attempt on the part of the enemy to break through our lines. When our voluntary withdrawal dislocated the enemy's plans of attack and compelled him to undertake another and unexpected advance, there arose yet another moment of strategical importance with regard to the conduct of the war. Long-distance reconnaissance again became a vital necessity, for we had to observe the enemy's concentrations with a view to ascertaining the likeliest direction of his main attack.

It was fortunate for the Air Force at this particular time that more importance was attached to its work than had ever previously been the case, 'The Hindenburg Programme' set out to equalise the numerical inferiority so manifest during the battle of the Somme, and the flying service was greatly reinforced in consequence. During the spring of 1917 we could at least feel ourselves equal to the Entente in quality of *matériel*, though indeed not numerically superior. The newly created units made it possible to carry out new work along with the old, From that time onwards until the end of the war the results of long-distance reconnaissance became one of the most important factors in the plans prepared by G.H.Q..

The tactics employed in long-distance reconnaissance followed the general situation of the war. The enemy were able to defend their line so well on account of their great number of fighting machines that it was hardly possible for any single aeroplane to break through. Owing to the small forces at our disposal it was impossible for us to escort our reconnaissance machines, or even to attempt to reach the objective by employing a formation of several two-seater machines. We therefore had to endeavour to effect our long-distance reconnaissance by employing very fast machines, which flew over the enemy's defensive patrols at a great height, and therefore had a better chance of escaping observation and of evading pursuit. For this purpose, of course, climbing power and speed were the principal considerations, and up to the very end the aircraft industry always rose to the occasion. The fact that in spite of the enemy's aerial defences, which grew steadily stronger and more wary, and in spite of the increasing difficulty of obtaining material, there was nevertheless no objective - even including the mouth of the Thames and the distant coast of France between Calais and Havre - which was inaccessible to our reconnaissance machines, proves the excellence of German workmanship and the general efficiency of the aircraft industry.

As a result of the great heights at which our machines were compelled to fly on account of the anti-aircraft batteries, more use was made of the camera. Even the most practised eye cannot pick out all the important details from the innumerable objects that are to be seen at a height of 18,000 or 20,000 feet, and furthermore the necessity of remaining in such dangerous circumstances for hours on end, during which period the attention has to be so concentrated yet so divided, causes a gradual relaxation of the nerves, and a loss of personal efficiency. Consequently the camera lens took the place of the eye for detailed observation, and the observer was only expected to acquire a comprehensive general impression of the situation which would assist him, after he had landed, to interpret the photographs he had obtained. The information so acquired would then be used to formulate the flying policy of the following day.

It was necessary to keep all rivers and canals that were navigable under careful observation, and information, as detailed as possible, concerning the enemy's railroad traffic had to be obtained. Even if the enemy moved their *matériel* by night, the accumulations of rolling stock at the stations and the dumps betrayed them. At first newly-erected huts were sufficient evidence that the enemy were concentrating their troops in preparation for some big offensive. Soon, however, this evidence lost its value, since the enormous number of huts which had been built for the earlier operations made it unnecessary for the enemy to construct any more for his later offensives. Before the end of the war the region on either side of the tines on the Western Front resembled a gigantic camp. Huts looked very much the same from above whether they had roofs or not, and even when large bodies of troops were moved, this fact, assisted by the refined methods of camouflage, made it almost impossible to detect any change from above.

However, the disposition of the enemy's aerial forces always gave reliable evidence on this point. Aerodromes, with their characteristic arrangement of large and easily visible hangars, and their incessant activity, could not be concealed even towards the end of the war. But the Allies were so strong in this respect that they were hardly even obliged to weaken the aerial forces on either side of the point from which they intended to launch their offensive. Nevertheless the concentration of flying units, when it occurred, was always a sign of preparation for a big attack. Experiments were made with dummy aerodromes, but it was found that they cost too much time and work to carry out on the necessary scale. In the early part of 1918, when both sides were endeavouring to decide the issue of the war by an unstinted expenditure of men and *matériel*, great importance was attached to the movements of ships on the English Channel and round about the harbours, while a good deal of attention was paid to the enemy's vast dumps and depots, which seemed large enough to equip the population of the whole world. The tankdromes lying far behind the lines became a focus for constant observation. Wherever the enemy attacked, he employed tanks. The movements of tanks, their testing grounds and places of assembly, invariably betrayed the point at which the attack was to be delivered. Finally, long-distance reconnaissance provided the far-reaching and hard-hitting arm of our bombing squadrons with excellent targets by locating *matériel* and ammunition dumps.

The work which we have described above was a very severe strain on the flying men. Among other things they had to endure the appalling cold, which at the height of 15,000 feet was often as low as -50 degrees Centigrade even in summer, and owing to the long periods during which they had to remain at these altitudes they suffered from the lack of oxygen. Many a poor fellow who had carried oat a long and successful flight far behind the enemy's lines lost his strength before his work was finished. Enfeebled and unable to concentrate his faculties, he would fall victim to some enemy fighting machine on his return flight. Others could not use their machine guns on account of frost bite, and, being defenceless, succumbed to the relentless attacks of the enemy. How often were the minutes anxiously counted as one calculated the amount of petrol which was left, when on the homeward flight one was engaged in some unexpected conflict against overwhelming odds, and our own lines seemed hardly to be getting any nearer! And who does not remember the feeling with which one listened for the slightest signs of engine failure after a long, long flight? But if the work was heavy, the reward was also great. Did we not have a constant pride in the knowledge that we were observing for the higher command, and that, far above the devastated battlefields, we were keeping watch for our comrades on the ground in their self-sacrificing and bitter struggle? No matter how hard the strife between spiritual willingness and the weakness of the flesh may have been, every man who engaged in long-distance reconnaissance flying during the war will secretly long for those glorious hours in his gallant, trusty machine, when, beneath the glare of the sun and bathed in the dazzling blue of heaven, it bore him safely along the irregular curve of the French coast to the grey mists of Paris, and thence back to the shimmering peaks of the Alps. German manhood, in its search for the joys of clamorous adventure in lands far distant and of every hue, was enticed to many other theatres of war; the sunny Adriatic and Macedonia's wild crags allured the adventurer; perhaps, even, he heard the call of the Pyramids, or far across the billows of the Black Sea was drawn into the mysteries of the East.

Not unjustly were our scouting airmen called the 'Cavalry of the Army,' when once trench warfare had laid that ancient and gallant service in its grave. The airman has inherited the daring spirit of the horseman to whom no horizon is too remote.

(DYCKHOFF.)

TACTICAL RECONNAISSANCE

We have already described how, in the course of time, tactical reconnaissance and the registration of targets devolved almost entirely upon the Air Force; how this work became more and more closely identified with photographic reconnaissance; how the camera and the photographic machine were developed; and how, in the last phase of the war, special photographic units were established. We have also estimated the tactical value of photographic reconnaissance. The following section deals more especially with the subject of artillery observation. A few typical descriptions will have to suffice for the illustration of our subject. The higher command required information concerning the principal alterations in the enemy's trench system and all the facts established by photographic reconnaissance which might throw a light on the intentions of the enemy, any rearrangement of his forces, extensions of his lines of communication, etc., while every detail appertaining to the infantry, artillery, pioneers, and trench-mortar units had to be registered with the utmost accuracy. Photographic reconnaissance presupposed a continual exchange of information between the infantry and the Air Force; only by such means could full use be made of it. Reports from the front line trenches and observation posts, periscopic photographs, the facts obtained from prisoners and by the infantry patrols; above all, however, the observations made from the balloons and the balloon panoramic photographs, had to be consulted for supplementary information. Tactical reconnaissance was perhaps the most dangerous work that the airman was required to perform owing to the incessant menace from hostile fighting machines and anti-aircraft guns, which sought, at any cost and by any means, to prevent the photographic machines from discovering any details of tactical importance.

(NEUMANN.)

CO-OPERATION BETWEEN AEROPLANES AND ARTILLERY

The artillery observation machine had to assist the artillery and do the work which was not possible by means of ground observation alone. This work consisted chiefly of discovering targets and of observing the effect of our own fire. By the word 'target' I mean anything which can or should be engaged by the artillery. The most important objectives are the enemy's artillery, strong points, saps and mining works, infantry camps, parks, railheads, the ascension places of their balloons, roads, billets and concentration points of the infantry, tanks, and transport on the roads and railways. Together with the aerial photographs, the information supplied by actual observation yielded valuable evidence, particularly on the question as to whether a position was occupied or not.

This fact had a particular advantage in that it made the immediate use of the artillery possible, whereas, even under the most favourable conditions, a few hours must elapse before a photograph could be turned to good account. At the end of this time, most moving targets would no longer be within the area shown on the photograph, and consequently could not be attacked.

The search for objectives became more difficult every day of the war, because both sides were compelled to withdraw all targets from hostile observation as much as possible. Many experiments in camouflage were made during the war, and, through competition with the enemy, the science rose from clumsy beginnings to refined maturity. Not only were woods, gardens, quarries, gravel pits, brushwood, hedges, and stacks of corn used as concealments, but special scenery even was made to screen

The submarine base, coastal batteries, and aerodrome at Dover (April 1316), taken from a German aeroplane, (a) Submarine base and several submarines. (b) Reservoirs, (c) Military Prison. (d) Coastal batteries of Langton Fort. (e) Barracks, (f) Infantry training trenches, (g) Aerodrome and 7 aeroplanes.

certain objects. Small copses were planted, avenues and covered ways were built, large nets plastered with twigs and leaves were spread over the spot which was to be hidden. Guns and trains, tents and barracks, even aeroplanes, were streaked with bright colours and thereby became difficult to see. Eventually all uniforms and the whole equipment were thus painted with protective colouring. Artificial clouds or smoke screens were used for temporary concealment, and dummy positions were extensively employed as a means of deceiving and diverting the attention of the enemy.

Hostile artillery was most easily located by observing the gun flashes and the puffs of smoke, while in winter gun positions could be spotted by the thawed patches of ground in front, Further evidence was given by the approaches which stood out particularly clearly in winter. It was only in the open warfare of 1914, and, to a certain extent, during the big offensives, that it was possible to recognise actual guns and troops, for on the latter occasions there was no time for lengthy camouflage preparations, while during 1914 reconnaissance was carried out from a low height, such as 3000 feet. Railway guns were, as a rule, easily seen from a very great height. Earthworks and fortifications could be recognised by the freshly-turned earth. Transport on the road was clearly visible in dry weather by the clouds of dust, while on other occasions the vehicles showed up against the white background of the road, and in winter they left tracks on the snow. Railway trains could scarcely be concealed on account of the smoke and steam from the engines. In spite of that fact, during the offensive of 1918, the enemy attempted to screen the line from Doullens to St. Pol.

The airman reported to the staff of the unit with which he was working, concerning any target that he might observe. This information could be transmitted by various means:-

1. By word of mouth, or by telephone, after he had landed at his home aerodrome or on the auxiliary landing ground.
2. By dropping a bag containing messages or the section of a map with suitable notes, or by smoke signals discharged over the staff headquarters of his unit.
3. By wireless. This method was by far the quickest, but suffered from the disadvantage that the enemy could 'listen in,' and could cause confusion by counter messages. It was therefore necessary to use some code or abbreviations which were unintelligible to the enemy. These abbreviations had to be changed frequently.

To obviate long and tedious descriptions the whole battle zone was divided into a series of squares, 1000 metres each way, and the horizontal and perpendicular lines were marked with numbers, or numbers and letters. These large squares were divided into twenty-five smaller squares, and these were quartered with letters. It was therefore possible to indicate an area of 100 square metres by using six numbers and a letter - e.g 2635.20.C.

Apart from this method of 'pin-pointing' by squares, each marked target would be indicated by some covering name, Christian names were used, or names of towns, rivers, etc. When a message was abbreviated it was, of course, necessary that the receiver should use the same abbreviations and map divisions as the observer.

Every wireless station had its special call consisting of two or three letters, a fact which made it possible for each wireless message to be directed to a definite address. Communication between the ground station and the aeroplane was effected by strips of white cloth in summer, or red cloth in winter, each strip measuring about 16 ft., by 2 ft.. These strips were laid out in certain figures, each figure indicating some specific abbreviation. Wireless telegraphy was also used for communicating from the ground to the aeroplane. Good results were obtained at night by using coloured lights for artillery control.

The work of the artillery observer can be divided into three main categories: directing fire at a target agreed on before the flight; at targets which the observer has picked up during the flight and indicated to the artillery for instantaneous engagement; and, finally, the control of drum fire (preparatory barrage, box barrage, creeping barrage, etc). The first style was commonly used against the enemy's artillery and supports. The artillery observation machine was therefore principally concerned with those targets that could not be observed by any other means, such as targets behind concealing woods or high emplacements, A systematic bombardment of the hostile artillery constituted an important item in the preparations for an attack, and for weakening the enemy's forces in defence. The second method was employed when the observer 'spotted' a target, reported it to the artillery by wireless, and immediately directed fire upon it.

In the case of drum fire he was principally concerned with the general position of the barrage and the filling up of any gaps or places where it was weak.

In order to carry out his work the artillery observer had to know, among other things, the exact position of our own batteries, of the lines, and of the message-receiving stations. He was not allowed to take any map which had been marked with notes on his flight, lest important information should fall into the hands of the enemy. Then again he had to memorise the whole region behind the enemy's lines. It was well worth his while to study all the latest aerial photographs before embarking on a flight. The following example will give a practical illustration of the manner in which the artillery observer carried out his work. His orders might be as follows: 'Direct the fire of a heavy howitzer battery 2/Fs.A.7 on the hostile battery at 3251.24.a as target No. 1, and the fire of the mortar battery 5/Fs.A.7 on the battery at 3452.11.a as target No. 2.'

As a preliminary the observer gets into touch by telephone with both the batteries with which he is to work. He informs them: 'I shall start at 6.30 A.M. and engage target No. 1 first, then target No. 2. My call is Ka.' The 'ready to fire' signal for both batteries will then be displayed on the ground station.

The machine starts, flies over the message-receiving station, and calls it up several times as follows: 'Ka Target No. 1,' in order to make sure that the wireless station is receiving his signals. The sign 'Received' is then laid out on the ground. As soon as the battery is ready to open fire another signal is displayed. The shoot can now begin. The machine flies towards the target and gives the order to open fire. The battery fires, and after a short time the observer will notice a burst in the neighbourhood of the target. The position of this burst he announces by wireless, e.g. '200 left 400 short.' The battery alters the direction and elevation of its guns, and after about two minutes the observer again signals it to fire, and announces the position of the bursts as, say, '100 right 100 over' In this manner shot after shot is observed until the shells are actually striking the target. At this point the general effect is reported, and the observer signals several shots simultaneously, e.g. '4 over, 1 direct, 2 over,' As soon as the battery is satisfied with the result it lays out the signal 'change targets' on the ground. The observer replies: 'Received, Target No. 2,' Then the ground station again displays the signal 'ready to fire,' and the second shoot is carried out in the same manner as the first.

Before the installation of the wireless apparatus the position of each burst was communicated to the artillery by means of coloured lights fired from the machine. A white light meant over, a red short, one green right, two green left. Later, the coloured lights were replaced by electric signalling lamps.

An effective means of weakening the enemy and of causing damage and moral effect was afforded by the practice of engaging moving targets. Special batteries were selected for this purpose, generally long-range batteries capable of rapid fire. These batteries were placed at the disposal of the artillery observer, whose work consisted of keeping an eye on the enemy and reporting all suitable objectives. Any target which seemed suitable to the observer he reported in the form of a question, and then waited for the signal 'yes' or 'no' to be displayed, or until he was informed by wireless whether the battery wished to open fire or not. The shoot, if agreed to, was carried out in the manner already described. Much good work was accomplished by co-operation between the Air Force and these special batteries. During the English offensives it frequently happened that infantry and cavalry which were ready to be brought up were attacked before they could take any part in the battle; as a rule they were scattered after suffering heavy casualties. More often still, the terrible tanks were damaged, and sometimes even destroyed, before they could advance to the attack. In Flanders we succeeded in driving back the destructive anti-aircraft battery near Ypres to the west bank of the Yser. Railway transport in the neighbourhood of the front line was impossible in fine weather owing to these batteries. During our own offensives, hostile columns preparing for a counter-attack, advancing tanks, and artillery were dealt with by the same method.

The work of our machines was rendered exceptionally difficult by the heavy anti-aircraft fire to which they were subjected. Some of the targets were a great distance behind the lines - 30 miles or more - and owing to this fact and the bitter opposition he had to overcome, it was seldom possible for the artillery observer to remain over the target for a long time. Work of this description was, therefore, generally carried out under cover of darkness. The artillery observer was also employed for directing our barrage fire. As a preliminary the observer used to mark out on a photographic map the area to be covered by the barrage, together with the direction of fix for each battery, and number of the targets. One after another the batteries were then controlled in the manner we have already described. Thus, for example, during the defensive operations in Flanders as many as sixteen batteries were controlled on one flight, an achievement which would have taken half a day to accomplish if the observation had been carried out from the ground.

The activity of the artillery machines and the damage they brought about compelled the enemy to devise special counter measures. Along with the anti-aircraft batteries they established a strong force of fighting machines in order to hinder and restrain the work of our artillery observers. Frequently the work could only be done after innumerable aerial combats, and many tasks were only possible under the escort of our own fighting machines. The indefatigable labours of these airmen and the self-sacrificing determination of the artillery pilots are to be thanked for the fact that, in spite of the enemy's numerical superiority, the German artillery machines carried out their work satisfactorily and completely, and gave to the hard-pressed infantry that support which was demanded of them.

A HOT TIME OVER ALBERT (JUNE 1918)

One wonderful June morning, when the sky was cloudless and the atmosphere unusually clear, I set out at 6 A.M. to register a shoot for one light and one heavy field battery, and also a 15 cm. gun. Archie bursts in the west were thickly dotted together, and announced that once again the Devil was about in the air.

We flew over the region of the Somme battle of 1916, a region which had been beaten and obliterated by the hammer-like blows of the War-God, Here, where once men had lived, there was not a ruin nor a tree to be seen. Only the sad multitudinous piles of rubbish faintly commemorated the sites of former habitations. On our way to Albert we flew over Bouchavesnes, Maurepas, and Maricourt.

An English squadron of eighteen D.H.9s flew over us at a great height, turned south, closely followed by our anti-aircraft fire, and dropped their belated Easter eggs on Cappy-sur-Somme, thereby enveloping that small village and its neighbouring aerodrome in thick clouds of smoke. According to official information and instructions, it was necessary to keep a sharp eye on all aircraft, in order to distinguish between friend and foe, and to avoid being taken by surprise.

The dump at Becourt-Becordel had for a long time been marked on the map in big white letters as 'Target No.1, awaiting registration,' and it was decided that a shoot could also be carried out on the sugar factory at Ribemont, In that position there was a battery which had bombarded the bridges over the Ancre, and had harried the progress of the morning rations to the troops in the front line. A slight pressure on the key of the wireless apparatus, and the four guns of my battery flashed in a small wood. Forty seconds later four shells burst in the garden to the east of the factory, some 200 yards short. The hostile battery, wishing to conceal its whereabouts, ceased fire, but we were not to be deceived by any such clumsy artifice. Two minutes later the next salvo placed two shells on the factory and two close by. After a bombardment lasting half an hour, the factory went up in flames, and the explosion of ammunition informed us that our friends, the Tommies, had stored all sorts of useful material on the spot. We were busy registering on our first target when from the west approached five hideous machines, dirty green in colour and ornamented with tricolour circles, but, on seeing the triplanes that were hovering over us, they came to the conclusion that we had better be left in peace. Their decision was wise, for the gaily coloured triplanes would stand no nonsense and were most disconcertingly accurate with their machine guns.

Next we went to our second target, a battery emplaced on the southern outskirts of Bresle, and proceeded to bombard them. This was paying them back in their own coinage, for we interrupted them in the process of shelling our own battery. The work seemed to last so long that we began to be anxious concerning our supply of petrol, for we had still a third battery marked on our map as being ready to receive our attention.

After two hours, however, we had finished with our second target, and signals were laid out on the ground to notify us that we should now register on 'Target No. 3.' This was the most important and also the most difficult target, namely the ammunition dump just to the east of Warloy. Unfortunately, at that moment, a formation of Albatross took the place of the triplanes, consequently the abhorred Sopwiths endeavoured to surprise us by diving out of the sun. Before we could get to work with our machine guns we were twice driven away from the front far back behind our own lines. A depressing feeling, not indeed unfamiliar - but today these disagreeable attentions were particularly persistent. Then the Albatross scouts took on these gentlemen, and soon one was punished for his audacity, going down in flames. The others, easily frightened, flew back over the lines, and I was able to continue my work.

The first shot fell right into the middle of Warloy, and caused a mechanical transport column which was standing by the roadside to retreat from the village along the road to the east with great rapidity. That pleased me well enough, for we could follow them up with our shells. The next burst, although, indeed, 550 yards short with respect to the ammunition dump, threw up a great cloud of smoke and dust only 120 yards from the routed column. At that the gallant motor transport warriors were at their wits' end. It was not possible for them to make the cover afforded by any dug-out, and their retreat was also cut off. They therefore left the lorries to look after themselves, and presumably retired to a place of safety.

I kept my position under the Albatross formation, and, feeling now perfectly secure, amused myself with the binocular, endeavouring to discover what had actually become of the column. After observing the fifth shell burst, I was very unceremoniously aroused from my interesting occupation by the sudden rattle of a machine gun in my immediate neighbourhood. In a flash the back gun was swung round towards this new aggressor; I had to save my skin from the attentions of two Sopwiths, which were blazing away like the very deuce less than 100 yards away. The radiator of our engine was riddled with bullets, and the water spurted past our faces as we went down in the tightest possible spiral, with the wires screaming and wailing. It was only thanks to the skilful flying of my pilot that we did not obey the summons to a better world, very much the worse for a few dozen bullet holes, for the two Englishmen, with their four machine guns, could out-manoeuvre us every time, and so the odds were greatly against us. Our spiral was so steep that I actually thought that our machine was out of control, and that the pilot was badly wounded. There was no time, however, for fears of that sort; we had got to escape, that was clear. We were then only 150 feet or so over Albert, but the pestering fellows would not leave us, and so we had to work our way still farther east.

But the good old engine could not endure being without water any longer, and it was clear that we should have to land among the shell-holes. Then at last our uninvited escort left us to our own devices, and went off to scrape an acquaintance with an observation balloon. Their advances, however, were not well received in that quarter. Finally, when we had reached Montauban, the engine gave out altogether. There was no time to select a landing ground, for our height was only 150 feet, and, in any case, each shell-hole bordered on its neighbour. My pilot let the machine glide as far as possible, and then, with only 15 yards of clear ground to land on, put the old L.V.G. down without a wire being strained, a few yards from a deep crater among the ruins of Montauban. Before assistance came and we were able to leave that place, we had the satisfaction of seeing one of our late adversaries come to grief in the distance among the smoke-clouds of the sugar factory at Ribemont. Two days later my L.V.G., with a new engine, was flying arrogantly again over the ruins of Montauban.

(FRHR. VON PECHMANN,
'ORDRE POUR LE MÉRITE'.)

CHAPTER III
BOMBING BY DAY AND BY NIGHT

THE PRINCIPAL WORK of aeroplanes consists of reconnaissance and artillery observation, and bombing must yield precedence to these duties. Although at the beginning of 1915 the newly appointed G.O.C. Air Force emphasised the importance of bomb raids, I and ordered that all machines were to carry bombs on every war flight, yet bombing remained very unpopular with most of the squadrons throughout the war, and became in reality a specialised branch of our Air Force. In September 1914, G.H.Q., organised the 'Ostend Carrier Pigeon Squadrons,' whose sole duty was the carrying out of bomb raids. It was originally intended to employ these squadrons principally for attacks on England, but this hoped for goal was found to be inaccessible on account of the great distance which separated the English coast from the nearest possible aerodrome. These Ostend squadrons were composed of the best and most experienced pilots from every branch of the Air Force, To increase their mobility they were quartered in railway sleeping carriages and carried out their first raids from an aerodrome in Flanders. From this base they undertook their first attacks on Dunkirk and other objectives behind the Fourth Army front. In the spring of 1915 they were removed to the Eastern Front and at the same time an additional squadron was formed which was known as 'The Metz Carrier Pigeon Squadron' after the name of their first aerodrome.

Shortly after our Army had broken through to Gorlitz, the Ostend squadron returned to the Western Front, having been equipped in the meantime with a newly-designed 150 or 160 H.P. C-type machine, in which the pilot sat in front and the observer behind; but even with this type it was not possible to attack England. On the 1ˢᵗ of January 1916 the Ostend squadron was renamed, being known henceforward as No. 1 'Battle Squadron' while the Metz squadron became No. 2 'Battle Squadron' and a few months later Nos. 3, 4, 5, and 6 squadrons were formed to carry out the same work.

No. 1 squadron was employed with excellent results in every undertaking of any importance and in various districts on the Western Front during 1916. Its railway carriage headquarters lent it exceptional mobility, and enabled the squadron to get on the move with the least possible delay. There was always joy among the infantry when No. 1 'Battle Squadron' with thirty or forty aeroplanes flying in well-disciplined and close formation, crossed the lines to attack the enemy; and many a gallant fellow in field-grey uniform waved greetings and good luck from his trenches to the squadron as it went on its way. The squadron was extraordinarily well trained in taking off and landing, and in a few moments the whole formation, consisting of flights of six or eight machines, would be in the air, and on its return would land with equal ease and celerity.

At the conclusion of the battle of the Somme No. 1 'Battle Squadron' was equipped with G-type machines, and sent to Bulgaria to take part in the campaign against Roumania. After the end of these operations it worked on the Macedonian front until May 1917, and then returned to France to participate in the great events which were expected in that theatre of the war.

This period constituted a turning-point in the history of all bombing squadrons. The design of our bombing machines had not kept pace with the opposing anti-aircraft guns and fighting machines, and, finally, poor climbing power and lack of necessary speed made it impossible for a bombing squadron to work by day, and so we were compelled to confine our attacks to the hours of darkness. Only occasionally, when particularly important operations were in progress, was a squadron sent on a war flight in the day time, but lack of practice in formation flying and tactics rendered such raids more rich in casualties than success.

A Daylight Bomb Raid

The objective to be bombed was usually selected on the day before the raid, so that pilots and observers might have an opportunity of studying aerial photographs of the target, so as to imprint its appearance from the air upon their memories. The following is a typical specimen of a squadron's operation orders for such a raid; 'The squadron will leave the ground tomorrow at 7 A.M. to attack the aerodrome at X. Flights will take off in the order 2, 3, 1, 4, 5. Assembly point over the town N. at 7.45 A.M. The leader will fly with number 5 flight, and his machine will display black-and-white wing-tip streamers.

'Flight No. 2 (single-engine C machines) will give the squadron a close escort and ward off all attacks. The target will be approached from the north, and will only be left when all machines have dropped their bombs.

'Every G machine will take a total load of 500 kgs. principally 12 and 50 kgs., short-fused bombs.

'N., Officer Commanding - Squadron.'

Preparations for such an undertaking necessitated a good deal of work: engines had to be overhauled and tuned up, tanks to be filled with petrol, and bombs fitted to their racks on the day previous to the raid. Before starting, the machines had to be brought out of their hangars, the engines run up, and each machine arranged in its order of leaving the ground.

The flying officers had usually prepared themselves for the flight some minutes before the specified time, and would give their engines, machine guns, and bomb releases a final test. The machines were placed sufficiently far apart not to get into each other's way when taking off, and punctually at 7 A.M. the first machine would leave the ground, the rest following at intervals of a few seconds. It was a rarely beautiful sight to see the squadron take off and climb into the sky, particularly when the beauty of the landscape itself made the spectacle yet more impressive. The memory of No. 1 'Battle Squadron' leaving the ground in Macedonia is one that can never be forgotten. Should one happen to

Trenches at La Ville aux Bois, 10 days before the attack. (April 6, 1917.)

be in the first machines off the ground, one could see the many others, both great and small, leave the aerodrome in the valley of the Vardar and laboriously gain height like a flock of strange birds of prey, silhouetted against that fair land with its green valleys, deep blue waters, and snow-clad mountain ranges spread out far below.

The climbing powers of individual machines vary considerably. The leader had to take that fact into account, and could not give the signal for departure until the last aeroplane had reached the height of its companions. Then the squadron was headed for its objective, the leader's machine in the middle of the front formation.

Thirty machines, death-dealing birds clutching many hundreds of bombs in their talons, manned by 100 German airmen, all of whom have been brought together only by a sense of duty and patriotic devotion, now embark upon their hazardous adventure. Possibly one or another of those young soldiers bethinks himself of his home and his sweetheart with her blue eyes raised to heaven in prayer for his safety.

But away with such thoughts: they only serve to weaken and dismay! Our leader grasps his control lever with a firmer grip, casts a swift glance at his revolution counter and altimeter, and keeps a sharp eye open for hostile aeroplanes. As yet there is nothing to be seen except forbidding white smoke puffs which indicate the proximity of the enemy's lines.

What an abundance of German determination, German devotion to duty, and German spiritual strength is symbolised by that squadron as, thousands of feet in the air, it approaches the enemy!

The 'Archie' bursts grow more numerous and still closer: already the woolly balls of smoke are surrounding the leading machines. The whole squadron becomes strangely agitated. Like the wind passing through a field of corn swaying it hither and thither, so now the machines swerve to left and right, as though in time to the explosions of the bursting shells. Individual machines follow a zigzag course in order to present a more difficult target to the gunners, but always endeavour to close in again upon the leader's machine. Suddenly the rattle of machine-gun fire is heard and a biplane plunges headlong past us, wrapt in flames from end to end, to be smashed to pieces on the mountain-side thousands of feet below. There was no time to notice whether it were an enemy or a friend, and every one who had been unable to see it clearly is worried and tormented by the uncertainty.

The anti-aircraft fire becomes still more furious, and one machine staggers and swerves violently as a shell bursts near by. After dropping its bombs upon some enemy position, the crippled machine turns and endeavours, damaged as it is, to reach its own aerodrome.

When about 30 miles over the enemy's lines, the anti-aircraft fire abates, and hostile machines are no longer to be seen: the squadron regains its formation and everything becomes quiet. Presently we know that Mount Olympus should become visible, and, sure enough, away on the right front its mighty, ancient head shows clear above the clouds. Many a pilot who has gone straight from school to war must involuntarily think of his old schoolmaster, who used to be inspired by the legendary glory of this mountain on which the gods of the ancient Greeks were throned, and whence they swayed the destinies of the world.

Once more a furious anti-aircraft fire is experienced, but we have reached our objective and every machine picks up its appointed position. Out in front the observer stands upright in his nacelle, peering tensely through the bomb eights for the mark to appear at which he should drop his bombs. Far below appears a sudden tremendous explosion, quickly followed by a vast cloud of smoke which rises from the ground to a height of many thousands of feet. Good shot: a petrol dump! Other objectives are hit: many aeroplane hangars become enveloped in flame and smoke. High up in the sky the gallant pilots determinedly turn and twist among the exploding shells and shrapnel. Their devotion to duty and contempt of death are rewarded by visible results. Again and again they approach the objective in order to drop their bombs with greater accuracy. Many a machine, shaken by the blasts of air from the exploding shells, groans and creaks in every part: fragments of shrapnel rip their way through its wings. But not one is crippled, and all escape from that Inferno.

After all the bombs have been dropped the squadron picks up its position again for its return flight, for it must still remain in good close formation so that it may be better able to defend itself against surprise attack. On the homeward journey hostile fighting machines endeavour to delay and cut us off. A brisk conflict ensues, but without any damage on our side.

After all have landed on their home aerodrome two officers claim the destruction of an enemy biplane. Every one smiles again, for all saw the machine go down but were unable to distinguish its nationality. And yet, alas! our success has not been gained without some sacrifice, for the victorious gunner who shot down the enemy's machine was badly wounded.

As a man wounded at a great height is liable to die from loss of blood, the pilot felt it was his duty to descend at once in order to save the life of his comrade, and landed therefore in the neighbourhood of a hospital.

The raid was attended by excellent results, A Bulgarian division at the front reported the explosion and fire caused by one of our bombs, a conflagration which was visible as a cloud of smoke even on the following day. Furthermore, the destruction of the enemy's aeroplane had been observed and greeted by the infantry with hand-clapping and cheers for the 'Germanskis.'

In May 1917 No. 1 'Battle Squadron' had to bid fair Macedonia farewell in order to return to the Western Front, and to take part in the great offensives which were to take place there.

The bombing squadrons were organised as follows: before No. 1 'Battle Squadron' was sent from the Western Front to Bulgaria in the summer of 1916, three flights were detached to serve as a nucleus for the formation of No. 3 'Battle Squadron' the number of whose flights was later increased to five. This squadron was assembled at Ghent, and was equipped with G-type machines, specially designed to carry heavy loads and travel at high speed. Its principal object was the achievement of the flight to England, On June 13, 1917, the first successful bomb raid was carried out on the English capital. In 1917 squadrons Nos. 4, 5, and 6 were organised, but the latter two were broken up after a short existence. With the exception of a special bombing squadron, S 32, all these units were used for night-bombing operations exclusively. Their pilots were the first to make a practice of flying and bomb-dropping at night, and they were specially trained for this work. The great success which this arm won in the summer of 1916 by the destruction of the ammunition dumps at Audruicq, will be described later.

The fact that bombing squadrons were now equipped with G-type machines, together with the increased efficiency of the enemy's defences, due to their improved and more numerous anti-aircraft batteries and fighting machines, made it necessary that bomb raids should be carried out under cover of darkness. No. 4 'Bombing Squadron' commenced night-flying operations at the end of 1916. In May 1917 this practice was adopted by No. 1 squadron, which had just returned from Macedonia. The result of the increasing importance of night bomb raids was a new organisation and reinforcement of the 'battle squadrons' which at the end of 1917 were included in the category of 'bombing squadrons.' The existing squadrons were reduced to three flights, and squadrons Nos. 5,

6, 7, and 8 were formed. No. 4 'Bombing Squadron' played a successful part in the Italian campaign.

In addition to the twin-engine G-type machines, the bombing squadrons were provided later with giant aeroplanes, with which at first one 'wing' and later two were equipped. These machines were equipped with four or five engines, each of 260 h.p.; their span was over 130 feet, and their net lift as much as 4½ tons. The weight carried consisted of eight or ten men, enough petrol for five or eight hours' flight, and a load of bombs weighing from one to two tons. In consequence of their long radius of action, giant aeroplanes were originally employed against remote objectives of strategical importance. Thus, for example, they successfully raided London, Dover, Abbeville, Calais, Rouen, and Boulogne. They were first employed on the Eastern Front in September 1916, and a year later appeared on the Western Front.

Bombing squadrons and giant aeroplane units came directly under the command of G.H.Q..

The objectives, however, were selected by the Staff of that particular Army Corps with which they were working, and depended on the situation of the moment. Before undertaking any operations on a large scale it was important that the enemy's preparations and the advance of hostile troops should be impeded by raids on important railway centres, ammunition dumps, concentration camps, etc.: in other words, upon targets lying some distance behind the lines. During the battle itself squadrons were used principally to give tactical support to our own troops by attacking objectives nearer to the lines, such as railway stations, camps, smaller ammunition dumps, staff headquarters, etc.; by delaying the advent of the enemy's reserves, and by wearing down the actual fighting troops.

There was never any question of attacking objectives other than those of military importance. The numerous rumours concerning the deliberate bombing of hospitals can only arise from the malice of theorists, either among the enemy or among our own people; they certainly never originated in the experiences of the night-flying man himself. It is impossible even on bright moonlight nights to recognise the red crosses of a hospital from an aeroplane. Also one must bear in mind the fact that bombs spread a good deal during their fall, and that it frequently happens, therefore, that objects lying several hundred yards away from the target itself may be hit.

Training pilots to fly big machines at night was a troublesome business, and unfortunately cost us many lives.

For the first time the nature and importance of night blindness was recognised. Pilots who flew brilliantly in daylight proved themselves to be quite unsuitable for night flying, for their eyes would not adjust themselves to the darkness. They also lost their sense of equilibrium in the air, and when landing were unable to judge their distance from the ground with accuracy. The proverb 'practice makes perfect' was also proved in this case, for by systematic training and a gradual increase in the difficulty of the tests put to night-flying pilots, a brilliant pitch of efficiency was attained. Eventually weather, with the exception of mists and fogs, was hardly taken into consideration, Flights were carried out without mishap on pitch-dark nights, without the help of moon or stars, and often through rain or snow.

As the night-flying airman gained in experience, his work was attended with a proportionally greater degree of success.

'Battle Squadron' 1 was the first to organise and carry out a bomb raid with full squadron strength. The first objective to be attacked in this way was Dunkirk, the most important dump and base of the British Army. On its various raids 'Battle Squadron' 1 alone dropped a total of 125 tons of bombs, equivalent to eight railway truck loads, upon this target. Bombing squadrons in the last year of the war dropped, on the average, 100 tons of bombs each per month, i.e. approximately the contents of seven railway trucks, reckoning each truck as having a capacity of about 15 tons. Because the 100 H.P. machine of the first year of the war, which, even when engaged solely on bombing, could only carry a 110 lb. load of bombs, and because the 150 and 200 H.P. types which followed were also incapable of carrying a serviceable load of anything beyond 220 lbs., it was left to the G-type machines and giant aeroplanes to prove the necessity and value of an increased net

Types of German bombs. From left to right they weigh respectively 110 lb, 220 lb. 660 lb.,27-1/2 lb. and just under a ton. The latter was the heaviest actually used in the war.

lift. A Friedrichshafen type or an A.E.G. could carry one ton; a giant aeroplane as much as two tons of bombs across the lines.

The efficiency of the night-flying squadron was not solely a matter of training the *personnel*, but was also concerned with several other factors such as organisation, technical *personnel*, the system of landing lights, etc. The experience which was acquired in respect of these factors also, enabled results to be achieved which were at first impossible, an example of outstanding importance being the increased efficiency duo to improved methods of using landing lights.

Aerial navigation at night was carried out principally with the assistance of the compass and stars, signal lights, and rockets, and, as far as it was visible, by the earth itself. Especial use was made of rocket batteries, which, at given intervals, discharged signal lights that, under good conditions, were visible for 50 or 60 miles. It is even more important not to lose one's way by night than it is by day, since a forced landing in the darkness is always a matter of grave danger to the flying man.

A Bomb Raid By Night

The following operation orders for a night bomb raid are typical:-

1. The squadron will attack the factory at J. at dusk.
2. Flights will take off in the order 1, 3, 2. Machines will start singly at Intervals of five minutes; the first machine of No. 1 flight will leave the ground at 6.30 P.M..
3. The rocket batteries at X. and Y. will give the direction signals, that at X. being four shots at intervals of three minutes; that of Y. being a shot every two minutes three seconds pause, then a second shot.
4. Direction lights and forced landing ground are shown on the accompanying sketch.
5. Direction of approach will be to the north; return, to the south of the direction lights.
6. Landing lights will be displayed at the home aerodrome on one green light being fired from the aeroplane. Special signals as previously arranged by the squadron.
7. 110 lbs. and 220 lbs. delay-action bombs are to be carried.
8. The squadron must make all preparations for a second flight.

N., Officer Commanding - Squadron.

It was not possible to fly in close formation at night owing to the difficulty of seeing one machine from another, and the consequent considerable danger of collision.

Let us accompany a night-flying machine on its flight. Half an hour before the time fixed for the start, the entire *personnel* of the aeroplane consisting of pilots, observer, gunner and mechanic, will be waiting by their machine to make the final preparations. Both the 260 H.P. engines have been run up for the second time, bombs examined and secured, and the instrument lighting set and machine guns tested. Everything is ready. The recording officer appears, and, having inspected the machine, signals with his lamp for the pilot to take off. There is a thunderous roar from the engines as the pilot opens the throttle; ponderously, and groaning beneath the weight which it has to bear, the gigantic black bird begins to move. It gathers speed; we skim across the aerodrome; a slight bump - we are in the air. The earth beneath disappears into the darkness of the night; the moon, that faithless friend, forsakes us and sinks beneath the horizon. Only the stars remain to light us upon our ghostly flight through the depths of the night. As though they feel particularly friendly towards us tonight, they glitter and gleam so brightly that we hardly need the moon at all. And then we think of the evil searchlights which will be even brighter and more dangerous!

The engines throb with their deep organ-like note. Long plumes of flame from the exhausts mark our passage across the sky. The pilot switches on his lighting set and casts a glance at the instruments; all is in order. The observer sits ahead in the nacelle, watching his compass and his map, and pointing out the course to be followed with his hand. The pilot obeys his directions and turns the machine in the given direction; the constellations, by which he is now flying, safeguard him from error.

We approach the lines. Searchlight beams, in ever increasing numbers, wander nervously to and fro. A broad barrier of light floats before us, showing that the enemy is still well supplied with *matériel*. We have got to get through that barrier. Several searchlight beams catch our machine and hold it fast. Suddenly all around us it is as light as day. The bursting shells creep nearer, until their explosions almost drown the roar of the engines.

Only by a sudden turn and rush of speed can we escape from the dangerous glare. The experience and skill of the pilot brings us through in safety and - Heaven be praised - once more we are swallowed up in the darkness! I turn round to watch another machine that is having a bad time with the searchlights and 'Archie'; probably some young pilot lacking in experience, I think to myself.

We near our objective. The machines ahead of us have stirred up the wasps' nest, and started the defences in full swing, Ring upon ring of searchlights encircle the objective, large ones, small ones, and some great enormous ones which are capable of reaching any height possible to us.

From all high points above the objective there is continuous flashing. Strings of coloured lights come up from the ground - 'flaming onion' barrage! A machine has got directly over the objective and dropped its bombs, A fire leaps up, growing ever larger; we can recognise the blast furnaces of the steel works in its light. Now comes our turn, and we plunge into that blazing inferno of light and flying metal. The illuminated blast furnaces give us a good mark. We are not yet discovered; the searchlights are still busy with the machine in front. We are flying at a fair height. The observer stands up in his nacelle, staring through his bomb sight, and makes a signal to the pilot. Now! He pulls the lever of the bomb release, and one bomb after another slips from the clutches of the machine.

The first explosion causes the defence to notice the fresh enemy. All the searchlights are suddenly concentrated on the space above the target. They try to seize us with their mighty arms and pull us down. We endeavour to escape into safety by a sudden burst of speed, but it is all in vain. A big beam succeeds in catching us, and holds us fast. Immediately all the other searchlights turn their attention to us. It is not possible to escape from their embrace. The anti-aircraft batteries blaze away and a moment later something happens - there is a terrific crash between the two left-hand planes. Then indeed we think that all is lost: but no, not yet! It is only a flying splinter that has struck the left propeller and shattered it. The pilot switches off the engine on that side; we must now get on with the power of the other one alone. By this time we have got so far from the objective, that both searchlights and anti-aircraft guns leave us and turn their attentions to our successor.

One engine alone is not sufficient to maintain the machine in horizontal flight, and we gradually lose more and more height. All the same we have succeeded in crossing the lines and passing their searchlight barrage without further damage, which is, at least, some consolation - we have escaped from the enemy. But what will happen when we negotiate our forced landing? Only 1600 feet up; the earth is black beneath us. Details such as houses, trees, small valleys cannot be distinguished, and only the boundaries of large villages, forests, and patches of water are visible. A forced landing now must result in a crash at least - perhaps something worse. The memories of those many airmen who have been burnt to death when negotiating similar forced landings, crowd irresistibly in upon our minds, while the back gunner continually fires off the specified signal rockets. Suddenly - Heaven takes pity on our plight - to our left blaze up the three familiar landing flares of an emergency landing ground. The distance, indeed, is still somewhat great in proportion to our height, but the calmness and skill of the pilot overcome this difficulty too. We land fairly between the white lights. Back on mother earth once again, thanks to our good luck, and our gallant pilot.

The machine is pushed to one side so as not to get in the way of any other, and we return to our home aerodrome in a motorcar. There we find much anxiety about us, and learn also that a second machine is missing. The airmen who have returned, and various other members of the squadron, have gathered round the searchlights on the landing ground, and are telling each other their experiences. The last machine to leave the ground has not yet returned. Out towards the west we see a green star suddenly appear in the air. It is a machine about to land. The landing lights are displayed, and the machine, with one flare illuminating its under-carriage, glides smoothly down, rushes ghostlike past us, and sinks noiselessly to earth between the lights.

All at once we hear the sound of a strange engine, an enemy aeroplane! Every light on the aerodrome is extinguished, and there is a wild rush for the dugout; those who do not reach it throw themselves flat on the ground. Already the bombs are bursting, and some of them fall on the aerodrome. The sound of the engine fades into the distance, and we leave our dug-out to search for the bomb holes. There are several of them in the centre of the aerodrome, 10 or 12 feet deep. One man of the searchlight party has been wounded by a flying splinter, The position of the landing lights is altered so that there should be no bomb holes in the path of any machine landing. Both bombers which were last to leave the ground have returned, but two are still missing. Some of the airmen report having seen a machine in a searchlight beam shot down in flames, and a second descend in a steep glide over the target. At that moment a telephone message comes through from an anti-aircraft battery: 'At 8 P.M. one of our bombing machines was shot down in flames over the Römerstrasse.' It must only be ours: a chill silence falls on the group assembled round the searchlight!...

The weather still remains fine and the report from the meteorological station predicting clouds has not been fulfilled. There are still four hours before dawn. Mutely the group disperses, and every man prepares for another flight. The words of the great philosopher Kant find here their application: 'The sense of duty within us, and the stars of heaven above us.'

The next morning the following laconic message is sent to G.H.Q.:-

In the night of the 18th-19th October the squadron attacked the given objective (the factory at J.) in several successive flights, and dropped altogether 14 tons of bombs. Several good hits were obtained, and a great conflagration was caused. One of our machines was shot down in flames by anti-aircraft fire, at X. over the Römerstrasse, and a second has not returned. This machine was probably compelled to land near the objective. Squadron aerodrome was bombed with seven heavy bombs. One man was wounded by a flying splinter.

(KELLER.)

NIGHT-FLYING MACHINES

From the beginning of the time when Man commenced to fly, the idea of flying by night was very truly 'in the air.' The problem was occasionally flirted with by short flights at dusk and in the moonlight, but nobody was willing to tackle it seriously. That was in the year 1911. The numerical superiority and technical efficiency of the French Military Air Service was manifest to the whole world, but even so, the Prussian War Office hesitated to take the necessary steps to improve the situation. However, at the beginning of September 1911 a scheme was submitted by the General Staff through the medium of Colonel Ludendorff, as he

The quays at Salonika on June 8, 1917: taken from the height of 13,000 feet.

was in those days, requiring that ten service and six home defence flying units should be established. The chief of the Imperial General Staff reported to the War Office in connection with this scheme: 'We shall not overtake France by methods like this. She has secured an advantage over us which we cannot overcome.'

This report led to an establishment and development of the Air Force, which equalised the inconvenient numerical superiority of our probable enemy. To accomplish this it was necessary to gain experience and training in the hitherto uninvestigated science of night flying. It was obvious that aerial attacks under cover of darkness, even though one could not accurately estimate their probable material results, would undoubtedly inspire our opponent with serious uneasiness, coupled with a wholesome respect for the efficiency and powers of our airmen. Also theoretically one was inclined to say that no efficient defence against aircraft at night could be reckoned with.

In the months of February and April 1913 the establishment of night-flying units was laid upon a broader foundation, and the preliminary trials were carried out at Metz. Our initial attempts were made without serious disaster, and it was demonstrated once again that bogies and prejudices soon disappear when one faces them steadfastly, although, indeed, the experiment was not popular in flying circles. It was not until the National Aero Association had been formed, together with the increasing competition that existed between flying men with regard to possible flight duration, that night flying was again inevitably taken up in 1914, although even then only by a few individuals.

The bitter necessity of war proved that we were right in calculating on the urgent necessity of night flying. In the winter of 1914-15 I was in command of my squadron at Ostende as Officer Commanding the bombing section of the Air Force. Although we only had 100 H.P. engines to put up against the 160 H.P. engines of the English and French, and were armed with quite inadequate small arms against tho machine guns of our opponents, we succeeded during September 1914 and January 1915 in carrying out four daylight operations on a large scale against Dunkirk, Nieuport, Furness, and La Panne. After that the enemy's aerial defences so increased in efficiency that it was impossible to undertake further work with any hope of reasonable success.

However, in order that we might efficiently carry out the work assigned to us, the attempt was made to deliver our attacks under cover of darkness. The first of these grandly conceived operations took place in the night of January 28-29 of 1915. We attacked Dunkirk with a squadron of fourteen machines, and, in spite of all the derogatory reports which were circulated concerning this operation, our efforts met with a striking success. This is all the more noteworthy because it was achieved without casualties or material damage. Progress began, although indeed slowly, to raise the efficiency of the flying men in this work. Late in the summer of 1915 the experience which had been acquired enabled us to lay down correct rules for the guidance of night flyers. As a rule it was unnecessary to carry arms, and, moreover, this practice reduced the load of bombs that it was possible to carry. The noiseless glide enabled us to approach the target very closely without being discovered.

Even though the number of nights on which it was possible to carry out successful operations was limited, it was soon found that night flying was applicable to other work besides mere bomb dropping. For example, particularly good results were obtained by locating batteries at night from their gun flashes. Again, the signal lamps that were indispensable to railway traffic, and the sparks thrown up by engines and steamers, afforded an easy means of observing movements of trains and ships. The sea-coast, fires, rivers, canals, lakes, bridges, large woods, railway lines, and dry roads provided an easy method of finding one's way by night. The enemy's searchlights, although used with a diametrically opposite purpose, assisted more than anything else to locate the objective that was to be attacked.

The winter of 1915-16 marked no progress in the science of night flying. Unfortunately its value was not fully appreciated by the higher command, and insufficient attention was paid to it. Various senior officers announced as their opinion: 'there is no inducement to undertake night flying, and no necessity.' Perhaps this view was inspired to a considerable extent by the fear that our opponents might resort to the same practice, and by so doing rob the Staff of their already scanty periods for rest and sleep.

It was not until the spring of 1916 that the indefatigable efforts of the General Officer Commanding the Air Force succeeded in obtaining due recognition of the importance of night flying.

During the nights of the 19th and 20th of February 1916, the united squadrons of the 6th Army participated in night attacks on Hazebrouck, Doullens and Amiens. On the latter raid eighteen aeroplanes took part, and returned undamaged to then base, having dropped three-quarters of a ton of bombs. This undertaking also confirmed the validity of the principles underlying our previous experiments, and led to further development in organisation and technique. The devastating results which even one of these night attacks effected can be better realised from the following example, which has already been described in the Press. Owing to the photographic work of No. 6 squadron, a very important position and railway junction was located on the St. Omer-Calais line. This position lay 36 miles behind the enemy's lines, and was claimed to be the main ammunition dump of the British Army. An attack by day stood no chance of success owing to the bitter opposition which was expected. Bombs would have had to be dropped from a great height, with but little chance of hitting the proper target, and the pilots would have been disturbed and distracted by the presence of hostile machines. Consequently it was decided that the attack should be carried out on the night of 20th July 1916. Only four machines of No. 40 squadron took part. Each of them carried one 45 lb. and ten 30 lb. thermit bombs, forty-three 25 lb. delay-action bombs, and ten incendiary bombs, the total weight being 1700 lbs.

The results of the bombing may be gauged by a comparison of the two photographs we publish on pp. 188 and 193, showing the objective before and after the attack. At least half of the total objective was utterly destroyed. The craters in the earth showed that a vast quantity of ammunition had been exploded. A letter that was captured, bearing the address 'Blendecques, July 22nd, 1916' stated that the explosion caused approximately 1200 casualties. Squadron 7 carried out a similar raid almost two years later during the night of May 20, 1918. The ammunition railhead at Blargies was bombed by one G-type machine, which attacked the target twice, dropping the first time thirteen 25 lb. bombs and two 110 lb. bombs, whereby numerous huts and ammunition trains were blown up. Since the objective was rendered easily visible by the resulting conflagration, various other machines of the same squadron attacked and completed the work of destruction. Once again the enemy's attacks, which had now increased five-fold in intensity, were brought to nought by the work of the night-flying squadrons. During the first quarter of 1917 four out of the seven existing 'battle squadrons' were allotted to escort duty, and of the remaining bombing squadrons, Nos. 1, 2, and 4, the last-named specialised in night flying. Night-flying pilots made use of the photographs, which had been taken to assist in the selection of objectives, for the purpose of discovering their whereabouts by night. These photographs, together with a well-thoughtout system of direction lights, the compass and the stars' enabled them to keep to their correct course when flying to and from the lines.

The experience of these squadrons was also of great use to our own anti-aircraft batteries and searchlight units. Between January and March 1917 a large number of specially constructed machines suitable for night flying were brought out on the Western Front, Until the end of 1916 night bomb raids of both friend and foe were approximately equal in number. Many attempts to engage the squadrons in aerial combat on their flight to and from the lines were without success.

On the night of February 10, 1917, the pilot and observer of a machine from Squadron 12 succeeded, for the first time, in engaging a hostile aeroplane with decisive results. This feat originated in a systematic investigation of the habits of the enemy's night-flying machines at their aerodrome at Malzeville. It was easy to discover the times at which the machines left the ground by the signals displayed. Our machine waited over the deserted aerodrome for the return of the enemy, who first made his appearance among the German anti-aircraft shells. Shortly afterwards our men noticed the red and green lights of a French twin-engined biplane. They quickly turned towards their enemy and opened fire at short range. After twenty-five shots from the synchronised machine gun, the hostile machine burst into flames and crashed to earth. This feat was confirmed by an artillery unit. Shortly afterwards the lights of a second French aeroplane were observed, and again our men succeeded in attacking from the rear. Shortly after they had opened fire the enemy machine descended steeply and disappeared into the darkness. According to the reports of French prisoners, this machine was also destroyed.

The incidents we have described above opened up entirely new prospects in connection with the successful combating of hostile night-flying aeroplanes, particularly when it was possible to attack them shortly after they had left the ground, heavy with bombs and a full load of petrol, and consequently clumsy in their movements. The probability of similar action on the part of the enemy was naturally taken into consideration, especially with regard to the rules affecting aerial navigation by night. Further aerial combats took place on the night of April 7, 1917, over Douai, and on April 13, 1917, over the

Heavy bombardment of Nieuport. Note the bursting shells.

enemy's aerodrome at Cramoiselle. A number of machines were shot down on the latter occasion, and we found a gun sight specially designed for night use.

Furthermore, in April 1917, a machine succeeded in descending by night to within a few feet of the ground over a French aerodrome, and in dropping a 130 lb. delay-action bomb close to the hangars, thereby causing considerable damage.

All the incidents which we have described were made use of in the summer of 1917 during a systematic investigation of the possibilities of aerial combat by night. The results of this investigation cannot be dealt with here; they do not come within the scope of this work. The relative value of bombing by day and by night again became a matter of debate after 'Battle Squadron' No. 3 had attacked England on seven occasions between May and July 1917, thereby challenging its title to be considered an island. On June the 13th and July the 7th, London itself was chosen as the objective, the latter raid being carried out at noon. The attacks made between September 3rd and September 4th against Sheerness, Margate, Chatham, and London took place under cover of darkness. After these undertakings the squadron announced:

'In a short time the increased efficiency of the enemy's defences will make it necessary for machines to fly at a height of at least 17,000 feet, or raids will have to be carried out exclusively by night-flying squadrons.' Thereafter all further attacks on London were made by night.

Each month some new work was found for the night flyers. On the night of September 2, 1917, St. Omer, which lay 30 miles behind the lines, was successfully bombarded by a long-range gun, and the observation for this shoot was undertaken by 235A Squadron of the 6th Army, which was able to confirm eight direct hits, and a resulting conflagration. The enemy's defence was very active and strong, and extended even as far as the gun itself, which was incessantly attacked by aeroplanes and thereby hampered in its work, while our machine, which had to remain over the objective for a long time, was continually harassed by numerous antiaircraft batteries and searchlights.

We can take it for granted that this bombardment was remarkably successful, for the wireless messages which we picked up from the same army on September 29, 1917 confirmed our claims. It was further established that the number of the enemy's machines engaged on artillery work by night had increased both on the British and French Fronts. Artillery observation at night, even for guns of medium calibre, was carried out on several occasions with excellent results on the front of our First Army. For this work accuracy could only be ensured when the objectives were of such a nature as to be easily visible by night, such as villages, woods, and badly concealed battery emplacements. Success depended principally upon the airman's ability to distinguish between the explosions of our own shells and the flashes of the enemy's guns.

The importance of the possibility of successful nocturnal artillery bombardments by aeroplane control can be measured by the fact that we ourselves, as well as the enemy, had been driven to the practice of moving troops, ammunition, and rations, and of carrying out our work of construction at night time, in the hope of concealing these operations from the eyes of the airmen.

The stages of development which we have now described, brought night flying to such a pitch during the summer and winter of 1917 that both sides engaged in almost incessant nightly activity, which concerned itself principally with billets, railways, and industrial centres. Because their tactical situations favoured such a policy, the enemy made a practice of promiscuously bombing several targets, while we, on the other hand, being restricted in our supplies of *matériel*, organised concentrated attacks within certain limits of time and space. Various opinions may be held concerning the relative merits of these two methods, but no one can dispute the greatly increased importance of the effect produced by night bomb raids on the general course of operations.

Our existing bombing squadrons, Nos. 1, 2, and 4, were very rapidly reorganised between November 1917 and March 1918, and those units (3, 5, 6, 7, and 8) which unfortunately had been disbanded, were now re-established.

At this period the raids made on Paris on 30-31st of January and the 8-9th and ll-12th of March 1918 were of special importance. The squadrons which took part in those during March - i.e. Nos. 1, 2, 5, and 7 - were under the general command of the Officer Commanding No. 1 'Bombing Squadron'. The experience gained on these flights made it possible for different objectives to be allotted to certain machines, and for a fixed programme to be formulated for the times of departure, and the out and homewards flights.

The general nature of the orders for an undertaking of this description was as follows:-

OPERATION ORDERS FOR AN AIR RAID ON PARIS

1. By order of G.H.Q. Squadrons Nos. 1, 2, 5, and 7, under my command, will attack Paris as a reprisal for the enemy's raids on German open towns.

2. Should good weather prevail, machines will leave the ground by 4 P.M. at the latest.

3. Order of starting: Squadrons Nos. 2, 7, 1, and 5. No squadron should take more than thirty minutes to leave the ground.

4. General Objectives for all squadrons: the northern quarter of Paris between the Gare du Nord and the Seine, special attention being paid to factories and stations.

    Special Objectives. - In order to effect as much damage as possible to the enemy's industrial centres targets of exceptional importance are allotted for special attention. It will be left to the discretion of the squadron commander whether he detaches three machines to attend to the target given him, or to reserve approximately one ton of the total weight of bombs carried by his entire squadron.

a. Objective for Squadron 2: the aeroplane and ammunition factories in the south-west of Paris (there are approximately ten aircraft factories and several munition works).

b. Objective for Squadron 7: the extremely important explosive and ammunition factory at Sevran, This factory occupies a site approximately 1100 yards by 650 yards.

c. Objective for Squadron 5; The same as that for No. 2.

d. Objective for Squadron 1: the munition works and electric power stations in the northern district of Paris.

5. Order and direction of flight:-

    Squadron 2 will start from its home aerodrome, and steer by compass. It will approach the objective and its special target from the south and depart by the south-east.

    Squadron 7 will start from the aerodrome of Squadron 2 and will fly by compass, approaching its objective from the south and departing by the south-east; the approach to its special objective will be left to the discretion of its leader.

    Squadron 1 will leave its home aerodrome and fly by compass. It will approach its objective from the north and depart by the north.

Squadron 5 will leave the aerodrome at Tupigny and fly by compass. It will approach its objectives from the north and depart by the north.

6. Order of landing:
Squadron 2 will land at its home aerodrome.
Squadron 7 will land at its home aerodrome, or, in case of necessity, at Tupigny.
Squadron 1 will land at its home aerodrome.
Squadron 5 will land at Tupigny should it be unable to reach its home aerodrome.
7. Squadrons 7 and 5 will meet by four o'clock in the afternoon at latest on the given day and at the specified starting-point.
8. The dropping of messages is prohibited.
9. Squadron 1 will give the orders for starting and landing.
10. No papers other than the pay book and identification papers are to be carried, and no notes are to be made on the maps. Wind lucifers will be carried.
11. Before the flight every man is to make him self acquainted with the orders concerning the necessity of withholding all military information.
12. All men are to make themselves thoroughly acquainted with the position, nature, etc., of all direction lights, searchlights, forced landing lights, and dummy aerodromes behind the 7th, 18th, and 2nd Army fronts.
13. In consideration of the extreme importance of this undertaking, every effort is to be made to reach the given objectives.

(SIGNED) KELLER.

The co-operation of a giant aeroplane squadron (No. 501), provided for in the original operation orders, was abandoned on account of the uncertain weather at that squadron's aerodrome. It is a remarkable fact that the March raid on Paris was carried out on a night when there was no moon whatever.

Meanwhile our enemies had not remained idle, and had developed every branch of night flying with as much energy as creative thought, although, indeed, as opposed to our own custom, they did not restrict themselves to honourable methods, but specialised in the use of cunning and insidious means of warfare.

On the 15th of February 1918 a hostile aeroplane appeared in the evening over the aerodrome of No. 2 'Bombing Squadron' at Aincourt and displayed the squadron's Morse landing signal As the squadron was at that moment ready to take off, the ground *personnel* came to the conclusion that they were dealing with a machine in distress, and displayed the landing lights. They were immediately attacked by machine-gun fixed, and six bombs were dropped. A flight commander of the squadron, who happened to be present on the aerodrome at the time, was killed by a bomb splinter, and several mechanics were wounded by bullets. The enemy made a second attempt to deceive us on the same night, also by calling for the landing lights of the aerodrome. However, this we succeeded in frustrating.

The increasing number of night-flying machines on all army fronts in April 1918 made it necessary to unify the regulations for direction and landing lights throughout the whole of the Western Front. During this time the 3.7 centimetre rocket pistol had become absolutely indispensable for firing the lights which, by their number and the intervals at which they appeared, gave pilots the necessary information as to their position and the course they should follow. Another method which involved the use of multicoloured lights, was successfully used to warn airmen of the approach of bad weather.

Before the offensive in the summer of 1918, which was to decide the fate of the war, the whole Army was able to appreciate the vast experience that had been gained in the science of night flying. Considerable success attended our efforts at combating hostile aeroplanes by well-thoughtout preparations, and by co-operation between the various defensive arms. The results of all our experience were condensed into a detailed code of regulations for the conduct of aerial fighting by night.

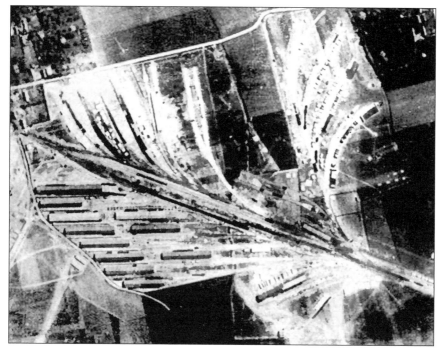

The ammunition dump at Audruicq before being bombed.

In July 1918 the weight of bombs dropped rose to a hitherto unheard of level. On the two nights of July 18 and 21, 1918, on the Western Front, 170 tons of high explosives were dropped. Allowing 15 tons for the capacity of each truck, this is equivalent to the contents of eleven railway trucks, the whole of which had to be transported by air. Owing to the fact that the means at our disposal were but slender in proportion to those of the enemy, this record could only be made by machines and airmen undertaking several flights in the course of one night. Thus, for example, during the night of August 21, 1918, No. 4 Squadron left the ground six times.

The impossibility of concealing preparations for operations on a large scale from aeroplanes, forced both sides to carry out all the preliminary movements of the troops under cover of darkness. This meant that the higher command was denied all information as to the movements and traffic behind the enemy's lines, as well as any preliminary reconnaissance of the actual battlefield, and the necessity, therefore, arose of improving artillery observation by night in the manner which has already been described. An important factor which greatly assisted the solution of this problem was the discovery of the possibility of taking aerial photographs by night. In the summer of 1918 this difficulty was overcome by the use of parachute flares and this method was so perfected that in September 1918 the photographic section of the Air Force detailed special squadrons for night photography.

Our review of night flying will not be complete without a survey of the work of giant aeroplanes, in the design of which those factors which affected night flying found exclusive consideration. Whereas every other type of machine had some part to play in daylight operations, this was not the case with giant aeroplanes. Their speed, climbing power, and manoeuvrability could not be sufficiently developed for them to undertake any useful work in daytime, owing to their great weight and consequent inability to avoid attack. The idea of equalising their chances, and, to a certain extent, overcoming this difficulty, by carrying a large number of machine guns, would have created an increase in weight which could only have been carried at the expense of their bombs or petrol. Their large radius of action, and the quantity of bombs carried, were the very factors which ensured the existence of giant aeroplanes, in the beginning, when they were in competition with the G type of machine, and for these reasons they were at once stamped as an instrument for night warfare alone.

Tests with these machines were first carried out in 1916 and the spring of 1917 in the Russian theatre of war, and excellent results were obtained by their use against the Riga-Petrograd railway and the island of Oesel In the autumn of 1917 giant aeroplanes were brought out on the Western Front, where they entered into brisk competition with those squadrons already engaged in attacks on England. Unfortunately during the summer of 1918 the limits which governed the use of giant aeroplanes, and distinguished them from all other types, were no longer clearly observed. Their work should have been confined solely to attacks on objectives that were inaccessible to any other type of machine, but occasionally, for political reasons, they were called upon to perform work of strategical importance. On no occasion should they have been required to undertake work of a tactical nature.

Thus, for example, on August 10, 1918, the R 43 was sent to attack Doullens and St. Pol, 15 miles behind the lines, although on the same night Staples and Boulogne were attacked by a squadron of G machines. The R 43 never returned. On the night of August 11, 1918, R 52 was sent to attack a small town called Bovais, a place exceedingly difficult to find, which lay 30 miles behind the French lines. The machine was shot down on the return flight, and its commander and crew of four were burnt to death.

A curve of development as steep as that which represents night flying cannot be without its corresponding depressions. Towards the end of May 1918, owing to the still existing call for day bombing, three machines from every flight were allotted to this duty. Human nature, like that of most of the lower animals, thinks it sees an enemy in the person of the Queen of Night, Perhaps it is not altogether by chance that none of our types of machines were ever called 'owls,' although the pigeon, the albatross, the condor, and various other species of birds are represented. In spite of everything, night flying will come into its own in the days of peaceful aerial navigation. The fact that the air is more suitable for flying at night than in the daytime, being calmer and possessing greater lifting power, is a great advantage, and in addition the practice of flying by night will be favoured owing to the necessity of saving every second of time in order that the day's work may be accomplished. We have seen something of this necessity reflected in the invention of the motorcar, the telephone, and the aeroplane. Let us hope that the achievements of war, which cost us the blood of our finest manhood, are not in vain, but will assist mankind in its progress towards the complete mastery of the air.

(SIEGERT.)

CHAPTER IV
FIGHTING EQUIPMENT

INFANTRY CONTACT MACHINES

IN DESCRIBING THE work of the infantry contact machines we touch upon what were perhaps the noblest and most self-sacrificing achievements of the young Air Force in the Great War. At the beginning of the war the Air Force was only designed for those objects which had been foreseen in time of peace, and was solely employed on reconnaissance work for the higher command. With the rapidly increasing sphere of aerial activity, and the necessity of giving the infantry direct assistance in their struggle, which was ever becoming more bitter, there arose that special demand which was satisfied by the infantry contact machines. Not only did the conditions of the war make this work necessary, but the airmen themselves were able thereby to satisfy an old wish that had long been cherished.

As is characteristic of all wars, and must always be the case, a kind of jealous competition existed between the various branches of the fighting services. The nearer troops are to the enemy, and the more heavily they are being pressed, the more they are inclined to depend upon assistance and reinforcements from behind. Confined as he is within the narrow limits of the front line trenches, where the view is restricted between parados and parapet, there soon arises in the mind of the infantryman the desire for co-operation and support. The infantry of old certainly respected the artillery since they could not dispense with their assistance, and both infantry and artillery imagined themselves superior to the cavalry and the Air Force which carried out their dangerous work farther afield, and of whose real assistance the infantry had no idea.

From the very beginning, but more particularly after the advent of trench warfare, it was the infantry that suffered most. They were called

The ammunition dump at Audruicq after the bomb raid carried out in the night of July 20, 1916.

upon to endure the severest hardship and to expose themselves to the greatest danger. They required a good deal of assistance in their heavy task. The flying men, all of them young and only recently taken from the ranks of the infantry, were able to feel with their whole heart for their late comrades. They knew how much they suffered and how heroically they fought. Many a man who performed his duty high up in the air, and saw beneath him those thin lines whence our infantry, in spite of cold and rain, rushed to the attack against ten times as many, thought of his own warm quarters, and longed to take part once again in the battles fought by his old friends.

It was first of all in the summer of 1916 - when our attack against Verdun, which had begun so brilliantly, came to a bloody end in the many devastated regions between the Forts on account of the lack of reserves, all of which had been used up in the battle of the Somme - that the infantry operations assumed a nature for which the previous methods of leading and support proved insufficient. From the moment when the infantry had left their lines to attack they were almost out of touch with the higher command and their own supports. Inexorably the enemy used to place behind them a curtain of fire on such a scale that it was impossible to keep touch with them. Even were it possible for determined runners to force their way across the almost impassable battle ground, they would hardly have any news to give, nor could they tell the exact position of the fighting troops. Our own preparatory fire and the defensive barrage of the enemy made the landscape almost unrecognisable, and entirely altered the appearance we expected from the map - sometimes whole villages disappeared, leaving no trace - so the infantry, incredible though it may sound, frequently did not even know their own position during the first crowded hours of their attack.

It often happened, therefore, that at the exact moment when the fate of the battle hung in the balance, the attacking troops had to decide on their own responsibility whether they should hold the ground which they had won or not, when so much depended on the assistance that could be given them. Disorganised by the pressure of fighting, weakened by casualties, they had to find what scanty protection they could in shell-holes or the remains of trenches, and they had to withstand the counterattack which the French would deliver from a region immune to artillery fire, and with fresh and untired troops.

It was a terrible situation for the higher command, who knew what the gallant fellows were suffering, and yet were unable to help them. How was it possible to send out reserves when nothing was known of the progress of the fight? How was it possible to direct the artillery fire accurately, and to spread out a barrage as protection to the fighting troops, when they had no information as to the position of the front line? An unfortunate characteristic of these operations was the lack of proper artillery support, and sometimes casualties were inflicted by our own fire. The same state of affairs existed when we were compelled to act on the defensive when the general situation of the war forced us to abandon our attacks. Again our troops suffered from the same cause.

The old-fashioned means of communication which were experimented with under these conditions, such as carrier pigeons, war dogs, etc,, failed utterly; the flying man was the only messenger that remained. The higher command and the infantry themselves, both of whom earnestly desired that observation should be kept over the French territory, simultaneously suggested to the flying units that they should make the attempt. The first primitive order referring to this scheme ran as follows: 'Fly low, reconnoitre the situation with your own eyes, return, and report.' It was as easy to say as it was all but impossible to carry out. From any height which afforded a reasonable field of vision, such as 800 to 1200 feet, there was nothing to be seen. There were no trenches, for the French artillery fire had left no time for their construction, and even those that had been begun were soon destroyed. The muddy uniforms of our troops were hardly distinguishable from their background of shell-holes.

From extremely low heights it was possible to pick out individuals or small bodies of men, but in very few cases could one form a general opinion of the situation from small items of information gleaned in this manner. The higher command became pressing and impatient in their demands, for the situation involved a terrible strain upon their nerves; the result was heavy casualties. If the enemy permitted our airmen to fly low, the machine was soon subjected to concentrated sniping and fire from the ground, particularly from machine guns, unfortunately only too often with disastrous results.

Great credit must be given to the Air Force for having carried out this work in spite of everything. They were inspired by an intense desire to help. The Air Force themselves suggested to those troops that were out of the lines resting, that they should carry with them strips of cloth, brightly coloured and easily visible, which were to be displayed on request from the aeroplane, and which could be easily recognised from above. The signal to display these strips was to be given by a specified machine provided with certain streamers, attached to the wings or tail, and flying low over the battlefield. The first experiments with this method were extremely successful. From a considerable height the front line of the infantry could be picked out against its background of shell-holes. The observer would throw out certain maps or aerial photographs marked with abbreviated symbols to the message-receiving station or staff headquarters, thereby enabling the command to form a general opinion concerning the situation, whether it were an offensive or defensive operation, and making it possible that the right means should be applied at the right time and in the right place.

This provided the beginning and the general line along which progress was made. Even this method, however, did not run quite smoothly at first, and the necessary experience could only be obtained after a lot of work and trouble for both the infantry and the Air Force. The fighting troops, exhausted by the pressure of battle, were mistrustful of the scheme, and only displayed the given signals with reluctance. As their most terrible opponent was the opposing artillery, they were naturally afraid lest its eyes - the enemy's aeroplanes - might discover their position should they display the signals. Further casualties were the result of this misunderstanding. But already mutual work between the infantry and the Air Force had sown the seeds of mutual sympathy and trust. An ardent desire to help on the one hand, and an increasing recognition of the practicability of this new method of warfare on the other, gradually brought into existence a feeling of true comradeship between the two services.

The result of the successes so hardly won before Verdun, during the battle of the Somme, and in the fighting round the Chemin des Dames, was made manifest to the whole Army in the autumn of 1917 during the operations in Flanders. Here it was that brilliant achievement, self-sacrificing resistance, and a splendid manhood rose to its greatest heights, weaving an immortal and imperishable crown of glory for our German soldiers during the dreadful hours and days of which our Commander, that man of iron, wrote in his memoirs: 'My head was full of schemes for fresh undertakings in the East and in Italy, but my heart was with our comrades in Flanders.' It was on that front that the infantry contact machine was found to be an indispensable weapon of modern warfare. The joint duties of contact patrol and 'ground strafing' earned them the comprehensive designation of 'battle machines.' In the last tremendous offensives in the spring of 1918, the final effort of our entire army, whole squadrons of these 'battle machines' preceded the infantry into battle, wore down the enemy's resistance, destroyed artillery emplacements, and showed our infantry the path to Victory in the truest sense of the phrase. The achievements of our Air Force at that time are indissolubly bound up with the invincible and victorious spirit which animated our troops during those last glorious days when the heroic German legions gave battle to the whole world.

It is obvious that the dropping of messages, a primitive means of communication already described, did not suffice to meet the requirements of operations which became ever greater in scale as time went on. In place of this method, which, besides being cumbersome, interrupted the observer in his duty of closely observing the tide of battle, we developed the wireless installation. Not only near the headquarters of the artillery and of the higher command, but also immediately behind the front line trenches, stations were erected whose duty it was to pick out the messages of the contact machines and to forward them to their appointed destinations. It soon became possible for the aeroplane itself to carry a receiving as well as a transmitting set, with which it could receive questions and orders from the ground while engaged in its work over the enemy's territory. As the infantry had learned something of the powers of co-operation with infantry contact machines from the flying officers during their periods of rest, and had come to appreciate its value, the divisional staffs now provided an Air Force liaison officer. The further trend of development led to the entire control of artillery of other calibres, such as trench mortars, 'minenwerfers,' etc., by the infantry contact machines, and for this purpose other wireless stations were erected close to the front line.

In the spring of 1917 the number of contact patrol units for a division operating in the main theatre of war was included in that of the 'working aeroplanes' (i.e., reconnaissance and artillery machines), and six or nine (and later twelve) machines were allotted for these duties. In addition every army corps reserve provided its own contact patrol service, which was recruited from the training centres of the infantry contact officers, A specialised branch of this work, developed towards the end of the summer of 1917, and which included the 'battle aeroplanes,' will be treated separately in a future section.

Towards the end of 1917 the advisability of continuing with contact patrol work was seriously debated owing to the heavy casualties suffered on this work through the enemy's very efficient aerial defences. The men were required to fly a slightly modified C type of machine, which, being quite unprotected, left them completely exposed to hostile machine-gun fire from the ground. Compelled by the exigencies of their work to fly up and down the same strip of ground at a very low altitude, they offered a most vulnerable target. In this hour of need the aircraft industry came to the rescue with armoured aeroplanes, the so-called 'trench strafing' machines, whose planes, empannage, and fuselage were constructed throughout of metal, while the pilot's and observer's cockpits were so heavily armoured with chrome-nickel steel, that even armour-piercing bullets fired at close range caused nothing more than slight dents. Machines of this type were known to return to their aerodromes bearing the marks of over thirty bullets, while their occupants escaped untouched. This type of machine thus enabled the contact patrol service to carry out its work satisfactorily and without heavy casualties.

(DYCKHOFF.)

SINGLE-SEATER SCOUTS

We have already described how, as a direct result of trench warfare, aerial fighting and a struggle for the mastery of the air came into existence; how the aeroplane itself came to be used as the weapon of offence, and how aircraft design and the science of ordnance were developed, under conditions of intense competition with our enemies, to satisfy those demands which were so incessantly made upon them.

The single-seater scout was the type specially adapted to aerial fighting. Its work consisted of clearing the air to enable the other machines to carry out their work, and of subduing the enemy's reconnaissance machines. The science of aerial fighting took its origin from duels between individual machines. Captain Boelcke was the first to achieve any success, which he did on the Western Front in 1915, with the assistance of the men whom he had trained in 'stalking tactics.' The fact that both sides possessed machines of equal efficiency, and that both were animated by the same gallantry and skill, although eventually numerical superiority remained with our opponents, led, in the course of 1916, to small groups of three or four fighting machines, and later to squadrons of twelve or eighteen machines, being used as one unit. With the organisation of the fighting squadron as the first tactical unit, there came into existence aerial tactics, that is to say, the scientific use by several machines of the third dimension of space for the purpose of approaching and attacking the enemy. These manoeuvres involved flying as high as 15,000 or 18,000 feet.

In 1917 a whole squadron engaged in aerial combat on the English front under the masterly leadership of Frhr. von Richthofen, This fighting squadron consisted of various formations of fighting machines, the total number of machines in the three or four formations being between forty and fifty. Squadrons of this description were under the sole command of the squadron commander, whose duty it also was to lead his squadron in the air. Fighting between individual squadrons, and occasionally between several squadrons together, on February 21, 1918 culminated in that bitter aerial battle which was fought by Frhr. von Richthofen's squadron near Le Cateau, This conflict lasted over thirty minutes, and involved as many as sixty or seventy machines, thirteen of the enemy's machines and only one of our own being destroyed.

The principal work of fighting machines consisted in destroying the enemy's powers of observation, whether carried out by aeroplanes or balloons, particularly when the artillery on either side was called into action. Whenever we succeeded in holding off the enemy's reconnaissance machines, their artillery became practically blind. Another point of equal importance was the necessity of possessing the mastery of the air during infantry offensives over those places where the fighting was hottest, in order that a close watch could be kept on the development of the attack. When telephone wires were cut as the result of the preliminary bombardment, the infantry contact machines became the sole reliable means of communication between the fighting troops and the higher command. Should the enemy manage to disperse our contact patrols, no communication existed to the rear of our lines, and if this happened when the enemy's fighting machines had succeeded in chasing away our artillery observation machines which were directing the fire of our guns against the enemy's barrage, it was impossible for us to send up reserves without a terrible loss of life and waste of time. When the machines of the escort squadrons, whose duty it was to protect our reconnaissance and observation machines from attack, were no longer able to carry out this work successfully, it became necessary for the fighting squadrons to be greatly increased in strength. It was of outstanding importance that we should hold the mastery of the air over the battlefield if we were to succeed either in offensive or defensive operations.

The enemy's observation balloons also had a bearing on this problem. Even if the enemy's aeroplanes were driven off the lines, the observation balloons still made it possible for them to keep an eye on the course of the battle, and enabled their higher command to counter our plans by making use of the information they acquired. It was therefore also necessary to render their opportunities for observation as few and as fleeting as possible by driving them down, or by pushing them back farther from the lines; or else to limit the heights to which they could ascend.

Naturally enough the enemy also attempted to obtain an insight into our position, movements, plans, and lines of communication, and to this end sent over photographic and reconnaissance machines at very great altitudes to enable them to break through our defensive patrols and reconnoitre the battle zone. It was the duty of our fighting machines to make this impossible. Since both sides endeavoured to obtain the mastery of the air when big offensives were afoot, by concentrating all their available units, the natural result was squadron fighting on a large scale.

During the last phase of the war decisive combats in the air were not restricted to daylight alone. We made special efforts to deal with the enemy's bombers who threatened our back areas and German territory, by arranging a system of co-operation between fighting machines and the anti-aircraft batteries and searchlights. For this purpose fighting pilots at the front worked with the home defence single-seater scout squadrons. These squadrons, which were organised similarly to the service fighting squadrons, acting on the information supplied by the aerial defence intelligence service, used to deal with any enemy squadron or individual machine which had succeeded in breaking through our defences at the front.

The work of our fighting machines is better known to the general public than that of any other type. Our fighting pilots in battle were like the knights of old, and the names of our fallen heroes will always be cherished with the gratitude, the love, and the admiration of the entire German people, and crowned with the laurels of immortality. It is only natural that the work of those hundreds of other pilots who gallantly did their duty day by day, but who did not have the same opportunities for individual feats of prowess, should not win the same wide recognition as that of the fighting pilots. All other forms of aerial activity lacked that romantic strain, that individuality, which seemed to revive the knightly deeds of ancient heroes, and which, albeit perhaps unconsciously, was doubly welcome to the German temperament, and still is cherished because of its soul-refreshing difference from our daily lives which, indeed, have little in common with romance and chivalry.

(NEUMANN.)

TRENCH-STRAFING MACHINES

The escort squadrons, originally established for the protection of our 'working aeroplanes,' were the precursors of the trench-strafing machines. Two or more escorting machines were allotted to the 'working aeroplane,' according to the importance of the flight and the vigour of the enemy's aerial activity. These escorting machines remained in the immediate neighbourhood of their companion, and concentrated their attention upon warding off hostile attacks. On particularly active sections of the line they were usually sent in formations, and, working in pairs, would carry out a watchful defensive patrol at some prearranged height, promptly attacking any inquisitive enemy who endeavoured to break through. As there were also numerous offensive patrols flying up and down the front, and as the enemy adopted the same system, the air was always filled with the droning of aeroplanes, either with the black cross or with tricolour markings. The manner in which formations broke up in the course of a general mêlée, and an aerial combat resolved itself into a number of simultaneous duels, gave rise to those 'battles in the air' which were so often reported in Army *communiqués* during the English offensive in Flanders in the spring of 1917.

The escorting squadrons were given the tasks of protecting our reconnaissance machines and carrying out actual observations in the neighbourhood of the enemy's trench lines; they were also required to report all movement on the lines of communication, the construction of light railways, and above all, whenever there were big offensives on foot, they were required to spot battery positions and, in conjunction with the infantry contact machines, to discover the exact locality of our front line.

Low-lying clouds made it impossible for strategical reconnaissance to be made during the September days of 1918. However, some glimpse of the enemy's back areas had to be obtained at all costs, for every day there was more danger of the English breaking through our lines at their point of attack near Cambrai. Single reconnaissance machines were constantly shot down owing to the low altitude at which they had to fly. They could only be protected by fighting machines on their outward flight, for on their return single-seaters were defenceless against attacks from behind.

The escort squadrons now rose to the occasion. Hying in close formation, and in spite of heavy fire from the ground, they fought their way through to a series of brilliant reconnaissance patrols. Many of them, indeed, never returned, but the enemy also suffered serious casualties.

The success which attended their efforts on this occasion laid the foundation of that work upon which the escort squadrons were principally employed later-attacks on ground targets. As a result of this new work, they were rechristened with the glorious name of 'storm squadrons' (i.e. trench-strafing machines). In the course of trench warfare it was found that even when our attacking infantry had succeeded in driving the enemy from his trenches, and at the very moment when their attack was successful, the assault was robbed of its principal moral effect by the failure of our artillery to provide sufficient preliminary protection against the enemy's counter-attacks. This fault was corrected with marked success by the trench-strafing pilots, who flew in front of assaulting troops at a height of only 150 to 200 feet, and attacked the enemy in his trenches with machine-gun fire and hand grenades. Again and again they would return and renew their attack with undiminished vigour.

In this connection the attack on Kemmel Hill will be remembered for all time. In the first grey light of dawn the battle squadron flew raging to the attack like a flock of gigantic night birds; lower and lower they descended, until they were only a few feet above the heads of the men in our trenches, and when with a thundering 'hurrah' the infantry went over the top, the aeroplanes overwhelmed the enemy's resistance with furious machine-gun fire. Our terrified opponents offered very little resistance; the wiser individuals among them held up their hands, and were taken prisoners by our victorious infantry.

However, the subjugation of the enemy's infantry did not finish the battle, for their back areas also had to be dealt with: their artillery, their support trenches, ammunition dumps, the reserves that were being hurried up to the front, their ammunition columns, lorries, trains, etc. This was a rich field for the work of the trench-strafing machines. The batteries as they blazed away, made welcome targets; they were attacked, and soon the gun crews ceased fire.

The enemy's reserves were situated in hollows and behind woods; it was the trench-strafing aeroplane's duty to discover their whereabouts. What disorder and what loss of *morale* they caused, as they attacked with bombs and hand grenades, and their machine guns reaped their bloody harvest! Even now, I can see in my mind's eye that American battery near Verdun, which was standing in readiness behind the small wood: the wounded horses reared, the rest bolted into the surrounding country, and the entire unit was scattered.

Strewn about in the neighbourhood of the front lines were a number of very dangerous machine-gun nests, whose positions were frequently betrayed by the smoke trails of their burning phosphorus bullets. The keen eye of the airmen searched yet farther afield for suitable targets: ammunition dumps, concealed in woods and difficult to discover, light railways, barracks, etc. Whenever columns could be seen hurrying up to the battlefield and crowded within the narrow compass of the roads through the woods, or on a bridge, then a well-delivered attack from the air might delay the arrival of the enemy's reinforcements for several hours, and thus decide the issue of the battle.

Should, however, the enemy's attack force us to take up the defensive, and perhaps even to retreat, then in this situation also our trench-strafing machines were the trusty supporters of the valiant infantry, and often enough they kept the onrushing enemy away from our hard-pressed troops.

Even though sometimes they were not required to participate in the fighting on the ground, their activity was in nowise diminished. They would then successfully attack the observation balloons, particularly on any section of the front where the number of balloons led us to suspect the enemy of planning an attack. The enemy's aerial forces also suffered heavy casualties from the daring attacks of these machines, which even penetrated as far as their aerodromes, some of which lay far behind the lines, although, indeed, the enemy - as a rule the English - were able to surpass us in this work. During July 1918 large squadrons of seventy or eighty machines would appear, and while two-thirds of their number remained at various heights to act as escort, the remainder would systematically attack our aerodromes one by one. Thus, for example, in the neighbourhood of Lille and Cortoyle, in the course of two days they succeeded in completely destroying three formations of fighting machines by bombs and machine-gun fire.

'Mosaic' photograph of Paris (St. Denis), showing the site of a bomb explosion.

In addition to their work during the day the trench-strafing machines strove indefatigably at night to shoot down the enemy's raiders on their homeward flight, particularly on bright moonlight nights, and to damage the billets, stations, and other objectives which lay behind their lines. It was naturally not possible for them to obtain the same decisive results by night as by day. However, like our bombing machines in their operations far behind the enemy's lines, single trench-strafing aeroplanes carried the war into the enemy's country by night with a very great measure of success.

ATTACKING THE SOMME BRIDGES AT BRAY AND ST. CHRIST

On the 6th of September 1917 we were compelled, to evacuate Péronne owing to the vigorous English attacks which were hurled against our lines, supported by a large number ox tanks and heavy artillery fire. From the grey light of dawn until late in the evening our trench-strafing machines were in the air striving to relieve our hard-pressed infantry, and they wore on the ground barely long enough for the machines to be prepared for the next flight. Then one morning a pilot from an infantry contact patrol arrived with startling news of a hostile force composed of every branch of the service which was approaching Péronne from the south in a long column along the west bank of the Somme, at the point where the bridges at Bray and St. Christ crossed the river.

It seems a heaven sent opportunity to the trench-strafing pilots, and a few minutes later twenty-four machines from our squadron start off on that fine September day. The prearranged height for assembly is soon reached: then the Halberstadts make straight for the lines, and soon Cambrai is beneath us. We have no difficulty in recognising the front lines, which are enveloped in a pall of smoke and dust. Without hesitation every machine plunges into that inferno, and it seems as though these gigantic birds rival each other in daring. The explosions of shell and. shrapnel are clearly visible against their dull background; thick black clouds of smoke roll across the earth. The iron song of the engine drowns all anxiety and soothes the nerves.

Only 1200 feet up; a rocket is fired as a signal, and the squadron splits into two lines, one behind the other. Two or three minutes later we are above the enemy. Nerves are strained to the uttermost, and with eager eyes we seek to pierce the thick clouds of smoke. We cast glances at the sky above, where great clouds, which seem to indicate the advent of bad weather, are appearing. Péronne, that devastated village, is blazing away on our left front; soon the shimmering ribbon of the Somme emerges through the haze, and a few seconds later we are over the objective. A quick glance at the map tells us that we have hit the right spot; there on the right lies Bray, and on the left is St. Christ. We see objects like thin cords stretched across the bridges. Not far ahead there appears a white puff of smoke, the first shrapnel shell welcoming our arrival; no damage is done. At a signal from the leader's machine we all descend in a steep glide upon the bridges!

One thousand feet, 800 feet, 500 feet - then - the heart beats until it seems that it must burst and every pulse in the body throbs. Down below on the bridge itself and the shore on either side are thick columns of men, horses, and wagons. A storm of machine bullets pours down upon them. At first no result is perceptible; it is almost as though we were shooting on some inanimate target; and then - men, horses, and lorries scatter pell-mell. Their only thought now is to save themselves by getting off the road, and we see them fleeing wildly in every direction. It is on the bridges themselves, however, that the confusion is at its worst. Teams break loose and jump into the river, men, beasts, and all; it seems as if the multitude were possessed by evil genii.

Our bombs and hand grenades whistle pitilessly down into the chaos, and I see more than one strike the very middle of the bridge. We are hardly 200 feet up, and it is possible to see every detail Again we return to the attack, and involuntarily one casts a glance at the villages on the east bank of the river, where, standing huddled up against a garden wall, arc between twenty and thirty horsemen. That in all probability will be the General Staff. Already the machine guns are chattering; the result is wild confusion, collisions, and a complete rout.

Suddenly two Sopwith scouts attack our machines from the left flank; after a short conflict I see one of them plunge down to destruction and the other hastily makes off. Twice again the machine guns rake the columns below, until almost every cartridge has been expended. After returning to our aerodrome to replenish our ammunition, we set off to the attack once more; again we met with the same success.

We had paralysed an entire English division; our infantry gained time to consolidate their new positions in peace. Our achievement was commended by an Army *communiqué* in words that will never be forgotten.

(HERMANN.)

CHAPTER V
THE GERMAN AIR FORCE ON THE WESTERN FRONT

VERDUN, 1916

WHEN G.H.Q. DECIDED to attack the fortress of Verdun, they also decided that the whole of that section of the front should be carefully reconnoitred. The front line trenches as well as all the back areas, which included the forests on the north-eastern front and the wooded region to the east of Varennes, received the closest scrutiny. In the course of that year photographic reconnaissance became easier and more efficient, and even capable of revealing objectives hidden in the depths of the forests, as well as making possible a thorough examination of the trenches, billets, and obstacles. The extensions of the trench system were compared with the existing records, and an estimate was arrived at concerning their powers of resistance; while in the back areas all camps, lines of communication, and aerodromes were reconnoitred as far as Bar-le-Duc.

At the beginning of February the reconnaissance machines became involved in the conflict. The preparation of a photographic map of the region to be attacked was undertaken by a special unit, assisted by the work of four squadrons which had hitherto been confined to the Verdun Front. At the beginning of operations three fighting squadrons were provided to carry out attacks on the camps and dumps behind the enemies' lines.

The attack itself started on February 21, 1916, under bad weather conditions and after a period of fourteen days of almost incessant rain. The effect of our barrage on the forest positions could only be observed from a very low altitude.

Halberstadt CL 4, a lightly constructed and compact 'trench-straifing' machine.

The long-range guns of the heavy artillery were brought to bear on Fort Douaumont and were controlled by observation from the air, the results of their work being confirmed by photographs. The fighting machines were used to harass all traffic on the roads leading into Verdun. At first the single-seater scouts were unable to accomplish much owing to the low-lying clouds, and during the whole of the Verdun attack there were never any formation or squadron fights in the air, for the French, contrary to the English, avoided aerial combats. The work of the artillery observation machines was the most important.

Each day the new batteries which the enemy brought up were discovered and engaged by our artillery. Unfortunately the infantry contact machines proved to be of little value, for the infantry did not as yet place sufficient trust in their service. Several hours used to elapse before information concerning the situation in our front line trenches could reach our artillery, and our course of conduct suffered in consequence. For example, our own guns were firing on the forts at Douaumont for hours after they had been taken.

The attack on the west bank of the Haas followed the same general lines as that on the east bank. It was principally a matter of a few important positions, and the artillery observation became particularly useful in dealing with them.

When the Somme offensive broke out in July 1916, the Air Force on

Fokker D 7. One of the moat efficient single-seater fighting machines designed during the war.

the Verdun Front had to be considerably weakened in order that they might be able to assist at the now scene of activity.

The principal work of those left on the Verdun Front consisted of keeping the closest watch on all concentrations of the enemy's troops so as to be prepared for those counter-attacks which were being delivered against the now weakened front. Thus, very early, we were able to recognise and discover the main direction of the French offensives in September and November by constantly observing their preparations.

In times of dire necessity aeroplanes were principally used as a means of communication, for carrying rations, ammunition, orders, etc., to the men in the frontline. Our fighting machines were successful in the attacks on various positions behind the enemy's front lines. Thus, for example, a bridge near Verdun was destroyed by bombs. The light of many conflagrations on the horizon often showed where ammunition dumps had been blown up by our aeroplanes. The bomb raids on the bases of the enemy's reinforcements at Vitry-le-François, Bevigny, and Bar-le-Duc were assisted by airships, which, however, were soon compelled to discontinue their work on account of the increased strength of the enemy's defences.

Although perhaps the Air Force did not play the same decisive role at Verdun as it did in later operations, the cause of this lies in the fact that they were opposed by French aviators, and that they were numerically too weak to be used as a unit in the battle.

All the same, one must remember that it was during the Verdun offensive that the Air Force developed from a purely reconnoitring corps to a combatant service. When the fighting was at its height there were at least half as many machine guns being used in the air as on the ground. Our airmen carried out all the reconnaissance that was demanded of them.

(HAEHNELT.)

THE BATTLE OF THE SOMME, 1916

The part played by the Air Force during the battle of the Somme has special claims to criticism. This battle was a wonderful training in everything appertaining to flying, and influenced the entire development of our Air Force in both organisation and design, as well as the methods of training *personnel,* up to the very end of the war. During the course of operations aerial policy came more and more to the fore owing to the numerous and vigorous attacks which were made by so-called experts both before and at the beginning of the battle.

A loud echo to these accusations was found in the debates of the Reichstag, Our war-worn airmen were hard pressed at the front during this period, and therefore, in the interests of the service, had to forgo offering any reply to these Parliamentary traitors. The airmen carried out their thankless work to the best of their ability but reaped no reward, thanks to the authorities whose 'expert' knowledge had been won, not in a pilot's or observer's cockpit, but at an office desk. Thus, eventually, both the Army and the general public were led to view the achievements of the Air Force in the spring and summer of 1916 from a very distorted point of view, which should now be corrected.

In accordance with the general scheme of this book, I shall abandon all statistics, graphs, maps, tables, and the like, which, as a rule, remain unread and carry but little weight, and base my argument upon the following considerations:-

1. The Report on the Work of the First Army in the Battle of the Somme, which was issued by the First Army Headquarters on January 30, 1917, and
2. My own experiences at that time and in that place.

The report begins as follows: 'The Battle of the Somme came as no surprise to the Second Army, which was operating on the same front. As early as February 1916 our airmen had observed numerous huts in process of erection on both sides of the Aisne in that region facing the north flank of the Army Front, Shortly afterwards the English divisions on the front north of the Somme were strengthened, and yet, according to the information obtained by infantry patrols, they were generally taken out of the line after a few weeks. Towards the end of April their number north of the Somme had increased to twelve, and facing them there were only four German divisions.'

Unfortunately the information obtained by tactical and strategical reconnaissance, between Starch and the beginning of the battle, is not included in this report, although one of the principal arguments advanced by our traitors at home was: 'Even before the opening of the offensive the Air Force had failed in its duty, and provided us with no information concerning the situation behind the enemy's lines.'

In March 1916 our airmen reported the movement towards the south of large bodies of troops from the French lines near Arras, and the erection of a large number of tents to the north of the Somme, all of which operations were protected by heavy artillery fire in order to restrain our observation. Thus, for example, on April 23, a Bavarian squadron reported two new hostile aerodromes to the east of Villers-Brettoneux, as well as a large training ground near Corbé. By the middle of May both these new aerodromes were provided with thirteen sheds instead of four, and thereby were able to house about fifty aeroplanes. In addition to this, the construction of countless hangars and sheds between the Ancre and the Somme was reported.

The presence of infantry training grounds and the laying of railways in the neighbourhood of Vecquemont was established by photographic reconnaissance. This information also showed us that the camps north of the Somme were intended for the use of the English, and those south of the Somme for the French. During May similar items of information were obtained by Squadrons 33, 32, and 59. In the light of these facts there could be no further doubt as to the region from which the attack would be launched and its general direction.

During the first two weeks of June there appeared signs of new communication trenches, running northwards to the front from far behind the lines, and round about the 'Hammer Wood.' The officer commanding No. 1 Bavarian Squadron reported to the general officer then commanding the 14th Reserve Army Corps that, in conjunction with the enemy's local aerial activity which was exceedingly lively, there could be no doubt that an attack would be delivered from that direction. The answer was to the effect that nothing was afoot on that part of the line, and that we need only expect an attack farther north, and near Serre and Hébuterne. Also his suggestion of the probability of an attack on the weak salient at Fricourt received no attention.

On June 17th a machine of the same squadron proved beyond doubt that the number of battery positions, dug-outs, communication trenches, and concentration points was greatly increased, particularly to the south and east of the 'Hammer Wood.' All aerial photographs were sent post-haste to the General Staff and to the headquarters of the 2nd Army Corps. On June 19th the information which had been acquired on these flights, particularly the fact of the existence of numerous trenches to the south of Maricourt, was confirmed by further reconnaissance. On July 17th I happened to be with No. 1 Bavarian Squadron, and took the opportunity of personally reading the report sent at 10.30 P.M. on the 22nd June to the General Officer Commanding the 14th Reserve Army Corps on the results of a reconnaissance flight. This report ran as follows: 'The enemy will attack - if at all - with Maricourt as his right wing, and not from Gommécourt alone. He does not wish to forgo attacking the salient at Fricourt owing to the tactical advantages it offers him.'

Squadron 32, having photographed Gommécourt, established the fact that it was in that neighbourhood that the enemy had made most

Fort Douaumont, Verdun. Before the German bombardment.

preparations for an attack by constructing earthworks. Also, Squadron 27 reported that, to the south of the Somme as far as the 'Römerstrasse' the enemy were making rapid progress in the construction of trenches for their attack.

It is only natural that the infantry were unable to estimate all this silent activity at its proper value, and this fact led them to misappreciate the work of the Air Force during the battle itself. Not only did our airmen have to contend with the overwhelming numerical superiority of the enemy, but they were also faced with a far more serious difficulty - the prejudices of the infantry and other branches of the service. The infantry had had no training whatsoever in the science of defence against low-flying aircraft, and, moreover, had no faith in their ability to shoot these machines down if they were determined to do so. In consequence of this they were seized with a fear almost amounting to panic, a fear which was fostered by the incessant activity and hostility of the enemy's aeroplanes.

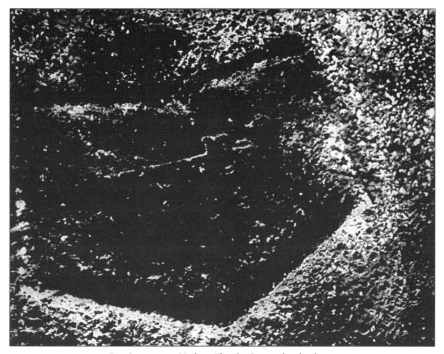

Port Douaumont, Verdun. After the German bombardment.

Although our infantry had a wholesome respect for the machine-gun attacks of the enemy's flying men, this work was considered of minor importance for our own machines, and this view is expressed in a *communiqué* of the First Army; yet, in the same *communiqué* we are told that the infantry were at first quite helpless against bomb attacks or machine-gun fire from above. As early as the beginning of April the G.O.C. Guards Corps had forbidden all bombing from that time onwards. The results of this prohibition may be estimated from the fact that while the enemy was free to attack us in this manner he had none against which to defend himself, whereas we had to employ much of our strength for this purpose. I am of the opinion that we could have found targets among the stores and ammunition dumps and *personnel* of our enemy, whose destruction would most certainly have delayed the development of their attack, and would at any rate have adversely affected the offensive operations of their aeroplanes. In official reports from the higher command I have read paragraphs such as the following:-

'Hostile aeroplanes are continually flying over our trenches at a height of only 150 feet, while the observer fires on our men, or, lying on one of the planes, signals with his handkerchief to the enemy's artillery.'

'An enemy aeroplane noticing a small white terrier emerging from a dug-out deduced the probable presence of an officer therein, and thereupon directed the enemy's artillery against it.'

'A hostile aeroplane flew over our positions last night. We could distinctly hear the conversation between the pilot and the observer.'

The irritation of the infantry found its expression in remarks such as: 'May God punish England, our artillery, and our Air Force!' or, a question passed from man to man as loudly as they dared: 'Has anybody here seen a German airman?' Yet none of these complaints were found to be justified on close inquiry.

As a result of this frame of mind, numerous orders were issued by the Army Corps, which further displeased the Air Force and led to undisciplined and unofficial replies.

On July 22nd, in spite of opposition, the photographic machines were sent up to fight an alleged hostile aeroplane, which eventually turned out to be one of our own Albatross machines. Our scanty defensive resources were being used almost all night and day, for fear of attacks from the air, although they effected nothing beyond using up petrol, wearing out engines, and so occupying the small *personnel* as to prevent them from doing more serious work.

Unfortunately the beginning of the battle of the Somme coincided with a period during which little improvement was effected in the design of our aeroplanes. The undoubted mastery of the air which, owing to the Fokker monoplane, we held at the beginning of 1916 in March and April, passed entirely over to the enemy's Nieuport, Vickers, and Sopwith machines. The monthly production of aeroplanes was not even sufficient to provide each squadron with the same type throughout. Thus, for example, Squadron 23 was composed of five different types.

In spite of these handicaps, I always found the Air Force during that period to be keen on flying, full of offensive spirit, and with a complete faith that things would eventually turn out all right. When the prowess of Boelcke and that of his followers, all of whom were flying the new fighting Halberstadt D 3, made itself felt, a reaction set in, and at the end of August the 1st Army Corps was able to report to G.H.Q.: 'We have received reports from various places on the front to the effect that our aeroplanes are now meeting with more success, and that the infantry are gradually recovering their faith in our Air Force.'

Having described the equalisation of the opposing forces and the beginning of a gradual intensification of the strength of both sides, this review of the battle of the Somme might well be brought to a conclusion, were it not that duty to our fallen airmen impels me to say a few words in answer to the invidious attacks which insinuate that our Air Force was 'over-decorated' particularly with the 'Ordre Pour le Mérite'. The Air Force was the only service whose honours could only be won in the face of the enemy, and one can still study the list of conditions which had to be satisfied before any of the three Air Force decorations could be granted. No emperor, king, prince, or general could wear those ribbons without actual experience of war flying. Together with the life-saving medal, these three decorations are the only honours which prove that its wearer, whether he be a pilot, officer-observer, or machine-gunner, has looked death unflinchingly in the eyes. The wound stripe itself no longer necessarily distinguishes its wearer as a hero, for an enemy's bomb in the night could have put him comfortably away in some base hospital or a bed at home.

In the whole course of the war there was no flying officer who won the 'Ordre Pour le Mérite' at an office table. Numerous victorious aerial combats - usually twenty or more - were necessary qualifications, and each one of these combats had to be confirmed with painstaking accuracy. What decoration of any other service is there whose wearer can lay claim to anything from twenty to eighty single-handed feats of daring and gallantry? And even if luck had favoured its wearer there was always some good reason for his wearing it. Of the seventy-two knights of the most exalted 'Ordre Pour le Mérite,' thirty-two have been buried in the war, and not one of them rested on his laurels. May their noble example live longer in the minds of the German people than the memory of the manner in which their honour was dragged through the mire of the battle of the Somme.

(SIEGERT.)

THE DEFENSIVE OPERATIONS OF 1917

In the winter of 1916, owing to the general situation of the war, it became necessary to prepare for those defensive operations which were expected. First among these preparations was a complete and exact reconnaissance of the many ramifications of the trench system and back areas along the whole length of the lines in order that the enemy's plans and direction of attack might be perceived in time, and for the general and comprehensive preparations for defence along the whole front to be organised. It seemed probable that the French would attempt to break through in Alsace, in order to improve their political situation by a local success; on the other hand, they could endanger all our war material by a push towards the industrial centres of the Saar, or, if they succeeded in reaching the railway from Longuyon to Montmédy, they could seriously threaten the reinforcements for the whole German Front by an attack from the direction of Verdun. Both here and in Champagne the enemy's preparations for an offensive were considerably simplified by the big operations that had been undertaken previously. Furthermore, there was the possibility of a combined offensive of the French and the English on the Aisne Front. The whole situation was therefore very uncertain.

All aerial reconnaissance was carried out with the same main object - the accurate observation of railway transport, particularly with respect to stations and their accumulation of rolling stock and material. By keeping an eye on the construction of huts behind the lines one could arrive at an estimate as to the strength of the enemy's forces in any given district, although errors were liable to creep in owing to the difficulty of distinguishing between dummy positions and huts which were actually occupied. Furthermore, the enemy's ammunition dumps, etc., were energetically sought for. Like ourselves, the enemy was compelled to concentrate his resources, and wherever he wished to attack, there he had to accumulate material.

We could not reckon upon any particular extension of this trench system for the purpose of his offensive, for as early as 1915 he had given us excellent indications of his plans in that respect by the construction of the 'Joffre' trenches. However, things were quite different with the artillery positions. Here, they were able to undertake a systematic alteration of the whole front with a view to deceiving us. Single-battery positions furnished with one gun only were used to assist the deception. But even in this respect it was possible to get some general idea of the situation, for the traffic observed in the neighbourhood of such battery positions was but scanty, and moreover there were usually no ammunition dumps in the neighbourhood. Another feature of the enemy's preparations for an attack consisted of laying tracks for the use of railway guns. By the construction of these railways one could estimate the direction of fire for these long-range guns, and could constantly discover the General Staff's plan of attack.

During this period it was equally important to screen our own observations, and we had to keep constant watch over our own defensive preparations in order to keep them secret from the enemy. In January 1917 the first signs of the enemy's preparations for an offensive were made manifest in the neighbourhood of Wychaerte, between Bapaume and Arras, near Roye, on the Aisne Front and in the valley of the Nesle. The 'Siegfried' operations, which were carried out between February and March 1917, were the enemy's preliminary movements for an attack on the Somme region round Bapaume, and this scheme of his along with the attack near Roye was thus eliminated. The preparations for this offensive on the Aisne and Champagne Fronts left no doubt in March as to the intention of the Entente to choose this section of the line. From a strategical point of view this also seemed likely: it was quite probable that they would make the attempt to cut off our salient by an attack in the north on the part of the English, and on the south by the French on the Aisne-Champagne Front.

Massed artillery positions before the English attack in Flanders in 1917.

In March we no longer entertained any doubts as to the main direction of attack, for the Air Force on these fronts began to concentrate and reorganise.

The principal duty of the artillery observation machines consisted of relieving the pressure upon our infantry by subduing the enemy's artillery. This work was carried out with great determination and success. The wireless installations close behind the lines proved of great service and assistance in the engagement of moving targets. At the commencement it was necessary to provide all single aeroplanes with an escort, since the general situation in the air was unfavourable to us. If the artillery observer wanted to carry out his work properly he had to be supported by some one who would look out for hostile aeroplanes and protect him from surprise. This co-operation between escorting machines and artillery machines was ensured by the fact that the escorting and artillery squadrons were amalgamated as one unit, and based at the same aerodromes.

The infantry contact machines were called upon to play an active part in the first days of the offensive. Part of our front line trenches had been lost, and our troops were scattered about in shell-holes, without any consolidation, and carefully avoiding definite trenches, since the enemy knew the exact position of these and concentrated his artillery fire on them.

In every group certain machines were told off to undertake fire control for our long-range guns. It was important that the same observer should always undertake this work, for it was only by specialising that the best possible results could be obtained.

The fighting machines at the beginning of the offensive were attached to various groups, and their operations came under the control of the Army Corps Commanders, Soon, however, it became obvious that this method affected the unity of the Air Force as a whole and led to a splitting up of the forces at our disposal. Generally there were never sufficient machines present at the places where they were required, and consequently, as time went on, fighting pilots were organised into groups which operated wherever the fighting happened to be most intense. By such means it became possible to establish defensive units, and the enemy's Air Force no longer broke through our defensive patrols by the aid of his numerical superiority. In fact, the enemy's numerical superiority was to a certain extent equalised by this method.

Similarly it was found necessary to pool *personnel* and *matériel* under the control of a central authority. It was only by such means that the best use could be made of the forces at our disposal during the long battle. One must remember that the fighting machines went from one big battle to another. An inactive section of the line was something that they did not know, and also it was impossible to allot any portion of the fighting service as reserves.

The work of the fighting squadrons was assisted by the officers in charge of the rocket batteries in many sectors of the front, who attended the wireless installations and sent messages to the group commanders which kept them constantly informed of the course of the battle. The pursuit of hostile squadrons was made considerably easier by the fact that the war maps were divided into large quadrilaterals, and by this means the position and direction of flight of an enemy machine could be signalled to a machine in the air at any given moment.

Bombing squadrons came under the direction of the army groups, and were used against depots, camps, and other enemy traffic centres. They achieved remarkable success by attacking billets, particularly in the neighbourhood to the west of Rheims.

The enemy's aerial activity was numerically the superior, but in no phase of the battle did it gain tactical advantage over us. Also aerial battles were not pursued so determinedly as on the English Front, as the French, although gallant, were not so keen. Long combats, such as were common on the English Front, were the exception on the French.

After the tide of battle had ebbed, our principal object was to screen the weakening of the German forces at the front from the enemy's eye, and to provide all our positions with the protection they required against observation from above. All objects which were not efficiently camouflaged were photographed, and the photographs were sent to the infantry for their information.

After the collapse of the French attacks on the Aisne-Champagne Front, they determined to abandon the offensive. However, fighting broke out with renewed intensity on the English Front, and most of the flying units were sent to the new scene of strife.

(HAEHNELT.)

THE GREAT OFFENSIVE, 1918

Whereas it was necessary for our defensive operations during 1917 to establish the Air Force upon as broad a basis as possible in order to meet the many various demands put upon it by the many places at which the enemy might try to break through, it was now necessary for our offensive operations to concentrate the Air Force so as to possess numerical superiority to start with. As a preparation and for the guidance of all flying units in the tactics of the offensive operations, a memorandum was issued in the winter of 1917 which shall serve as the foundation of this section. Its distribution was so well timed that the entire Air Force was concentrated from the beginning, and organised with one definite object in view.

Even when preparing for our defensive operations in 1917 we still kept in view the probability of a future offensive. The construction of aerodromes, each equipped with the same number of hangars along the whole strength of the Western Front, was carried out until our strength was easily distributed along the whole front. It became absolutely necessary to screen the concentration of our flying units, which might easily have been betrayed by the construction of aerodromes. Also notices of the movement of units could not be given too early, lest the enemy's espionage system should acquire information concerning our plans of attack.

Large depots were organised on the Western Front for the supply of spare parts, and similar depots were set up on various other fronts with a view to misleading the enemy.

In order that the observers might become thoroughly acquainted with every possible area in which they might have to operate, squadrons were assembled upon the various fronts from February onwards, so that they might have an opportunity of learning the battlefield. Our advance itself was conducted in such a way that those squadrons lying some distance behind our lines, and thus outside the radius of the enemy's reconnaissance, were the first to be moved. From these bases in the back areas a few necessary reconnaissance flights were made, but any concentration of aircraft along the front until the day of the attack was strictly prohibited. Wherever it was necessary for units to be moved up to their positions near the front lines, all material was stowed away in hangars, shelters, etc.

It was important for the purposes of secrecy that the enemy's reconnaissance machines should be kept away from the region through which we proposed to advance. Scouts were therefore continually patrolling those sectors, in order to chase off hostile aeroplanes which attempted to break through. Newly-arrived squadrons were not allowed to fly over the lines, lest the enemy should learn of our concentration through an increase in the casualties.

The enemy attempted to carry out the reconnaissance which he desired by employing exceptionally strong squadrons. The result was very intense aerial fighting. Our fighting machines were concentrated under the command of von Richthofen. Small groups of our fighting machines rarely engaged in aerial combat, since they desired to conserve their forces. As an example, on February 21 there occurred the first big aerial battle, in which altogether sixty or seventy aeroplanes took part. The English fought obstinately and the fight lasted for over half an hour, thirteen of the enemy's machines being shot down, while we lost one only.

Those reconnaissance machines, which were already operating over the region which we proposed to attack, had an excellent opportunity of studying the aerial photographs taken by various units, and of obtaining exact information concerning the future battlefield. The trench-strafing squadrons, which, as yet, had not been formed into groups, were concentrated behind the lines, and practised the attack of ground targets with machine guns and bombs.

Instruction in the methods to be adopted by other branches of the service were worked out in every detail by explanatory operation orders, illustrated by photographs. These orders were distributed even among the regiments, and specified aerial photographs among the companies and platoons.

It was not until forty-eight hours before the offensive was due to begin that the entire Air Force was made ready to take the air, and was told to await the orders to attack. Heavy clouds hung about the front of the 17th, 2nd, and 18th Armies on the day of the offensive itself, making it impossible for trench-strafing machines to assist in the infantry attack, or for reconnaissance machines to carry out their work until about 11 A.M., when the clouds lifted, and it was possible to give the higher command a very clear report on the progress of the battle. It was not until the evening that it was possible for the trench-strafing machines to attack the artillery in order to subdue them and to hinder their retreat. This work met with exceptional success, and a quantity of heavy artillery fell into our hands.

On the following day the duty of the Air Force lay in reconnaissance and registration of the reserves that were being hurried to the scene of activity. Wireless stations close behind the lines assisted in the work of engaging these targets with heavy fire.

After the first front line had been broken through, we advanced rapidly. As the closest possible touch had to be kept with the infantry, it was essential that they should be followed by aeroplanes, and only by such means was it possible to transmit orders and messages, for the despatch riders and runners, owing to the rapidity with which we advanced, were not able to carry out the heavy work imposed on them.

In order to preserve the individuality of the various flying units, their transfer to aerodromes in the devastated area was effected in groups by convoys of lorries. Aerodromes were first reconnoitred by a photographic machine, and were then divided up among the groups, so that each group would be self-contained within its own sector. Special aerodromes were provided for the fighting machines, and on the third day of the attack the enemy's aerodromes which had been closest to the line were used by us. Practically all material found on these aerodromes had been destroyed by fire.

The achievements of No. 1 lighting Squadron must be attributed principally to the initiative of its commander, Frhr. von Richthofen. His aerodrome was always so far forward as to be within range of the enemy's artillery, and the great success with which he met is to be attributed to the fact that he always sought to keep on the heels of the enemy. Unheedful of weather conditions, he camped out in the open in the cold spring months, with all his men and mechanics under canvas, hard by his machines. As a result, the Air Force rose to a pitch of efficiency never previously attained. Many a machine was badly damaged, and many men were injured, through forced landing among shell-holes in the devastated region. On the other hand, casualties due to enemy action were very small, thanks to the activity of our fighting machines.

We have already discussed the work of the reconnaissance machines. When the advance came to a standstill they were again required to take over the work usually associated with trench warfare. The trench-strafing machines worked indefatigably from all heights, and on every section of the battle front, directing most of their attention against the enemy's reinforcements. They specialised in attacking the narrow roads and bridges of the Somme, and the results of their work were seen in the evacuated region after the enemy had retreated. In co-operation with the artillery they frequently caused great confusion at such points. Throughout the whole of the offensive the infantry contact machines were working incessantly over the lines.

Although the expenditure in *matériel* and *personnel* during the battle was very great, yet up to the very end the units could be maintained at full strength, thanks to the Aircraft Supply Depots that had been provided.

From every army aeroplane park an intermediary depot was pushed forward into the sector worked by the squadrons to be supplied. This method was of particular importance in order to maintain the supply of petrol, of which a vast quantity was used. Tank lorries proved to be insufficient, and enormous iron containers were constructed from material obtained in the Belgian factories, so that supplies of as much as 100 tons could be sent up at a time.

The bombing squadrons were principally under the command of the army groups. During the night following the first advance, and in the following nights, railheads and railway junctions behind the lines were attacked, while later on reserve camps and ammunition dumps were selected as targets. In this work No. 7 'Bombing Squadron' achieved remarkable success. In spite of unremitting activity by night, this squadron refused to rest, and made a practice of carrying out day bomb raids with C-type machines, and bombing all camps and magazines in the neighbourhood of the battlefield. While on their outward and return flights they used to attack the enemy's lines of communication with machine guns.

The fighting on this new front was of the most bitter description, and the war in the air became intense when the French as well as the English had concentrated on the new battle front. Thus the tide of battle ebbed and flowed until August 8th. On this day, a misty morning, the enemy put down intense barrage fire upon the Somme Front. As soon as we realised the extent of this early morning attack, squadrons from all fronts were concentrated so rapidly upon this section of the lines, that by the time the mists had risen, a sufficient aerial force had been assembled. The day that was to be a critical one in the course of the whole war, proved the most, successful in the whole of our airmen's history. On the evening of that day eighty-three crashed enemy machines were counted behind our lines. Our airmen had raised the level of the whole German fighting forces by their assistance and gallantry in the battle.

(HAEHNELT.)

Chapter VI

German Airmen In Many Theatres Of War

Italy

WHEN THE GERMAN 14th Army in the valley of the Save was assembled round about Laibach and Krainburg towards the end of September 1917, and the Army Commander proceeded to verify his information concerning the district and our enemy, it became obvious that the existing Austrian maps of the Julian Alps, and the mountainous regions of Tolmein, Karfreit, and Civigale were quite unreliable. There was actually nothing in existence except a map on the scale of 1 to 200,000 sufficiently good to be used in case of necessity as a source of information concerning the plains, but it was hardly of any service for the tract of mountainous district.

Thus the General Staff was faced with a difficulty at the very beginning, a difficulty which at least must result in serious delays. An exact knowledge of the lie of the land is an essential preliminary condition for any advance, particularly for the artillery, and this exact knowledge should be acquired without loss of time. Owing to the lateness of the year, the probability of heavy snowfalls up in the mountains, and more particularly to the fact that the enemy were planning an attack on the plateau of Doberdo, it was imperative that we should make haste. The object of our intended offensive was to counter the attack in question, and to relieve the pressure on our allies at Trieste. It was, however, clear that to order the divisions to advance to the attack without any accurate knowledge of the peculiarities of that mountainous country was a particularly hazardous course of action.

The squadrons of the German Air Force attached to the German troops in this district helped the General Staff out of their dilemma in the shortest possible time, A few days sufficed for our fighting pilots, with the daring and experience they had acquired on the Western Front, to drive all the Italian airmen from the air, particularly as the Italians had hitherto only been confronted by the Austrian Air Force, which was at that time provided with inferior machines. Consequently our reconnaissance machines were ensured command of the air over the battlefields, and were therefore able to carry out their work unhindered. Before long they had completed a photographic survey of the districts on both sides of the lines, and had provided the General Staff with a complete picture of the enemy's railway system, the distribution of his forces, and the disposition and strength of his flying units. The reconnaissance of the enemy's aerodromes proved especially useful later on when our advance had been successful, inasmuch as it provided our squadrons with bases which they could occupy forthwith, and consequently greatly increased the promptitude with which they could be employed in case of emergency, as it obviated a search after possible landing grounds in that region, which, although comparatively flat, was bad flying country owing to the extensive cultivation.

Thanks to the improved map, the positions which the artillery were to occupy when they advanced could be selected beforehand, targets could be allocated to individual batteries, and the batteries themselves controlled by aerial observation. This achievement had to be effected in the face of heavy odds in the air against an enemy who was at any rate partially equipped with better machines, and under conditions of great difficulty which, among other things, involved flying 40 miles or more from the base in Carniola to the front over impassable mountains, and without any possibility of intermediary landings or forced landing grounds. In addition to that, both luck and the atmospheric conditions were not particularly favourable to us; only occasionally were there any fine days before the attack began, and even in the very beginning we had suffered many misfortunes and had lost much men and material through the activity of the enemy and through flying accidents.

Our plans for the offensive involved the Air Force being given work of decisive importance as soon as the advance commenced. The penetration of the Italian line to the north of Tolmein was carried out successfully against an enemy familiar with all the possibilities of mountain warfare after two years of hard fighting. Although against greatly superior odds, it was successful after only a short struggle. The advance then developed with almost ideal swiftness and without delay. The Province of Udino was opened up with incredible ease by our divisions as they swept irresistibly forward, although, indeed, they encountered but little resistance, while the individual objectives of our attack fell one by one to a well-thoughtout enveloping movement. Our forces advanced to the attack on October 23, 1917; on the 28th they had reached the Tagliamento, and behind them along every road there lay huge quantities of *matériel* which had fallen into our hands, and represented the entire supplies of several of the enemy's armies.

The limits of advance which had been assigned to our small forces were greatly exceeded. The fact that the enemy, when once he had been thrown back into the mountains, offered hardly any resistance, but surrendered a large area to us, led our General Staff to believe that the Italians intended to hold them at the Tagliamento. It did not seem advisable to press the enemy with the forces that we had at our disposal, and it was considered that our gains were already more than sufficient. Then our airmen established the fact that it was the enemy's intention to make a stand behind the Piave. Previously, between the 2nd and 6th of November, our airmen had been engaged in observing the almost unbelievable confusion among the enemy, and had thereby supplied much valuable information to the General Staff. Acting on the information thus acquired, we were able to consolidate our position in the whole of that wide province between the Tagliamento and the Piave.

When winter arrived it brought with it trench warfare on the Piave, and all its characteristic work associated with trench warfare, which did not differ materially from that which was carried out on the other fronts. As a matter of fact, it was difficult for our forces, small as they were both on the ground and in the air, to hold their own over so large an area. The enemy was soon reinforced by French and English forces which were hastily hurried up; the old game that we had played on the Western Front was begun all over again; one against ten. In spite of all difficulties we achieved remarkable success even then. On December 26th, every machine attached to the Army carried out a concerted raid by broad daylight into the heart of the enemy's country, and attacked the aerodrome at Trevignano from a very low altitude, partially destroying it. The violence of the enemy's antiaircraft defences was unable to prevent us from displaying the black cross even as far afield as Verona.

In conclusion, it is worth remarking that the beginning of December 1917 witnessed some excellent work on the part of No. 4 'Bombing Squadron' which was attached to the Army. Particularly good results were obtained when a section of this squadron, with indefatigable zeal, started seven times in a single night, in order to celebrate the Kaiser's birthday. Padua, Mestre, and Treviso were their principal objectives, and their work was considerably assisted by the clearness of the bright southern nights. In Padua and in Venice, the grandchildren of the present generation will still be told the story of those Northern 'Barbarians,' who, like the storm-wind of the North itself, swooped down on their black pinions and carried terror and destruction in the stillness of night along the sleeping plains at the foot of the Alps.

(DYCKHOFF AND HOMBURG.)

FLYING IN THE EAST: THE DARDANELLES

'Too many cooks spoil the broth'; example - Turkey. The Turkish Army had been reorganised by the German Military Mission, the Turkish Navy by the English, while the Turkish Air Force had been under the tutelage of the French! Such was the position shortly before the outbreak of the Great War, nor should the zeal with which England and France had made use of Turkey's reverses in the Balkan War to attack German influence in the Near East be overlooked; then, when they failed in this object and Turkey entered the war on our side two weeks after its outbreak, England and France endeavoured to cripple those two principal factors in the defence of the Dardanelles, namely, Turkey's Navy and Air Force. The technical *personnel* of the *Goeben* and *Breslau* discovered that there was hardly any serviceable piece of machinery on board the Turkish ships. The cunning English had distributed vital parts of machinery among the various factories at Constantinople, ostensibly for the purpose of repairs, with the result that even after many weeks of work there were still quantities of material missing.

Things were much worse even in connection with the Air Force over which the French had exercised so friendly a supervision. When I first visited that enormous and ideally beautiful aerodrome to the north of San Stefano in January 1915, I found among the vast quantity of unserviceable rubbish in the shape, of aeroplanes only two machines with which the daring Turkish pilots would risk five minutes' flights over the aerodrome in dead calm weather. These two machines, an 80 H.P. Gnome-Deperdussin and a 40 H.P. Blériot, were the pride of the Turkish Air Force. Neither of them could properly be termed 'flying machines,' much less 'service machines'; and the pride of the Turks in such awe-inspiring contraptions, although now and then it is true they flew without smashing, shows how cleverly the French knew how to make use of the weakest side of the Turkish character, self-satisfaction, for their own ends.

Captain S., who was sent to Constantinople in February 1915 in order to reorganise the Turkish Air Force, was faced with a task indeed. The most important thing was to hurry up aeroplanes from Germany as quickly as possible. Since the direct route through Serbia was blocked, and Roumania was hostilely 'neutral' - so much so that they refused to allow the Christmas parcels for the crews of the *Goeben* and *Breslau* to pass through their territory - there remained only one method, namely to fly the machines from Southern Hungary to Lom Palanka on the Danube in Bulgaria, and to bring them thence by railway to Constantinople.

In March 1915 an attempt was made to bring six machines to

The Suez Canal where it enters the Bitter Lakes.
In the left bottom corner the tenta of an English camp can be seen.

Constantinople by this route. Three of these arrived at San Stefano, but were, of course, too late to take part in the defence against the great attack on the Dardanelles in March 18th; however they had at least arrived. Then Bulgaria also suddenly bethought herself of her 'neutrality,' and therefore seized the three remaining machines as they were on their way from Lom Palanka to Sofia. It now became necessary to risk flying from Herculesbad to Adrianople, and the flight was successful with but very few exceptions - an excellent testimony this to the efficiency of our aeroplanes at that time. Of course it was not possible to carry spare parts or supplies on these flights, for all the available 'lift' had to be applied to carrying the necessary quantity of petrol.

The first German machine appeared on the Dardanelles in April 1915, The conditions under which our men had to fight were as bad as possible. Quite apart from the fact that they had the honour of opposing ten times as many enemy machines, an honour which was later afforded to our men in every other Turkish theatre of war, they were frequently obliged to fly 60 miles or more over the sea in a land machine, since the islands of Imbros and Tenedos constituted the most important objectives for our reconnaissance. Also, co-ordination between the flying squadrons and the General Staff, so greatly to be desired, was, owing to the difficulties in communication, almost impossible, since it took four hours on horseback to get from the aerodrome to Staff Headquarters, and small reliance could be placed on the Turkish telephone service. The Turks remarked with considerable bitterness that when a German machine was attacked it turned as though to flee. We had much difficulty in making them understand that the B-type aeroplane must first turn away from an attack in order to obtain a good field of fire.

This unfortunate impression on the Turkish mind was finally destroyed in February 1916 by the arrival of three Fokkers, who in one week shot down six of the enemy's machines. Then once again the gallant B-type machines, possessed the mastery of the air, and were able to annoy the English with cameras and bombs. The ships presented a most enticing target, but one which was exceedingly difficult to hit. Their zigzag course made it almost impossible, and yet we succeeded twice, at Smyrna and in the Gulf of Saros, in obtaining direct hits on transport steamers. Night bomb raids were also very popular, particularly on the big English aerodrome in the island of Tenedos.

On one of these occasions two of our airmen got into very serious difficulties. The pilot had descended to within 120 feet of the ground, the observer had bestowed his blessing of bombs, and when he settled down contentedly for the homeward flight with the feeling of having done good work, the pilot shouted to him despairingly that the engine control had jammed. There they were, in the night, only 120 feet above the enemy's aerodrome - an extraordinarily unpleasant situation! With astonishing coolness and agility the observer climbed down upon the plane, found that the control rod to the throttle had worked loose, and that the throttle itself had automatically been closed by its spring. He therefore held it open himself and was obliged to remain standing on the plane throughout the whole of the homeward flight, which lasted nearly an hour. The machine landed safely.

When the English evacuated Gallipoli, the Dardanelles theatre of war became less important; most of the machines, which were now able to reach us from Germany without difficulty, were sent to other theatres of war.

(Bormann.)

Flying In the East:
The Sinai Front and Palestine

The route from Homburg to Bagdad was open, and it behoved us to make use of the advantage afforded us by the defeat of Serbia and the relief of the Dardanelles, Thus the idea of undertaking the campaign against the Suez Canal was resumed, but on a bigger scale than in 1915. For this purpose a German squadron was despatched to take part in the campaign, and they were, therefore, the first flying men to carry out their duties in the heart of the desert. Their preparations were commenced in January 1916 with true German thoroughness. It was clearly going to be an experiment, and the technical equipment of the squadron had to be adapted to tropical conditions.

The fourteen C 1 Rumpler machines, with a 150 h.p. Mercedes engine and enlarged radiators, turned out to be excellent, as also the technical equipment and the spare parts with which they were supplied. I can now think with pleasure of the handy crates in which Daimler delivered their spare engines, and which could be transported on camels, in contrast to the methods of other firms later on in the campaign, who packed our spares in enormous crates which could hardly be dealt with by cranes. The squadron were provided with mechanical transport for carrying their supplies, but were denied motorcars for themselves, because the 'experts' declared that they could not be used in the desert, a logic which even today I utterly fail to understand. Another expert declared that in the desert it was only possible to fly at night, or at the very most at early dawn!

The question of replenishing supplies was vital. The overland route was the only possible means of supplying the Sinai Front. From Constantinople onwards the distance to Beersheba was approximately 900 miles by railway, and Beersheba was the base for the canal campaign.

The authorities in Constantinople did not seem to appreciate the difficulties of transport, or to take the necessary precautions to meet them, for the foresight which was displayed at the changing places was very limited. At Bozanti, Gelebek Mamouré, Islahije, and Bayak material accumulated in a most disquieting manner, with the result that there was much congestion and confusion. During the rainy season floods caused delays of eight or ten days in our transport system. The lack of rolling stock, the inefficiency of the locomotives, and the difficulty in obtaining fuel owing to the lack of wood and coal were also incessantly causing trouble.

Nor were these the only difficulties. Hitherto we had been carrying on war in the enemy's country, and had been accustomed to order, Here, however, we were in friendly territory! It is obviously useless to give orders unless one can exact unconditional obedience. It was, however, but very rarely that the transport officers were able to do this. Moreover, we had to take into consideration the Oriental character, and the easy corruptibility of the Turkish mind. Also they had no appreciation whatever of the value of time. 'Jawasch, Jawasch!' (slowly) represents an ideal life to the Oriental. All hurry, all haste they consider to be coarse, and odious to their souls. They are naturally pachydermatous, and no doubt the climate has a lot to do with this mode of life. Finally, there were a large number of Germans who only too readily fell into this contemplative and philosophical way of thought and living.

The English were in a far better position. Driving obliquely out through the Sinai Desert from the Suez Canal, they had undertaken the construction of a railway which was to effect junction with the old cultivated territory of Egypt. Along its whole length this railway was accompanied by a water supply carried in a cast-iron pipe of about 12 inches diameter. Pumping stations and regulator taps were distributed along the line. The sea provided them with an alternative route, to Alexandria and Port Said. This route could be all the better employed by the English owing to the fact that our U-boats were hampered in their activity by the shallows near the coast.

Before the Canal campaign proper began, General von Kress undertook a very thorough reconnaissance with powerful forces. At Easter 191G he pushed forward as far as Katia; overwhelmed the English camp, and took about 20 officers and 1200 men prisoners. Two machines took part in this expedition, both of which belonged to No. 300 Squadron, who advanced a detachment to Beersheba.

During this undertaking El-Arish, which lay about 90 miles from the Canal, was used as an intermediary landing ground, and later on the whole squadron was stationed at that place, while General von Kress also made it his headquarters. The flying men now began to appreciate the immense difficulties of carrying out their work in the desert. From Beersheba onwards all the supplies, from the petrol down to the smallest spare part, had to be brought up on camels, which were compelled to follow the old caravan route owing to the scarcity of wells. When our aerodrome was in process of construction, the English airmen carried out a very vigorous and daring raid. At eleven o'clock in the morning they dropped their bombs, and, having descended to within 100 feet of the ground, attacked us with machine-gun fire. However, they inflicted but little damage.

The Canal expedition began towards the end of July before our expeditionary force was numerically complete. We hoped by this means to ease the pressure of the battle of the Somme on the Western Front, However, the English no longer contented themselves with merely defending the Canal but had pushed forward about 15 miles towards our positions on our main line of advance. Our attacks did not surprise them, and they carried out some really excellent counter-attacks with such effect that the Turkish troops were compelled to withdraw to positions to the west and south-west of El-Arish. The attack which the

211

Senussi were expected to make on the Egyptians to the west did not take place. The resulting ferment among the Arabs made it necessary for the greater part of our expeditionary force to be employed in that district, so that only a weak contingent was left to meet the English attacks which were expected in the desert. The plans of the English were clearly revealed by the fact that they began to construct a railway from the Canal through the desert of Sinai.

Our reconnaissance now principally concerned itself with the progress of this railway and with observing the enormous camps along the Canal. It was only possible to fly on every other day owing to lack of petrol. In order to increase his offensive power, Lieut. Henkel, an observer gunner, added a machine gun firing forwards, mounted for the pilot's use close by the engine. By this means the first English aeroplane was shot down.

Since the aerodrome only lay 7 miles from the coast, we had to reckon with the possibility of being bombarded from the sea. This was actually planned to take place in the early hours of September 17, 1916. In the night of the 15th-16th we experienced bomb raids, and on the 17th, shortly before dawn, the alarm signal rang out again. Owing to the false accounts given by the Royal Flying Corps concerning the pretended results of their recent bomb raids by night, English seaplanes came so close up to the coast that one could hear them at their landing station. In no time our airmen - either in their sleeping suits, or at any rate but very lightly clad - were in their machines. A Sopwith was shot down in flames, another was compelled to land, and the rest fled. We followed up our success with a continuous raid, lasting throughout an hour, with bombs and machine guns against the monitors and seaplane carriers, which eventually retreated at full speed to the north, so that our Rumplers were unable to follow them farther. We had thereby scored another success, which raised our spirits yet higher.

The rainy season was upon us, so we took the opportunity to move from El-Arish to Beersheba. This move was not known to the English for several days. The squadron reached Hafir to the south-west of Beersheba in three night marches, with 300 heavily laden camels. In November

1916 a long flight to Cairo was carried out from this aerodrome, the total distance being over 480 miles. This flight was completed, but not without an intermediate landing, as, owing to the anti-aircraft defences on the Canal, our machine had to make a detour on its return, I took it for granted that a feat of this description, which involved attacking them 180 miles behind their lines, would astonish the English to no small degree, and, in fact, that they would doubt the reports coming through to their aerodrome from Cairo.

Having started from Beersheba at 7 A.M. on November 13th, Lieut. Falke and Lieut. Schulteheiss landed at El-Arish, replenished their petrol supply from a companion machine, and continued the rest of their long journey. At four o'clock in the afternoon they regained Beersheba, after having landed at El-Arish as before. They had successfully bombed the station at Cairo, had obtained valuable photographic information as well as observing the transport on the Canal They also took an interesting photograph of the Pyramids at Gizeh. The flight from El-Arish outwards was in a direct line. The return flight was made to the south of Suez. Not a single English machine was seen. We learnt later from prisoners, that the English pilots on the Canal, when it was reported to them that a German aeroplane was over Cairo, had naturally assumed that there must be some mistake, and had therefore remained in their quarters!

Meanwhile the English were systematically proceeding with their railway construction. They were building at least 700 yards of line per day, and later, for a short time, they doubled this distance. They mapped out a kind of schedule by which the railway was to reach certain points of military importance on certain days. This railway, so to speak, formed the key to our plans, but we were unable to harass the English successfully in their advance. A cavalry division was always guarding and patrol ling the districts about 15 miles ahead of the railhead, which had reached the district we had evacuated in front, of El-Arish on December 20, 1916.

I had long accustomed myself to the thought of evacuating Beersheba since the General Staff became more and more inclined to confine themselves to the defence of Palestine. A quantity of material which was not required at the moment was therefore removed to a kind of aircraft depot at Damascus. A detachment was also sent there to assist in putting down an insurrection of the Druses in Horan. It turned out that their mere appearance in the air was sufficient to effect this. In order to retreat beyond Beersheba one had the choice of two routes: eastward across the Dead Sea into the district to the east of the Jordan, or northward across the plains of Palestine. There was some talk of an aerodrome near Aman, but personally I inclined to the belief that the northern route would be selected. On this route there turned out to be a suitable aerodrome near Ramleh on the railway to Damascus and hard by the road from Jaffa to Jerusalem; this aerodrome was occupied early in March.

After a local reverse near Chan-Junis in January 1917, and since it was fully realised at the Turkish headquarters that the English objective was Palestine, it was decided that we should take up the defensive in that section of the front between Gaza and Beersheba, In this district the lines of communication were very bad, but from Beersheba, which was rightly assumed to be the key to the position, a well-built road ran across Hebron to Jerusalem. There were only a few wells in existence, and sites for new wells were eagerly sought for and their construction put in hand. Although the country during the dry season was everywhere passable to every kind of transport, the situation was entirely altered during the rainy season. The wadis became raging torrents, and on either side of the road one had to wade tediously through the sticky mud. It was rarely possible for horses, and never possible for mechanical transport, to move under these conditions.

Towards the beginning of March the English railhead approached Chan-Junis. In the meantime there had been a change in the *personnel* out East. The old 'lions of the desert' had returned to Germany, and new flying men, experienced in the fighting on the Eastern or Western Fronts, had taken their place. Furthermore, in barely three weeks we had succeeded in transporting eight new Rumpler C 1 machines with fixed synchronised machine guns from Constantinople to Damascus.

In order to safeguard the further construction of their railway the English had to take Gaza, On the morning of March 20, 1917, when they bad deployed their cavalry to envelop the town and wished to press forward upon Gaza with their infantry, there resulted some sharp fighting to the south. The cactus thickets over which it was impossible to see, proved a very serious obstacle to the success of the first infantry attack. Reconnaissance from the air was impossible to the enemy owing to the presence of German airmen. On the evening of the first day of the battle, the enemy had indeed succeeded in penetrating at various points, but the resistance had not yet been broken. On the next day two Turkish divisions which were hastily brought up gave us some breathing space. The English did not wait for their attack, but withdrew. Four weeks later they made another attempt of the same nature, but this also was in vain.

According to the assertion of His Excellency Djemal Pasha, the Air Force had saved the situation during the first battle of Gaza, and the service they performed during the second battle of Gaza was certainly no less. The movements of the English from their positions were promptly reported by our machines, the position of their flanks was observed, and our General Staff were kept constantly informed concerning the course of events. Since the officer commanding, General von Kress, had no modern means of communication at his disposal other than three wireless stations, and as the first battle of Gaza had been conducted on the lines of open warfare, it was necessary that all orders and reports should be carried by our aeroplanes. Consequently, if the General wished to change the disposition of his troops, he took with him in his car a tablecloth which could be spread out on the ground. As soon as this cloth was displayed a Rumpler promptly landed in his neighbourhood. By this means the Staff were able to keep the troops well under control. During the afternoon, sections of the Air Force were told off to carry out bomb raids on the enemy's cavalry concentrated at various points on the plains, which afforded them no cover whatsoever. Some of the prisoners that we captured told us of the destruction effected by these raids.

About this time the English abandoned the plan of campaign which they had hitherto followed.

On the edge of the desert itself trench warfare made its appearance, and thereby provided our airmen with a field of activity than which nothing could be more comprehensive or possess better prospects. Long-distance reconnaissance was frequently carried out in flights of over six hours' duration, as far as the Canal itself. The reinforcements which the English were constantly bringing up, partly by sea and partly by railway, made it necessary to effect bomb raids from very low altitudes. Prisoners reported to us that, as a result of our vigorous attacks on railway trains, transport on the railways for a long time had to be confined to the hours of night.

It was well known that a water-pipe ran alongside the railway. Lieutenants Felmy and Falke had for a long time kept their eye upon this as a target. When the second battle of Gaza began, these two officers landed 90 miles behind the English lines, blew up the conduit, and returned home with a large piece of cast-iron pipe by way of a souvenir. The English were compelled to retire from the battle they had lost without even the comfort afforded by water.

This first successful experiment called for repetition, and four weeks later they blew up the water-pipe again. This time, however, they wished to include the railway itself, the telegraph system, and the electric power cables in the destruction. The second feat was as dangerous as the first had been easy. Their machine had landed some distance to the side of the position which they intended to blow up, on the site of a patch of salt water which had been dried up by the sun. The engine of the machine was still running. It happened by chance that the pilot had hung his fur coat over the observer's seat The two men themselves were working hard laying their stock of explosives, and were concentrating all their attention upon the west, whence a cavalry patrol was approaching them at full gallop. Suddenly a shot rang out! A second patrol had approached unnoticed from the rear among the sand-dunes, and was actually between themselves and their machine! In a flash the safety devices were withdrawn, and there then began a race for life. Actually the pair reached the machine without being hit. The English patrol had imagined the fur coat to be an object of danger, and had encouraged

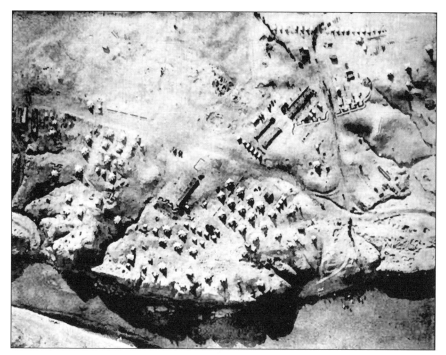

English Camp on the Tigris.

themselves by putting a bullet through it.; Once in the machine, the airmen were masters of the situation.

The daily reconnaissance and artillery control occupied the full time of our airmen henceforward. For a long time past the average odds up against us was 5 to 1, but in February and in the first part of March 1917, owing to changes in the *personnel* and breakdowns in transport, the odds were as high as 12 to 1. The fact that between Easter 1916 and the end of September 1917 not a single machine was lost, while sixteen English machines were shot down or forced to land, proves that our airmen rose above all difficulties, that the technical *personnel* was all that could be desired - in short, that every man did his duty.

There was no rest-camp for aviators in the Holy Land, such as has been erroneously reported. In the days of most urgent necessity, from the middle of March to the middle of April 1917, over 210 hours' flying above the enemy's lines could be recorded by our airmen. Few as they were in number, they succeeded in retaining their sense of superiority.

Ruins of Shamarra, built by Caliph Al-Mulasim, son of Haroun at Rashid.
English infantry tranches are clearly visible.

A remark which throws some light upon the situation is that of an Australian flying officer who had been shot down. When he saw our Round Table assembled in the refectory of the Spanish Monastery at Ramleh, he asked in an astonished voice: 'But, where are the rest?' and would not believe that this was the whole of that German squadron which was accomplishing so much work.

On the reconnaissance flights photographic information had to be constantly supplemented by actual eye observation, a kind of work to which observers were quite unaccustomed in 1916 and 1917. Furthermore, conditions made it necessary that our machines should land in the immediate neighbourhood of the Staff which was so eagerly awaiting their reports. At first, however, the great heat of the desert destroyed a very large number of our photographic plates, for more than once the gelatine coating melted in the warm water.

The beginning of trench warfare and of systematic artillery control made photographic reconnaissance all the more necessary since the maps of the region upon which we were working, namely, a map whose scale was 1:800,000 and another very inaccurate map of 1:250,000, were quite useless for the purposes of trench warfare. Lieutenant Jancke conceived the happy thought of producing a map consisting of mosaic photographs to the scale of approximately 1:100,000, which should be used as the basis for constructing a really accurate map. This work was successfully carried out after weeks of wearisome labour in spite of the primitive means we had at our disposal.

Under the leadership of their new commander, General Allenby, whose influence was most apparent, the English adapted themselves more and more closely to the conditions of desert warfare. Their luxurious tents, which had previously distinguished the camps along by the Canal, and bad made it possible to estimate the strength of the forces occupying them, disappeared. They took to a kind of bivouac shelter, consisting of shallow trenches over which they stretched canvas as a protection from the sun. It was a long time before it was possible, even with the assistance of our aerial photographs, to arrive at a correct method of estimating the number of troops that were covered in this way. The exact strength of the cavalry, however, could be assessed to within one squadron, since the horse lines could not be concealed, and later on we could also estimate the strength of the infantry to within a battalion. It was much more difficult to deal with the artillery and the machine-gun units, but the tanks betrayed themselves by their broad peculiar tracks in the desert sand. During the offensive in the autumn of 1917, Gaza was bombarded by heavy batteries in forty different positions on the land side alone. In addition to this they experienced the results of artillery fire from the naval forces. The unfortunate coastal directions, i.e. north and south, enabled the enemy to enfilade our positions which ran approximately east and west from the sea. On the other hand, if they were located too far from the coast, it became easier for the English to effect a landing.

The southern sun, which used to blaze down so hotly upon that theatre of war in a manner to which the Europeans were quite unaccustomed, and the lack of water considerably reduced the mobility and usefulness of our forces. In that torrid climate there is a dry season from April until the beginning of November when the rainy season begins. During the dry season an almost continuously ideal weather condition obtains for the flying man; the sky shines blue day after day. Perhaps occasionally the early morning hours may reveal fog and mist along the coast, but that is all. When engaged on long-distance reconnaissance one was generally quite safe against any unpleasant surprise in the shape of thunderstorms or big cloud formations. On the other hand, the rainy season brought with it furious rain which frequently lasted for days on end and was usually associated with heavy thunderstorms, during which period all flying was out of the question. However, the snatches of fine weather during the rainy season reminded one of our fairest spring days at home.

The intense temperature of the air and the eddies close to the ground made themselves felt. Should one leave the ground at noon, the machine would rock and bump very considerably, but from approximately 2500 feet upwards the atmosphere was comparatively calm. Naturally, these atmospheric disturbances were more marked over the mountainous districts, but even then they inconvenienced an experienced pilot but little, though for beginners it was not advisable to fly during such hours of the day.

In torrid regions there is no dusk; as soon as the sun has sunk it becomes rapidly dark, and in the morning it grows light just as quickly. When the full moon was shining it was unnecessary to illuminate the landing ground, although the dummy aerodrome was always brightly lit up. On such bright nights, machines generally made use of secret landing grounds in the neighbourhood; the aerodrome itself was empty, a precautionary practice which the English also adopted.

At first we suffered severely from the heat. The rapid changes in temperature, cold nights and hot days, resulted in all sorts of chills, owing to the primitive shelters with which we were provided, and a chill almost always ended in dysentery. A large number of men became infected with malaria when travelling, but in the desert itself, when far away from all water, there were no germs. The strain upon the *personnel* was such that, as a rule, they had to be sent home after nine months. It was surprising how old veterans who had been out for two years or so would suddenly fall ill, after having held out for so long, but with the exception of a few bad periods, the health sheet could be marked 'good,' thanks to the precautions of the doctors.

Also the mental experiences of the men were important, owing to the effect of isolation in the desert. That 'loneliness,' which His Excellency von Ludendorff speaks of in his *War Memoirs*, we also experienced. Yet it is typical of a case like this that the majority of those old 'lions of the desert' should ever and again feel within their bones a longing for those sunny lands once more.

(FELMY.)

FLYING IN THE EAST: MESOPOTAMIA AND IRAK

At the conclusion of the Dardanelles campaign in February 1916, all machines were sent to Irak, with the exception of a sufficient number to carry out the necessary reconnaissance for the protection of the coast of Asia Minor against any landing of hostile forces.

The situation was briefly as follows: The 6th Turkish Army had been told off to hold Bagdad. General Townshend, with about 13,000 men, had been shut up in Kut-el-Amara in the course of his advance on Bagdad, by eighteen Turkish Army Corps. English reserves, which were being hurried up to his assistance, were held off at Fellahieje by thirteen Turkish Army Corps, The Turks were in the minority, and their equipment left much to be desired. Had the English succeeded in making a successful sortie from Kut, the position of the 6th Turkish Army would have been excessively dangerous. In order to escape from this situation, the Turkish higher command considered the advisability of withdrawing from the neighbourhood of Kut-el-Amara without fighting, and in order to reassemble their scattered units at a position where they would be able to defend Bagdad.

At this critical period there appeared the long-awaited German squadron which brought with it a Fokker fighter. The airmen threw themselves into their new work with enthusiasm, and the *morale* of the troops on the ground was thereby greatly improved. Hitherto they had been obliged to remain inactive and watch English airmen fly over Kut daily, and drop bags containing provisions. The situation was now reversed. Day and night the 'Parasol' monoplane hummed over Kut, dropping bomb after bomb upon the crowded troops below, who previously had been secure against all bombardment since the Turks had lacked ammunition. Before long I had succeeded, in the course of a few days, in shooting down three English machines, and thereafter no aeroplane carrying provisions appeared over Kut.

Meanwhile we had erected a kind of aircraft depot at Bagdad with such scanty means as we then possessed. A very large number of propellers were used owing to the enormous heat, which made them split. We even succeeded in cutting and gluing propellers of our own design. Everything that might be turned to account for industrial purposes in Bagdad was made use of for the construction of aeroplanes; an entire machine was actually built, and flew remarkably well. We also carried out successful experiments in connection with petrol distillation. One of our greatest difficulties was the manufacture of bombs, but with the assistance of cast-iron pipes inserted one inside the other, filled with high explosives, and detonated by a cartridge, we succeeded in producing an efficient substitute. The beleaguered division, which consisted principally of Indian troops, suffered in *morale* as a result of the daily bombing. The Indians pressed more and more for surrender, and before long the appearance of large fires in Kut informed us that the enemy was destroying his material and had made up his mind to capitulate. General Townshend then surrendered his sword to the Turkish Commander.

This victory was worthily associated with that of the successful result in the Dardanelles campaign. The airmen who used to fly over Kut can be proud in the consciousness that it was due to their activity that this success first became possible.

It was not for long that the 13th Army Corps was able to rest. It is true that the Russians could no longer prevent the fall of Kut, but they now threatened Bagdad from the east by advancing through Persia. The only machine out of seven which arrived at Bagdad in a serviceable condition was put in readiness for this new work. The rest of us had to be content with the old machines, and our only new acquisition consisted of an aeroplane which had been copied from the English R.E. type. The English greeted its first war flight with admiring recognition, in that they dropped a parcel of aeroplane spare parts together with this note: 'We congratulate the newly-arrived bird upon its success. Herewith are a few spare parts, which, no doubt, will soon be required.' At that time a very singular exchange of letters was in progress, which relieved the monotony of desert warfare in a most welcome fashion. The limit was reached one day when the English airmen proposed that we should all land at some neutral spot to meet over a cup of tea, and exchange new papers and gramophone records. However, we were unable to see eye to eye with them in this conception of warfare. Those who know the English are aware that, in spite of events like this, they would always fight in the air with the greatest determination and keenness. No doubt our machine guns and bombs provided them with plentiful antidotes to boredom.

The English prepared for their new offensive in the late summer of 1916. Photographic reconnaissance showed that, in addition to railway construction, they had established new camps at concentration points on the Tigris, There was an increase in the steamer traffic, and new types of machines made their appearance. With the material then at our disposal it was useless to think of offering a resistance to this new attack. One request for more aeroplanes and the necessaries of war followed on another; but it was a long way to Constantinople, In vain did the handful of Germans endeavour to accelerate the arrival of supplies. All such demands were rendered nugatory by that peculiarity of the Turkish temperament about which we have already complained. If it be Allah's will that we should be victorious, then victory shall be ours, even without new aeroplanes; but if Allah hath ordained otherwise, then nothing can help us. Kismet! all is fate!

And indeed Fate overtook us. The English attacked in November, when the cool season set in. Against their machines of the latest type we could only pit our old worn-out aeroplanes, which had been exposed to all weathers without even the protection of canvas. The planes were warped; one vaguely remembered that there had once been such things as altimeters and revolution-counters. The wheels had no tyres; their rims were bound round with rags. With these machines our pilots fought the unequal contest, defying death. The first victim was our Fokker, which fell before the onslaught of four English machines. Our own aeroplane, which we had built ourselves, and armed with a Russian machine gun designed for land purposes, flew daily behind the enemy's lines with many a trick and ruse, since we dared not allow ourselves to be attacked. Damage received during the day had to be repaired at night by moonlight. For three months the unequal struggle continued; for three months the Turks held out. As long as they heard our own machines buzzing over their heads, they fought like lions. And then, at last, at the end of January 1917, the English broke through our lines.

The army retreated in wild and indescribable eon-fusion. The airmen had to fight a rearguard action. Every piece of their transport was lost along with all the rest of their *matériel*, and consequently the machines, for which there was now no longer any petrol, had to be burnt. And still the retirement continued. In order to relieve the pressure of the pursuing English forces to some extent, our airmen blew up bridges, drove locomotives, in short did every kind of technical work which was required. There was still no rest; Bagdad itself was captured, The rest of the Turkish Army eventually reassembled at Mosul, and the German airmen, with their proverbial thoroughness, began the work of reconstruction. It was indeed a Herculean task.

In the meantime I myself had been to Germany to speed up the delivery of fresh supplies. I returned to Irak in April 1917 with nine new scouts. In order to confound the English by the unexpected appearance of a new type, I covered the 300 odd miles from the railhead of the Bagdad line to the front in one day. But even this rapidity was no use. On the same day an English machine appeared at a great height and dropped a tin of cigarettes with the following message: 'The British airmen send their compliments to Captain S., and are pleased to welcome him back to Mesopotamia. We shall be pleased to offer him a warm reception in the air. We enclose a tin of English cigarettes and will send him a Bagdad melon when they are in season. *Au revoir*. Our compliments to the other German airmen. The Royal Flying Corps.' The English secret service had again done a brilliant piece of work. However, I succeeded, without any particular surprise, in chasing down several Englishmen who had promised to give me such 'a warm reception in the air.'

The English did not press far beyond Bagdad. Their principal object had been to restore their prestige, which had suffered seriously owing to the fall of Kut, by the capture of Bagdad. Consequently, in the summer of 1917, the Turks had rest and time in which to recuperate.

In the fighting which ensued, the question of holding the Bedouin Arabs became more and more important. They seriously threatened our lines of communication, for not quite the whole of Islam had declared for us against their 'oppressors,' the English, and the so-called Holy War only existed in the imagination. In reality the hatred of the Arabs for the Turks and the English respectively was fairly well balanced, as they considered both to be intruders who were draining the resources of the country. Although indeed the Turks, by levying a monthly tribute of from 500 to 1000 pounds in gold from the most influential tribal leaders, guaranteed a kind of benevolent neutrality, the tribes only obtained exemption from raids because they had nothing more to lose. On the other hand the Bedouins were always very partial to us German airmen, particularly after I had succeeded in shooting down an English machine close by the camp of the big Shammara tribe. Many German airmen who had been compelled to land behind the English lines were brought back into safety with true Arab cunning.

Just as in 1917 at Bagdad, the English offensive of 1918 also began in the autumn, only this time matters moved fasten The forces at our disposal had been decimated by a terrible famine, brought on by Turkish indolence and the bitter feeling among the population of the country, who were no longer cultivating their fields, owing to the vigorous system of 'requisitions.' Numbers of horses, camels, mules, and donkeys were lost, and the result was a catastrophic disorganisation of our transport system. It was in vain that the German airmen fought with the courage of despair; it was in vain that they used to fly across the lines in the face of eight or ten times as many hostile machines, for which, day and night, petrol and other necessaries were being provided, as well as for their mechanical transport.

At the very last moment our squadron broke away from the enemy, and, since their retreat to Aleppo was cut off, arrived after infinite trouble by way of Mardin, Malatia, Sivas, and Amasia to Samsun on the Black Sea.

All was now lost. This was particularly tragic to us, who saw ourselves now condemned definitely to remain upon the defensive, and by way of *matériel* had to content ourselves "with any scraps that were left over from the Western Front, The thought that in spite of all self-sacrifice it was impossible for us to achieve any definite success, demanded the highest qualities of devotion to duty and self-forgetfulness on the part of the German warriors. Many, who came from a European theatre of war to report for duty in Turkey, before long turned their back upon that unhappy country. A few remained true to the Crescent - true until death. Many a gallant German heart now lies beneath those hot desert sands. To them, the heroes of Irak, these lines are dedicated.

(SCHÜZ.)

Chapter VII
Seaplanes

Seaplanes Over the North Sea

ABOVE ALL, IT was the duty of seaplanes to co-operate with the naval forces. They had to serve as eyes to the naval commander, to surround our own bases with a protective screen to report the arrival of hostile aeroplanes without delay, and to protect our own forces, when engaged upon operations, against any surprise attacks. Not only, however, did they have to ward off attacks, but it was also their duty to prevent hostile machines and airships from reconnoitring over our harbours and observing the movements of our shipping, more particularly of our mine-sweepers. Submarines had to be conducted to suitable objectives, protected from hostile aeroplanes in the neighbourhood of our coasts, and assisted by pilotage into our harbours during bad weather.

Other tasks were; attacks with bombs or machine guns against ships or land targets, removing the navigation marks of the enemy, and controlling the artillery fire when our coasts were being bombarded. From what has now been said it will readily be seen that the North Sea and the English Channel were the principal scenes of seaplane activity, and that the North Sea, being the field upon which the High Sea Fleet carried out most of its work, required the most rigorous watchfulness.

At the beginning of the war there were only two seaplane stations on the North Sea: Heligoland with six machines and but a few men, and a station had been begun at List, on the Island of Sylt; otherwise, except for an empty shed at Wilhelmshaven, there was nothing ready in the way of accommodation. The senior naval officers had no means of judging the probable usefulness of the seaplane, and in maritime circles the confidence of the fliers in their weapons was laughed at.

Heligoland, being the base farthest seaward, was expected to seek out and announce the enemy's fleet, the advance of which, on England's declaration of war, was expected any moment. The first order received, 'Reconnoitre over the sea to the farthest limit possible with your machine,' gave plenty of scope for work. During the first few days, therefore, both men and machines were used unsparingly; every flying officer hoped to be the first to report: 'There they are!'

They never came. Bit by bit the machines were crashed, and the pilots went to the Baltic in order to fetch spare parts. Those who were left flew with double determination. In order that they might penetrate still farther westward and northward, petrol stations were established in Borkum and List, and during fine weather the very last drop of petrol was used in flying. Still there was nothing to be seen. Gradually there dawned the realisation that the English fleet did not mean to come out to an open fight at sea. It would not meet us in fair fight, but preferred to blockade us far from the German coasts, and thus began the dishonourable process of strangling us by starvation.

Only occasional sorties by light cruisers, destroyers, and submarines, and the very rare appearance of a flotilla of warships, disturbed the peace of the North Sea. In order that the enemy's ships, with their unexpectedly high turn of speed, should be discovered immediately, it was necessary to be exceedingly watchful and to fly in any weather. We had also to cover our own sorties, to protect from surprise our mine-layers which used to proceed as far as the English coast, and to keep the fairways clear for our submarines. Thus there began a systematic service of reconnaissance and protection; seaplane stations were hastily erected, and *personnel* and *matériel* strengthened. New stations arose at Borkum and Norderney, while those which had already been built at Heligoland, List, and Wilhelmshaven were enlarged. The work was exceedingly difficult, for, with the exception of Wilhelmshaven, all the stations were on islands, and every scrap of material used in their construction had to be carried thither in ships.

We steadily worked towards such a state of efficiency that reconnaissance had no longer to be carried out along individual

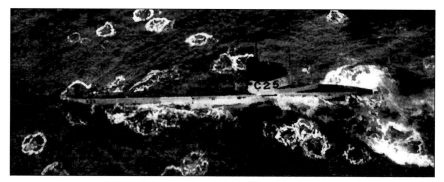

English submarine, C 25, attacked by German seaplanes. The water is ringed by bomb explosions.

sections and at various times, but could be continued from dawn to dusk unintermittently along the whole district. During long summer days this was a serious matter. Our machines used to fly in almost any weather when it might be possible for the enemy to make a sortie. But in spite of invariable devotion to duty, owing to the long distances and the difficulty in obtaining the necessary numbers of men and machines, it was not until the last year of the war that we succeeded in making the air service so comprehensive, that, although even then the watch that was kept was not incessant, the reconnaissance was really satisfactory.

The duties of the North Sea flier were not only difficult but also thankless. The 'silent heroism of the North Sea airmen' has become proverbial with our Navy. The machines used to fly hour after hour, in autumn and in winter, often in danger from mist and storms, without ever catching a glimpse of the enemy. Some airmen, after 400 hours' flying, still had no encounter to report; many of them never returned from sea. Often enough a machine was compelled by engine failure to descend on the water, and the occupants wore condemned to drift about for days without any provisions until they were picked up by a passing steamer. Sometimes, when the sea was rough, the wrecked machine would capsize, and its crew have drifted for days lashed to the floats. It was not easy for the airmen to keep their spirits up. Both pilots and observers, particularly the beat, used to leave the North Sea for other theatres of war where they could take part in aerial fighting and bomb raids. And yet the work had to be done; the North Sea had to be patrolled day in and day out and all individual aspirations merged in unenvious recognition of the achievements of German airmen at the front without the possibility of emulating them. Thus the days when there had been some encounter with the enemy, who, as a matter of fact, would usually beat a retreat as soon as they were sighted, were days of rejoicing.

And even when the enemy should fight, the airmen continually had to deny themselves the pleasure of attacking, because it was far more important that they should report their information. This process, in the early days of the war was round-about and took up a lot of time. As a rule, the machine had to return home and report thence to the commander of the naval forces either by wireless or telegram; only rarely did they have an opportunity of communicating directly with our ships at sea, by means of signalling them or by dropping messages. The first step forward was made when the wireless set was mounted on aeroplanes, at first only in the form of a transmitting set. The observer required both experience and good luck in order to send through his message quickly and accurately. It was not until the wireless receiving set was also installed upon aeroplanes that we had the satisfaction of knowing when these messages were understood.

The North Sea observer had to know something about almost everything. He had to be able to navigate correctly for six hours on end by means of compass and chart alone; find his way back across the sea to a small island without any marks to guide him, and in spite of varying air currents, knowing full well that any mistake might hinder him from reaching his base before dark, and mean death or internment to him. He had to know the types of the enemy's ships and something about the tactics of naval warfare. He had to be well acquainted with the seaplane wireless set; he had to know how to drop bombs and use machine guns, and moreover he had to be an accomplished seaman in order to cope with the difficulties of a seaplane when compelled to land during bad weather. The work of the North Sea airman was not only dangerous and monotonous but also responsible, for upon a single report might depend victory or defeat in a naval engagement.

During the first two years of the war, machines were sent out singly. As long as they had no wireless set they were given up for lost if they did not return from their work. As a rule it was impossible, owing to the conditions of the war, to search for them, and their salvation had to be left to chance. When the wireless sets were mounted on aeroplanes, it was possible, should the machine be compelled to land through engine failure, to give the signal for distress and position while they were gliding down to the water. Their position was then known, and any of our vessels which happened to be in the neighbourhood could be sent to their assistance. But even then it was difficult to find them on the vast surface of the ocean, and, in spite of the rockets which they fired, the search was not always successful; it was, however, some comfort for the airman to have a chance of being rescued.

Later on, when we possessed a sufficient number of machines, reconnaissance used to be carried out by pairs. They then were able to help each other, and at least, provided the weather was reasonably clear, the serviceable machine, if unable to land and pick tip the occupants of the machine in distress, owing to a rough sea, could return home with an exact reckoning of the position of the wreck, and send help. The use of machines flying in pairs also had this advantage, that should, for some reason, it be impossible to use the wireless, reports could be delivered by one of the machines. Naturally it also happened, and unfortunately not rarely, that both of the machines were missing, and that, although the signals of distress could be heard, nothing was ever found. In those eases one had to assume that one machine had been compelled to descend, and that the other had gone down to rescue the two men who were in danger and had been destroyed by the heavy sea. Nevertheless, the method of sending out machines in pairs gave the airmen a sense of security, and therefore increased their efficiency, particularly during bad weather.

The regions of the four North Sea seaplane stations had hard-and-fast boundaries, and were divided into sectors, which were flown over according to the plans prepared beforehand. The station at List supervised the regions in front of the Danish coast; Borkum, that of the Dutch coast; Heligoland and Norderney were obliged to look after the open sea to the middle of the North Sea, The two last named, therefore, had the most unfruitful and at the same time the most difficult work. As a rule the enemy would attack from the west or north just out of sight of the coast, and so came within the sectors of Borkum and List, which were frequented also by cargo shipping and the trawlers, which could, therefore, save the machine and its occupants should they be compelled to land. On the other hand, in the middle sector, not only the enemy's warships, but neutral cargo ships and fishing boats also, were rarely to be seen.

The nature and importance of the work carried out by seaplanes over the North Sea can best be understood by taking the last year of the war as an example. At that time submarine warfare was the most important factor in the conduct of naval operations. The seaplanes, therefore, in addition to protecting the other naval forces, had to see that the submarines could emerge and return in safety. The English sowed a broad girdle of mines round the circumference of the Bight and endeavoured to make the whole area impassable by that means. Consequently our mine-sweepers had to be continually at work clearing paths across the mine-fields through which the submarines could safely be guided in and out. It followed also that the mine-sweepers were obliged to go far afield, sometimes even as far as the neutral waters of Holland, Behind them there used to be forces of destroyers, cruisers, and ships of the line. They were defenceless except for guns of a small calibre, and hampered by their lack of speed, so that as soon as the enemy's ships appeared they were obliged to beat a hasty retreat.

It was therefore the duty of the seaplane not only to reconnoitre as far as possible and to warn the mine-sweepers of the approach of ships in time enough for them to retreat in safety, but also to hold off the enemy's machines, which were particularly active and interested in observing our mine-sweeping operations and in discovering the positions of our fairways. Except in cases of urgent necessity, mine-sweeping was never carried out without preliminary aerial reconnaissance or without the escort of aeroplanes.

Sometimes seaplane-carriers were sent to accompany the mine-

Hansa-Brandenburg: single-seater fighting seaplane. A monoplane with 150 H.P. Benz engine.

sweeping flotillas, and on those occasions the machines they carried took over the escort work. An advantage of this method lay in the fact that the long flight up to the scene of activity could be dispensed with, and consequently almost the whole time during which the machine could remain in the air was usefully employed; a disadvantage was the difficulty of finding the carrier ship again in the event of the visibility becoming bad. In such cases it was almost inevitable that the machine would have to land owing to lack of petrol and, actually, distressed machines have been known to drift after many days from the Dogger Bank as far as Norway, and to be picked up there with their occupants still alive.

The English were particularly anxious to discover the localities which we were sweeping for mines, the clear paths for our submarines, and how the vessels were piloted in and out. Seaplanes were told off to obtain this information. The distances that had to be flown were great, as was also the region that had to be watched, but on the other hand the airmen used to be able to see over a large area of the ocean in fine weather. England ruled the sea, and consequently was usually able to search for and salve machines which had landed, and under favourable weather conditions could even move up machines on destroyers or torpedo boats, and thereby diminish the distance they had to approach by air. We could always be certain that whenever our minesweepers were observed at their work, the area which they had cleared would again become infested with mines during the nest few days.

It was also the duty of the North Sea air service to hold off all enemy seaplanes. For that purpose formations of fighting machines were necessary, since the English aeroplanes generally appeared in groups of three, and therefore we had to put up against them at least three or, even better, five aeroplanes. The labour of watching over so large an area of sea was colossal, and the number of machines at our disposal was limited. At the end of the war there were only twelve units, each consisting of five machines, for the whole of the North Sea, It would have been desirable to increase their numbers, but this was impossible owing to the limited extent of our seaplane stations and the lack of aero-engines, of which the Navy was only allowed a certain number every month by the Army. The pressure of work was enormous whenever the enemy, his aerial observation having escaped the notice of our fighting machines, succeeded in making the whole of our mine-sweeping operations void. The work of these fighting machines was not easy, and was as fruitless as that of the reconnaissance machines. It was rare for any conflict with the enemy to take place in 100 flying hours, and yet the danger of flying over the sea was doubled by the fact that the machines were unseaworthy, since they had been designed for fighting purposes, and usually went to pieces if landed on the sea even under normal North Sea weather conditions. In order to restrict the losses as far as possible, seaworthy reconnaissance machines were usually sent with each formation of fighters, to pick up the occupants of a fighting machine were it compelled to land, and bring them home or at least keep them above water long enough for help to arrive. However, this accompanying machine used to limit the work that could be carried out by the fighters, since the latter, owing to their greater speed, were obliged to throttle down considerably to keep in touch with it. In the event of an aerial combat the accompanying machine would remain close at hand, observe, take photographs, and announce the result by wireless. In this way it was sometimes practicable not only to call up reinforcements to the scene of the fight from the home station, but also to bring up machines which happened to be in the neighbourhood.

At length, on November 9, 1910, the torpedo fliers get the weather for which they have wished so long.

In the hangars all is activity. The final preparations are made, although the machines have been ready to take the air for weeks past. The torpedoes are once more tested and carefully slung underneath the fuselages, then one after another the machines are lowered to the water with a big crane.

At 2 P.M. three torpedo-carrying machines and their fighting escort start. Their orders are: 'Attack cargo ships off the mouth of the Thames.' They have soon disappeared from sight, keeping close up underneath the clouds in order to escape the notice of the enemy's machines as long as possible. As it is clearer off the mouth of the Thames, the course is altered to 'port' following the leader, and laid for the Downs, over which a broad layer of fog still hangs. At 3.45 P.M. the Sunk lightship is passed.

A few minutes later a merchant ship, then another, then a third, and finally a whole convoy emerges from the fog. In order to get a good view of the ships, the machines fly on a zigzag course. The convoy is protected against submarines by trawlers and a torpedo boat. The enemy is still unconscious of our presence.

3.49 P.M. The formation is within range of the hindmost steamer. Three torpedoes drop in quick succession. The machines turn sharply away, while the torpedo men eagerly follow the rapidly disappearing wakes of their missiles on the surface of the water. Suddenly one, and a few seconds later another, column of water leaps up at the side of the ship. She heels slowly over on to her side and, three minutes later, has disappeared.

Completely surprised, the torpedo boat, the trawlers, and the merchantmen open fire with futile shells and shrapnel on the machines as they are disappearing into the fog. At 4.55 P.M. all the machines are safely landed at their base. The formation leader reports: 'One ship of about 2000 tons sunk by two torpedoes.'

(MOLL.)

THE 'WÖLFCHEN'

Wölfchen was the name of the seaplane which accompanied Captain Nerger on his world-famed cruise on the *Wolf*. This seaplane was a Friedrichshafen design, was fitted with a 150 H.P. engine, and was provided with a wireless installation and bomb-dropping apparatus. From November 1916 until February 1918 the *Wolf* and *Wölfchen* were at sea, and the seaplane contributed a good deal towards the success of the voyage. In fifty-six flights it displayed the Iron Cross to all the oceans of the world - to the Pacific, the Atlantic, the South Seas, and the Indian Ocean.

The repairs which had to be effected during this long voyage were very numerous, but, with the aid of the spare parts that were carried on board, and, to a certain extent, by making use of material taken from captured steamers, the machine was always kept in a serviceable condition, and ready to take the air whenever it was required. Very frequently it had to be completely taken to pieces, and as often reassembled again. These operations were exceedingly difficult owing to lack of space, but could not be avoided lest the ship should be recognised as an auxiliary cruiser by the aeroplane on its deck. Also the machine had to be protected as much as possible from any damage which might be caused by exposure, particularly in the tropics.

Here are a few extracts from the *Wölfchen*'s log book: -

PACIFIC OCEAN

On May 24, during reconnaissance flight, New Zealand was sighted 60 nautical miles to the west.

June 2, 1917. - Orders. Hold up the merchant steamer which has been sighted north of Raoul Island and bring her to S.M.S. *Wolf*.

The ship had suddenly appeared while S.M.S. *Wolf* was lying close up to the island, engaged on repairs to her engines and trimming her bunkers. *Wölfchen* started at 3.30 P.M. and flew north. On reaching the

'Wölfchen' on board ship.

steamer we spiralled down to within 200 feet of the deck and dropped the following message in English:-

'Steer south to German cruiser and do not use wireless. If not obeying orders, you will be shelled by bombs.'

The second time we flew over the steamer, we dropped a bomb only twenty yards from her bows. She changed her course at once and steered for S.M.S. *Wolf*, escorted by the *Wölfchen*. After our threat, she dared not use her wireless.

It was the New Zealand ship *Wairuna* (3900 tons) bound from Auckland to San Francisco. The ship and her cargo were worth many hundred thousand pounds.

June 16, 1917. - Orders. Hold up the four-masted schooner which has been sighted in the west, and bring her to S.M.S. *Wolf*.

Wölfchen started at 3.50 P.M. and flew west. We spiralled down from a height of 600 feet to within 250 feet of the ship. Our first two attempts to drop a message on the deck failed. Owing to the drift of the vessel, both fell some distance to the leeward. At our third approach a bomb was dropped from a height of 250 feet, close by the bows. The ship at once hauled down her top-gaff-sail, and displayed the American flag. *Wölfchen* ordered the vessel to steer S.E., and intimated that she would be bombed if she did not follow. At once she turned in the given direction, and the machine, circling overhead, led her to S.M.S. *Wolf*.

It was the American four-masted schooner *Winslow* (567 tons), with a cargo of coal, provisions, petrol, and wood from San Francisco. Unfortunately the petrol was useless for flying purposes.

Owing to bad weather, *Wölfchen* was again dismantled and stored away on the afternoon of June 11.

INDIAN OCEAN

September 25, 1917. - Orders. Investigate a patch of smoke which has been sighted, and report on vessel, course, and distance.

It was the Japanese boat, *Hitachi Maru* (6700 tons). The *Wölfchen* received a further order to support S.M.S. *Wolf* in holding up the vessel, and to bomb her if she committed any hostile act.

At the first shot from S.M.S. *Wolf* the steamer turned hard to starboard, apparently with the intention of escaping. Thereupon a bomb was dropped 30 or 40 yards ahead of her bows, and almost at the same time S.M.S. *Wolf* opened fire, so that the seaplane was led to assume that the steamer was resisting. We therefore flew up again and dropped another bomb from a height of 700 feet, which fell into the water close to the port side. The force of the explosion blew two men overboard. At that the steamer hove to, S.M.S. *Wolf* ceased fire and the *Wölfchen* ceased bomb-dropping, but flew over and round the ship until the prize crew had gone on board.

We landed close by the vessel and discovered that the nuts on the propeller bolts had worked loose, and that in consequence of the lash on the propeller shaft the engines could no longer throw true against the cranks. Having communicated by signals with the ship, we were towed in our aeroplane back to S.M.S. *Wolf* by motor boat.

(MOLL.)

Chapter VIII
Anti-Aircraft and Home Defences

THE CITIZEN OF Berlin or of Breslau hardly knows the meaning of the words 'Home Anti-Aircraft Defences,' although the inhabitants of the Rhine districts and Southern Germany understand them better. From Cologne to Freidrichshafen on the Baltic, many towns, some of them large like Cologne, Frankfurt, Carlsruhe, Freiburg, Stuttgart, and smaller ones like Bonn, Coblenz, Treves, Offenburg, etc., have experienced the moral effect of bomb raids, suffered grievous losses in human life and damage to houses, and have therefore learnt to know something about that splendidly organised Home Anti-Aircraft Defensive System which was developed from 1916 onwards.

The first bomb raid took place in the winter of 1914-1915. The objective of the raiders in December 1914 was the open town of Freiburg, and in March 1916 the powder factory at Rottweil. There shortly followed a regular series of attacks on the industrial centres round Diedenhofen and Luxemburg, and finally in 1918, those wicked attacks on the Rhine towns and Southern German towns which have been sufficiently talked about in the Press. The raid which penetrated farthest inland was an objectless and unsuccessful attack on the region around Dortmund, and a similar attack on Munich. There was even a threat of an attack on Berlin.

Our system of anti-aircraft defences was inaugurated in 1916, and put into operation in the valley of the Saar, from Saarbrücken to Dillingen, and it was also used round about Diedenhofen and Luxemburg in order to protect the chemical, powder, and explosive factories at Leverkusen and Schlebusch. Balloons of 160 cm. capacity and kites were sent up to heights of 6000 and 9000 feet respectively on a cable controlled by an electrically-driven winch. Other cables hung free from the balloon and kite, and were invisible to the airman on account of the latter's speed. In the event of a machine flying into one of these cables, disaster and death were the inevitable results.

The cables holding both balloons and kites were sufficiently strong to withstand a wind velocity of 8 yards per second. From the reports of enemy air men in 1917, we learnt that this protective measure greatly hindered them in carrying out their work, and was oven the cause of the raids being partly abandoned. On tho 24th January 1918, the first machine to be brought down by flying into the cables at a balloon station was accounted for at Diedenhofen.

(GRIMME.)

ANTI-AIRCRAFT BATTERIES IN ACTION DURING THE BATTLE BETWEEN THE SOMME AND THE AVRE IN AUGUST 1916

On August 8th, in the grey light of dawn, thick mists lay along the Somme and the Avre. Shortly before midnight the English and French had commenced operations with a very heavy artillery barrage. Shell after shell wailed down upon us, sometimes of the heaviest, sometimes of light or medium calibre - a truly murderous gunfire. Nothing could be seen 100 paces away.

Close up behind the front line the light guns mounted on motor tenders await developments. Telephonic communication has for a long time been cut off, and most of the runners fail to get through the barrage; even if they succeed in doing so, they mostly seek in vain for their guns, for the only way of surviving that murderous hail of fire is by constantly changing positions.

Suddenly we hear the deep rumbling note of an engine-tanks! Crowds of tanks are bearing down upon us! They must have easily passed over our front line infantry positions in the thick mist. It is a case for rapid action. With feverish haste the gun crew direct their weapon against the nearest monster. A brief command - 150 yards is the range - and the shell speeds forth on its errand. Too short! the sights are raised; again we fire; and this time the shells strikes plumb upon the body of the Colossus. A sheet of flame leaps up; the petrol tank has been penetrated and blazes brilliantly. There the monster lies motionless. The crew as they jump out are shot down by our infantry, who have assembled in the neighbourhood of the battery.

Slowly, very slowly, we yield before the overwhelming odds, vigorously beating off the enemy whenever he appears too near. Tank after tank is laid low, crippled and motionless, shattered by the German explosives. The mobile motor batteries hurry here and there, relieving the hard-pressed infantry and giving them safe passage.

In a wooded area where the infantry have been collected together in close columns for the attack, the shells of an anti-aircraft battery scour the region clean from barely 500 yards' range, dispersing the enemy before they have advanced fifty paces. Here, one battery alone has destroyed seven tanks during the morning; there, maybe, a battery has cut up a daringly planned cavalry attack. The infantry, fully appreciating their value, relies upon the protection of the batteries against the onslaught of the tanks and of the hordes of the enemy. The number of victims that the anti-aircraft batteries have bagged from the air is also large; seventeen machines fell to their guns alone on the 8th August 1916. A glorious day indeed for 'Archie' on the Somme and the Avre!

(GRUNOW.)

'DIE WACHT AM RHEIN'

The meteorological stations report the weather conditions on Northern France, Belgium, and the Rhineland as follows: 'Cool; clear, moonlight, a slight east wind over the whole district/ The home anti-aircraft defences count on the probability of an air raid. The balloons and kites ascend to a height of 5500 and 6600 feet respectively. At midnight a report comes through from Coblenz, Bonn, and Cologne, that a squadron of unknown nationality, at least five machines strong, has passed over Treves at a great height, flying down the Moselle, but has dropped no bombs on Treves itself; the searchlights have been in action but have not been able to find the enemy (probably on account of the latter's height), Coblenz, Bonn, and Cologne wait in a state of breathless excitement to discover against which of them the attack is to be made. The whole of the Rhineland is enveloped in darkness; there is only one region which cannot be darkened, and that is the bright ribbon of water where the Moselle and the Rhine are shining in the dazzling moonlight. It is useless to expect that they will miss their objective, particularly should it be Coblenz, since it lies at the junction of these two 'flying ways.'

The anti-aircraft staff officer has given the alarm. Batteries, searchlights, machine guns, all are manned by their full crews. Only the fighting squadrons remain quiescent, it being impossible for them to attack the raiders until dawn. Now there comes through a report from the listening station at Coblenz: 'Engines can be heard at a great height.' And immediately after that, innumerable anti-aircraft guns thunder and lightning their barrage over the town. The machine guns remain silent. The searchlights blaze forth, but as they cannot find the enemy, they are extinguished again. Then there follows the first pause in the barrage fire in order that we may listen again - already a report had come through from the listening post: 'The sound of the engines is fading away down the Rhine.' The raid is therefore not against Coblenz - hence the great height at which the squadron is flying - and shortly the town and the surrounding districts become calm again; the population breathe freely once more and leave the cellars and shelters which they have sought in spite of the injunction - 'Pay no attention to air raids.'

Things turn out in the same way at Bonn, and so the last doubt has now been removed that Cologne is to be their objective tonight. Not long afterwards the infernal noise of the exploding shells of the Cologne anti-aircraft defences mingles with the shattering reports of heavy bombs. Five searchlights have caught the enemy's machines in their beams of light; some of the batteries are firing as at target practice; no matter how they may twist and dive, the searchlights always pick up the enemy again. Now it is time for the machine guns to play their part; they chatter and their blazing bullets leap up into the night. Twenty minutes have passed, and already quietness reigns again completely. The hum of the engines has faded away into the distance, anti-aircraft batteries and machine gunners compute their expenditure of ammunition, the searchlights have been extinguished, the balloon and kite barriers above the explosives works at Leverkusen and Schlebusch remain aloft as if with a feeling of contentment that this time also, as on every previous occasion since their appearance, the enemy has not dared to attack the factory.

It appears that the target has been the important southern bridge at Cologne which, however, has not been damaged. It is true that in its neighbourhood and round about, twenty-eight bombs have fallen, but the only damage is the destruction of a house, two deaths, and four badly wounded and slightly wounded individuals. On the other hand the enemy have lost two machines, of which one was utterly destroyed with both its occupants.

Although Cologne, Frankfort, and Mainz had been attacked about the same time, the night was remarkably uneventful in Southern Germany, and the expectant readiness and nervous tension were unnecessary. Already, before morning dawned, several fighting squadrons were ready to leave the ground - indeed every minute was precious - and precisely at 3.15 A.M. a report came through to the effect that a squadron was approaching Stuttgart. That squadron should never reach its objective. Thanks to the excellent work of the Air Force Intelligence Service, two fighting squadrons had time to cut in between Stuttgart and the Trench squadrons so as to climb above the latter, and, assisted by direction shots fired by the anti-aircraft batteries - shells whose explosion is visible for some distance and serves to indicate to our airmen the direction of the enemy - had determined to attack. A veritable aerial battle resulted. Before long the enemy turned to flee after three machines had been shot down in dames. The French lost four more during the pursuit, and eventually escaped with two only, thanks to the appearance of some cloud banks.

The various branches of the Air Force on active service never had to work so completely together as those on home defence duty. Airmen, batteries, airships, searchlights, machine guns, intelligence and meteorological services, all worked together in sympathetic co-operation, and all these sections were unified in the course of their successful labours, as the founder of the home defences intended. Germany's Air Force protected Germany's homes.

(GRIMME.)

CHAPTER IX

A GLANCE INTO THE FUTURE

THE DREAM OF a German Air Force has faded away. Henceforth it will survive only as a memory and in heroic story. For that very reason we shall be able to consider in an unprejudiced manner: -

a. the further military development of our late enemies, and
b. the peaceful conquest of the aerial ocean, together with those problems and objects with which friend and foe are equally concerned.

The last military struggle on land, unique as it was in its tremendous scale, has been fought out - at any rate, the last on a European terrain. It is absurd to think that any military domination, to the extent which existed five years ago, can be reborn to any of the Central Powers, including Russia, since they all have been shattered. For reasons of national psychology one can understand that France, desperately hurt though victorious, is determined not to relax the terms imposed upon the Central Powers for a long time.

The sole surviving efficient power on the continent is separated from Germany by land-frontiers only. Thus, on account of that fear for the returning strength of her neighbour - a fear as inextinguishable as it is groundless - it is in France, as contrasted with England and America, that the further development of aerial forces will most certainly be brought about. The third arm will stand in the foreground of the picture at the expense of both the Army and the Navy.

Immediately up against aerially defenceless frontiers, there will stretch from the sea to the Alps an almost unbroken line of aerodromes for fighting aeroplanes, all utterly unproductive from any cultural point of view. Farther back, in a second zone, there will be the bombing squadrons and infantry contact machines organised into groups, and ready, on account of their power for rapid and concentrated destruction, to supersede the complicated and tedious system of advancing troops and artillery. In addition, there will be the so-called 'working aeroplanes,' comprising those branches of the service that are permanently attached to the army, i.e. artillery observation and photographic machines, together with the observation balloon units, France will make great efforts to avert all prospects of a future war on the European continent, although the possibility of such a war exists only in her imagination.

The situation will be quite different should France compete with her present allies in an extra-European scramble for supremacy on the sea, in the air, and in the matter of colonies.

The world's history began with fighting round the Mediterranean. The entry of America into the war was the signal for fighting on the Atlantic, which led inevitably and logically to a mutual blockade by the belligerent countries. The solution of this problem was no longer to be looked for in the use of Dreadnoughts and submarines alone after the first ocean patrols had been accomplished in aeroplanes and airships, although France had hitherto undertaken no patrols of this description. Sea-going craft and aircraft engaged one another in combat.

'The world is my demesne' is the motto upheld by our merchant seamen in the face of our late adversaries. They must extend it and add; 'My demesne is not only the world, but also the space above it.'

England knows how intimately the possession of one of the most powerful battle fleets is related with commercial and colonial prosperity. She will have realised from the day when, under the operation of our Air Force, she ceases to be an island, that the possession of the English Channel, the Dardanelles, or the Straits of Gibraltar can only be maintained by a simultaneous mastery of the air which lies over these vital points in world-supremacy. Furthermore, a system of air communications encircling the whole globe, a system such as is projected by England, can only be evolved under the protection of a strong Air Force, America and Japan will have to follow the same order of ideas.

But in the very carrying out of their aims for the economic exploitation of the air they hide a recognition of warlike requirements. It is not a dove of peace, but the bird of war, which has laid its egg in the nest of the still Allied and Associated Governments. That which shall develop from this egg will betray only too clearly its warlike origin. The phoenix which shall arise from the ashes of our naval and military Air Services will bear quite a different character. Armour is a hindrance to a swimmer. The aeroplane and airship that have been developed purely for commercial purposes, and without any secondary object, will be immensely superior in their performances to those machines burdened with armour, or designed for the mounting of offensive weapons.

A contemplation of the future of aerial warfare would be incomplete without a glance at the art of anti-aircraft defences, which grew, during the war, from nothing to a condition almost of perfection. In contrast to aeroplanes and airships with their light armament, there will be a marked deterioration in anti-aircraft gunnery, due to the fact that practice under war conditions, when live shells are used against machines actually controlled by men, will not be possible. No ingenious substitutes or cunning systems can supply that practice which the war offered. The gradual loss of experienced anti-aircraft gunners will lead naturally to a correspondingly increased reliance on the attacking and destructive powers of the flying squadrons.

All nations which have to reckon with the fear of further inevitable hostilities in the sharing of the spoil won in a plundering peace, find themselves faced with this question: 'Is it better to construct commercial and industrial establishments underground, or so to develop air power that it becomes unnecessary to do so?'

No matter what the decision may be, those energies employed by other nations in the pursuit of offensive or defensive measures will in

Germany be free of this bondage, and can display themselves in the service of true civilisation. For our flying, therefore, there shall dawn a day of resurrection. Our former enemies have taken care that this shall not happen too quickly. Fourteen paragraphs of the Peace Treaty form the tightly-knotted meshes of the net which has been cast over the young eagle's head. Only Article 201 shall here be quoted textually, to commemorate the enemy's recognition of German inventive genius and German productivity:

'During the six months following the date on which the present Treaty comes into force, the manufacture and the importation of aircraft, parts of aircraft, engines for aircraft, and parts of engines for aircraft, shall be forbidden in all German territory.'

By the time that this work is published, the period of quarantine placed upon our pestilential aerial activity will have nearly elapsed. The design that is bound up in this six months' embargo, and whose object is quite obviously to exclude us from the outside market, and to leave the Allied aerial traffic unhampered by competition from Germany, must and will miscarry. Together with Austria we constitute geographically a Continental centre, while France - and even more so England - can never represent lanes for European aerial traffic, but only termini for arrival and departure. This helps us to a definition of the expression 'aerial traffic' generally.

It seems to me more than questionable whether the aerial traffic of the future will be such as is imagined by the general public, whose ideas are too much bound up with purely terrestrial considerations. The masses couple the idea of 'traffic' mainly with the notion of a 'railway,' more even of a steamship service. Out of an exaggerated development of this conception there arises the mistaken idea that aeroplanes will take the place of the express train or the liner, just as the locomotive took the place of the horses of mail coaches. No apprehension need be felt on that score for another fifty years. Aeroplanes and airships will get over the defects inherent in other means of transport; they will make up for deficiencies and fill gaps - just as in equipment for aerial warfare the captive balloon retained, and probably will retain, its full value as a means of observation along with the aeroplane.

But above all, aircraft discloses new possibilities whose development lies outside the limitations of wheeled methods of transport.

The aeroplane is no immediate competitor to the fast night trains, such as the express from Berlin to Frankfort. Not yet can it challenge a means of transport that is reliable in any weather. Countries which possess a dense railway system need anticipate no fundamental changes in their traffic organisation for the nest ten years, even though letters and parcels should be forwarded by air. During the war wireless telegraphy and telephony, micro-telephony, telewriting, and high-speed telegraphy attained such a capability and certainty of operation that much of the work which originally seemed reserved for aeroplanes can be accomplished by their means.

And now, after having outlined in so negative a fashion the possible future uses of aircraft, we might profitably consider those problems which depend entirely upon aircraft for their solution. One such problem, for example, is the development of vast areas of land, 800 miles or more in extent, that possess an insufficient railway system or suffer from lack of water. Consequently we can say that the most favourable prospects for future development lie with those districts to which the geographical term 'trans' is applicable: i.e. trans-Siberian, transoceanic, trans-African. A prospect such as this leads one to believe that the trans-oceanic flights, which at present are so rare and phenomenal, will in the future be resolved into a regular service. That which stands as a record for today will be quite a normal performance tomorrow. Let us now consider the future in the light of what we have gained. The world's record flight for duration is over twenty-four hours without any intermediate landing; the record for speed is nearly 180 miles per hour. Thus it will be possible to reach Bombay, New York, or Irkutsk from Berlin in one continuous flight. The flight of our L. 59 proves to all thoughtful people the results achieved in aerial progress through the problems brought up by the war.

A few words on the future prospects of the airship. I regard the airship merely as the precursor of the aeroplane. In due course the latter will overcome its inferiority in flight duration and useful load as compared with the airship. Nevertheless, so far as the immediate future is concerned the importance of the airship will again be very great. But its traditions, its impressive dimensions, and its ability to keep in the air all day long with thirty or forty passengers must not make one forget that its lifting power only increases in proportion to its size, and that there is in practice a limit to the latter. The gusts of a ground wind increase the dangers which are already involved in the going up and landing even of small airships. Changes in temperature, sunshine, and atmospheric 'bumps', under certain circumstances may become dangerous. Even the size of sheds and base equipment becomes uneconomic, Finally, until we can seriously depend on filling with helium, the proximity of internal combustion engines to an inflammable gas will hardly encourage intending passengers.

The giant aeroplane, which is destined some day to supersede the airship, was in a purely experimental stage at a time when the airship had already been highly developed. Any comparison between them at the present moment is therefore apt to give a false impression. For that reason one is led to believe that in the matter of airship design we are approaching the end of one period, while another begins with the building of giant aeroplanes. Perhaps for crossing the ocean the airship is still superior to the aeroplane. The airship, too, will be the first to accomplish a non-stop flight round the world. It will still play its part in the vanquishing of space, but it is the aeroplane alone which can, must, and will gain the victory which shall be won over the problem of time.

Now let us return and consider the possible uses to which aircraft may be put in the immediate future, and the various problems of business, science, and research towards which the aeroplane or the airship can contribute either wholly or partially some solution.

Both airships and aeroplanes will entirely revolutionise the science of surveying by undertaking topographical work from the air. The extent to which they may be employed upon this work can be estimated from the fact that up to the present only a seventh part of the total surface of the earth has been surveyed. Aircraft will be used for the production of town plans, and maps for tourists, cyclists, motorists, or airmen, and to carry out the preliminary work in connection with plans for railways, canals, and colonies. They will supply accurate information concerning any river beds and portions of the coast which, owing to periodic variations in the currents are continually altering the conformation of their banks and shoals.

Then again, for advertising purposes the aeroplane will be found useful not only for taking pictures, but also for dropping propaganda leaflets.

But the airmen will extend their activity even beyond the very wide limits which we have already outlined. Aeroplanes may be of great service to the high sea fisheries for the purpose of observing and reporting on the approach and course followed by large shoals; by keeping an eye upon the nets, and even by supplying rapid transport to the consumer. Then again, there are banks of shellfish to be looked for and watched, and expeditions to be sent out to destroy ravaging whales and seals. One must not forget the possibility of establishing communication between wrecked ships and the mainland by aeroplanes flying across the breakers (dropping life lines, transporting tackle, etc., and supplying provisions).

Airmen will also prove useful allies to the police force on land. Thus, for example, they might take photographs of traffic centres at various times of the day to assist in compiling statistics, or be used for dispersing forbidden assemblies without bloodshed by continually flying over the crowd at a low altitude. The sound of the propeller would drown all speechmaking.

But even now the business possibilities of aircraft have not been exhausted. They include so many different ideas that it is difficult to combine them all into one comprehensive catalogue. Thus, for example, one might mention the possibility of using aircraft for special transport work such as carrying fresh flowers, or even for sending pay to troops in strike or riot areas; for the control of long transcontinental telegraph cables from malicious damage or destruction by storms; for the transport of specially topical cinematograph films, and as a means of combating forest and prairie fires, where the damage caused is so often unnecessarily heavy owing to ignorance of the point of origin and progress of the fire. In connection with this work aircraft could take photographs or drop fire-extinguishing bombs. Again, aeroplanes could be used for keeping watch over enormous areas of the country, specially over the herds of cattle in Australia and South America.

Flying will be used to save time in business on journeys which would otherwise have to be made on the backs of donkeys or camels, and for visiting many places widely scattered apart, particularly in the East, where the continual good weather and excellent facilities for forced landings - as in Egypt, Palestine, and India - lend themselves to work of this description, Furthermore, aeroplanes could easily locate and destroy dangerous packs of ice in rivers and canals, or melt snowdrifts in railway cuttings and sunken roads by employing 'flamethrowers.' They could lay telephone wires along short distances, when it is of urgent importance that communication should be established without delay (as, for example, from the scene of a railway accident to the nearest telegraph stations), and could take the place of mountain railways, cable railways, and rack and pinion railways whenever it was possible to land on the summit.

I have already discussed the future prospects of airships which will be called upon to assist in vanquishing space. The victory over the problem of time, which is so intimately related with that of space, will go to the aeroplane. Such a victory cannot be obtained by theoretical or philosophical juggling with ideas, but by a sober endeavour ultimately to fly round the world in twenty-four hours. The machine will ascend from Döberitz in the early dawn, and thunder its way towards the morning star at a speed of 600 miles per hour. No matter where the pilot may cast his eye backwards, should it be across Ireland, Newfoundland, Vancouver, Vladivostok, or Moscow, everywhere he will see the image of awakening day, everywhere time will be the same. Perhaps even this event may be brought about by employing unoccupied machines directed on their way by wireless, or to which the necessary power is transmitted by wireless, as I suggest will ultimately be the case with the aerial mail, which will be carried out by aeroplanes controlled only by electric waves, and containing no men.

It is not by chance that the era whose end will see this complete consummation of humanity's struggle against the forces of nature has its beginning now, when the nations are beginning to recognise the value of world peace. The first trans-oceanic in the month after the end of the war stamped the next twenty-five years as a period for the reconstruction of international goodwill. During five years of research our German Air Force prepared the way for the conquest of the space, and it is the same power, indestructible like energy itself, which shall carry on the work to its completion.

(SIEGERT.)

THE END